'Armand Hoff' is the pseudonym of an ex-burglar, thief and
playboy who wishes to remain anonymous. He has now reformed
and is a respectable businessman in the Netherlands, where
no-one knows of his past.

The Panther
Armand Hoff

Mayflower

Granada Publishing Limited
Published in 1977 by Mayflower Books Ltd
Frogmore, St Albans, Herts AL2 2NF

First published in Great Britain by
Frederick Muller Ltd 1975
Copyright © Armand Hoff 1975
Made and printed in Great Britain by
Hazell Watson & Viney Ltd
Aylesbury, Bucks
Set in Monotype Plantin

*All characters herein are fictitious and any
resemblance to actual persons living or dead is
purely coincidental.*

Contents

I	'Oh, My Father . . .'	7
II	An Afternoon When Childhood Ended	40
III	Parisienne Variety	62
IV	Cote D'Amour	69
V	The Night I Nearly Murdered Heidi	90
VI	The Role of Robin Hood	127
VII	Victoria	137
VIII	No-Man's-Land	151
IX	Mireille, Jeanine, Madeleine, Yvonne, Manon, Yvette . . . and the Maquis	176
X	Love With Mother and Daughter	192
XI	How Lucky Can You Be	212
XII	On the Run in Africa	221
XIII	'So You Won't Talk'	232
XIV	Career of Crime	245
XV	Secret Agent	256
XVI	The Panther Strikes Sweden	271
XVII	The Panther is Captured	281
XVIII	Lust for Freedom	296
XIX	The Running Stops	311

Panther's dedication to his son:

The free choice of a man selecting his mate does not really enlarge the minute contribution towards what eventually grows to become his offspring.

Perhaps this is what causes his never ending surprise each time he realizes what actually being a father means.

Your mother marrying me and the coming of you afterwards were the two greatest miracles that ever happened to me.

Both gave me an entirely different outlook on life and also were the main causes for the writing of this book. Not because I felt the belated need for confession or even justification of my former life and sins. No, none of that, but simply a father's attempt to reach out for his son.

You'll not often find it an agreeable tale but at least it is an honest attempt to explain what happened a long time ago, before you were born.

After all, birthright entitles one to the knowledge of who and what one's parents were and even more so in your special case. As the bearer of my name sooner or later you are bound to be confronted with my past. The world may still try to make you suffer for my sins and what better protection against prejudice than the simple truth?

Also, if this account of my mistakes should prove a help to you in evading some others, no one could accuse the Panther of sending his cub into the jungle unprepared.

Should you find it in your heart afterwards to still think kindly of me, the Panther may rest in peace at last.

I

'Oh, My Father . . .'

I wasn't at that extraordinary funeral. While he was dying I was working as a 'masseur' in Paris, in a parlour that was really a brothel for frustrated women. When the news of his death reached me I was in the familiar surroundings of a French prison, serving a sentence for a country house jewel robbery.

He was the architect of my life. I was his epitaph – the one they didn't put on his headstone.

Let me tell you about this ranting evangelist who cornered me into being a self defensive liar almost as soon as I learnt to speak.

My father was a bible-thumping Dutch priest. When he died, over five thousand people attended his funeral to pay their respects. To me the man they mourned was anything but a saint. I could not forgive, let alone forget his ruthless harshness nor his cruel brutality just because he was now dead. At that time my hatred was still choking me. It almost seemed a legacy like the scars of his thrashings I am carrying on my body to this day.

Even more strongly than the most unforgettable experiences of sensuality with women, I can recapture for instance the anticipation and the agony of that braided leather dog lead lashing my naked young body until at times the blood ran like sweat down my legs. God, how I feared and loathed him.

However, I do owe him just one thing.

If he held some responsibility for the fact that by the age of sixteen I was familiar with reform school, with prison cells, with the bedrooms of whores, had taken part in armed hold-ups and had become an accomplished housebreaker, he was also responsible for the gymnastic training which was to lead to the Swedish police nicknaming me 'The Panther'. When they had their dragnet out for me because, having once broken into the Royal castle at Sofiero and into the Queen's bedroom, they had evidence that the climax to my series of audacious robberies in their country was to be the theft of Her Majesty's diamond necklace with its row of flawless stones.

That's right. When luck ran out and they caught me they recovered loot I had stolen from the home of Prince Bernadotte, from the home of Thorsten Krueger, brother of 'the Match King', and from a Consulate in Stockholm. The climbing contraption I used is now an exhibit in the Stockholm police museum. And but for some boys playing Cops and Robbers I would have had the Queen's diamonds, too.

That was ironic. When I'd been their age, it hadn't been a game. It had been for real, a self-testing of courage to overcome the cowardice my father was battering into me – my sanctimonious father!

Religion was his real disease. He caught it when he was thirty, a big, strong man full of lustful appetites suddenly stricken by a debility which the doctors diagnosed as diabetes.

This was back in 1910. Among the supposed causes of diabetes in those days were intemperance, excessive drinking and over indulgence in sexual pleasures. The caps all fitted. Diabetes was a serious matter and my father was a frightened and desperate man. Then God, in the form of a hospital visitor, showed him the way to save his immortal soul.

The hospital visitor was a crusading member of the Darbinistic sect, founded by an Englishman, John Nelson Darby, in the nineteenth century. And my father was ripe for the role of repentant sinner.

Maybe it paid off. Certainly he lived another thirty-eight years – but they were harsh, bitter years of conflict, of illness and pain and of constant outbursts of rage.

When he came out of hospital he joined the sect.

He gave up alcohol. He gave up fornication. He disciplined himself against solitary sexual relief. Pleasure and sin became synonymous to him. For the rest of his life he suffered much physical pain but no greater than the mental agony he underwent in trying to cast the devil out of his soul. But the devil mocked him, not only in his own soul but challengingly and tauntingly from within all those around him.

He fought this adversary wherever he found him. And nowhere did the devil seem more vulnerable and accessible than in me, his own son, conceived in sin, in lust. Sermons for my immortal soul, thrashings and rage for the devil my physical body harboured and was possessed by!

He crucified all his children, but I was the chosen battleground for his dedicated fight against human weakness and wickedness.

He was still a young, handsome looking man when he left hospital, snatched from death, so he fervently believed, to crusade in the name of the Lord – a tall, distinguished looking fanatic with a powerful voice, and a welcome recruit to the evangelist sect which shunned all pomp and ceremony. With a small allowance from the sect and a tiny pension from the Government, he began his religious career by visiting the sick and aged; bible in hand.

Although the sect had its churches, the Darbists were very much missionaries. During the summer months my father toured the countryside, setting up his tent in a village or small town, staying for a week in each place before moving on, holding services under canvas, whipping up religious hysteria with his passionate denunciations of the evils of the flesh and finally baptizing his quota of converts.

These baptismal services were to be the only part of his religion for which I was to develop a secret enthusiasm. They involved total immersion in a large tank of water and men and women alike wore long white cotton gowns for the ceremony but were otherwise completely naked.

During the brief period of total immersion the gowns had a tendency to float upwards and outwards to become like gigantic water lilies on the surface of the water. A small boy, kneeling down and pretending to pray like the rest of the congregation, once he knew the strategic position to choose for his devotions, could enjoy the forbidden sight of the male and female genitalia of that town's most respected citizens.

My father relaxed and almost warmed to me on occasions when I was responsible for bringing other boys of my own age to such travelling circus services. He never once suspected the nature of the attraction.

This tall, austere young priest with his good looks, his passion and fire, and his resonant voice was a great success. He packed them in, especially the women – one of those women was my mother.

My mother, from whom I remember hardly any evidence of love for myself, must have loved my father. They must have courted, however unimaginable it is. They must have talked of human love. For when he was thirty-five and she was twenty-eight, despite opposition from her family, they married.

There was no money in religion – certainly not his kind. Indeed, throughout his life until he died, heavily in debt, he subsidized his evangelical work with hers!

For my mother's family were wealthy and when, soon after

the marriage, her parents died half the fortune she inherited automatically became his. The consequence was a big, but inevitably gloomy house in The Hague.

When I was born I already had two brothers, Louis and John, and a sister, Carol.

John and Carol, the latter with whom my mother, a domineering martinet, still lives at the age of eighty-five, were the docile ones. Louis and to lesser extent my second sister, Ann, who was born three years after myself, were like myself the thorns in my father's flesh. But Louis was either cleverer or luckier than I, so I was the whipping boy.

I had a third sister, of whom I have only a single memory. But that single memory is the beginning of remembered events.

My grandmother lived with us, we had a governess, Jaantze, and there was a succession of maids, none of whom seemed able to endure the oppressive atmosphere of our home for long.

I was four when my mother had her sixth and final pregnancy. I knew vaguely, but without any understanding, why she was confined to bed. The situation was a repetition of that of a little over a year before when Ann had been born.

This time it was different. The doctor came and went frequently. There were strange nurses in the house. My father was remote and seemed unaware of us. My grandmother seemed sad and anxious. The servants talked in whispers. There was a sense of something unknown being wrong and I remember watching from a hiding place in a cupboard under the stairs, my father opening the front door to a drably dressed stranger carrying some kind of heavy crate which they took upstairs, going into the room adjoining my parents' bedroom.

Some time later, when the house was quiet and the man had left, my father came to the room where my brothers and I were waiting for our evening meal.

I remember him standing in the doorway, coming no farther. I remember being frightened because I thought one of us must have done something wrong and would be punished – and it might be me.

'You boys come with me,' he said, and turned on his heel. I remember the lack of warmth in his voice, although it was only afterwards that I knew it should have been there.

I remember the stairs of our home as being so high that, at four, I had to still almost crawl up them, smelling the dust embedded in the pile of the elaborate carpet.

I lagged behind my two brothers who silently and obediently followed our father, and by the time I reached the room the three of them were already standing looking down into a small, oblong box of polished wood which had been placed on an occasional table. The purpose of the box had no meaning to me, and when I reached it I was too small to see what it was that they were looking at in such silence.

'Now you can see!' said my father, lifting me up by the armpits in a manner that made me feel more uncomfortable.

I remember that the tiny head of the dead baby, all to be seen of her, seemed blue and red speckled. She was somehow only half human and there was that complete stillness of the flesh by which, with sensory perception, one recognizes death from life. She was dead in the way I had only seen animals to be dead.

I felt sick and terrified. There was an unknown, unfamiliar smell in the room. I struggled desperately in my father's hold, and he put me down.

'She was your baby sister,' he told us. 'The Lord in his wisdom and mercy has seen fit to call her to Heaven to take her place among the angels for she has lived and died without having sinned. Blessed be the Lord. Amen.'

'Amen,' we all echoed obediently, I in a shaking, uneven voice.

'You may now go down for your suppers,' my father said, dismissing us.

There that early memory ends. It was only afterwards, in retrospect, that the insensitivity of confronting a small boy of four in this way with the reality of death was really quite unbelievable.

But this was the kind of father he was to his family.

Yet the picture is distorted if it shows him to be humourless. He could roar with laughter as easily and as terrifyingly as he roared with rage. His humour was, of course, sadistic and cruel.

Right back as far as memory reaches, something as timeless as awareness of night and day, hunger and thirst, I remember the old-fashioned brass car-horn which he kept locked away in a cupboard with the dog lead whip, his cigars, his private books and papers – his secret things one can only imagine about. It had a rubber bulb which when squeezed caused a sudden, sharp shock of sound.

Oh, yes, my father played games with his children, but they were his games, for his laughter, not ours.

He would lurk behind a door, or in the darkness of a corridor, in a cupboard or cellar. When one of us approached, he would blow that terrifying toy. The tension which existed when he was in the house, and even knowing what might be expected, never prepared me for it. I always shrieked with fright. He always roared with laughter at my terror.

We were all of us, his children, frightened of the dark. I do not remember a night, as a small child, going to bed without pulling the blankets over my head in order to feel a measure of safety.

There is always a point where fear turns to hatred, and there is no going back on a hatred that has its roots in fear. Hatred of my father dates from the age of six, and from the reasons why I ran away from home for the first of several occasions.

My brothers and I were playing in a street near our home. A tradesman's van was passing, its coachwork immaculately washed and polished. The temptation was too great for me. I scooped up a handful of mud from the gutter and threw it at the van. Unfortunately I missed the van but hit the driver full in the face.

The man was understandably furious, reigned his horse and leapt down from his seat. My brothers and I were too well trained not to recognize the futility of flight from adult anger and we made no attempt to escape.

He grabbed me by the collar and asked Louis, as obviously the oldest boy, for my name and address.

'I'll soon find out, you know,' he said.

So Louis told him, and since our house was near I was taken back home by the driver for my father to 'deal with me'.

Believing I knew what that meant I was already whimpering when I was confronted by my father on the doorstep. He listened to the story of my 'criminal assault' and I could read in his face that he was thinking hard about how most effectively to give me what he usually called 'the lesson of my life'.

I saw his nostrils flare, and when his eyes met mine he almost smiled.

'Take him to the police,' he said abruptly to the driver.

'But . . .' said the driver, looking down at me as I cringed away from the heavy hand that still gripped my coat collar. 'But, he's only a kid.'

'He's a little devil,' said my father, with a strange note of satisfaction in his voice. 'Take him to the police! I insist on it. That'll give him the lesson of his life. Much more effective than another thrashing from me. That'll put the fear of God into you, won't it?' he added, bending down to bring his face and his piercing eyes close to mine.

Then he motioned Louis and John to pass him and go into the house, and finally shut the door in the faces of the driver and myself.

'Well, if that's what he wants . . .' said the driver, as he began to lead me away.

But he was obviously disturbed by the outcome of the affair, and the grip on my collar was not as tight as it had been. At the corner of the road I wriggled free and ran for my life. I realized afterwards that no heavier footsteps had echoed in chase after mine.

No child running away from home, for any reason, thinks very far ahead, or other than emotionally. I made the first of the many decisions I was to make not to go back to my father's house.

I ran, then walked, then sauntered, then loitered. It grew late, it grew dark, it grew cold. My determination did not waiver, but practical considerations began to add to my fear.

When a police patrol found me, I was in an alleyway, in a doorway huddled up under sheets of corrugated cardboard which I had taken from an office waste-bin. They were not, as I had first believed, looking for me because of the incident with the van driver. They hadn't been told about it. I had simply been reported as a missing child.

I was taken back home where, without any welcoming warmth or relief at my safety, I was ordered to bed. Jaantze brought me some hot soup, but I knew that she had smuggled it to me.

But it is none of all this that makes the early adventure remain so clear in my memory. Not only were my feelings for my father now resolved into the positiveness of a hatred with which I could combat fear, but from the moment of recognizing him as my enemy I had begun, for the first time, to defeat him. The threat of the police hadn't materialized. I hadn't been thrashed. I had got away with it, and ended up drinking hot soup in bed – an unheard of luxury.

It was not a battle which, as a child, I could possibly have won. But I had my victories to chalk up. What was more, my father actually contributed to the toughening-up process I began subjecting myself to.

Up to the time of running away I had been miserably aware of myself as a cowardly little boy. But in running away from home I had discovered that I could have courage, too.

I wanted desperately to be brave. I wanted to be like the heroes in the boys' adventure stories I was beginning to read surreptitiously. I wanted to prove myself to myself and to others, especially the other boys in the day school which I had started to attend. The exploit with the van driver had become known and for the first time I was conscious of being treated with some respect by my classmates.

One day when I was about ten, our class was taken to a museum. The guide had just been showing us a case of antique silver coins, which he said were valuable, when his attention was distracted. One of the boys remarked that the coins would be worth stealing, that it would be easy, that one missing would never be noticed.

'Go on then!' another boy challenged him. 'Take one! I *dare* you!'

He drew back, irresolute. Several of the other boys began to laugh at him scornfully. I recognized an opportunity to show that *I* had courage that demanded admiration.

'He's scared!' I said. 'But I'm not.'

And I pocketed the coin. My life as a thief had had its beginning.

Of course, I couldn't keep the coin. On the following Saturday I took it to a small, side street jewellers. I said it had been left to me by my grandfather and I wanted to sell it to buy a birthday present for my mother.

This seemed a believable story to me, and I was rather proud of it. I realized later that the man in the shop couldn't possibly have believed such a story and that I'd probably been lucky enough to walk into a shop that fronted for a fencing business. He must have decided that there was no risk to him in buying the coin from me at very much less than its worth.

He gave me enough, however, to buy an airgun. Three of the boys who had been there when I had stolen the coin, and who had waited outside the jewellers when I sold it, accompanied me home with my new acquisition. My parents were out, and I said that we could play with the airgun in the garden.

My father kept pigeons, and his favourite was an East Indian bird. One of the boys, who couldn't have hit a tree trunk from ten yards if he had been trying, shot and killed the bird.

We were all very scared. The unfortunate marksman suggested that we should throw the body of the dead bird away.

'Our cat might find it and bring it back,' I said.

'Then we could bury it,' said another boy.

'The gardener would be sure to dig it up when he comes,' I said. Then I had an idea. 'I know,' I said. 'We'll burn it in the kitchen stove. The maid is out, Jaantze is having her afternoon nap, and my grandmother never comes into the kitchen.'

We took the dead bird into the kitchen. It lay on the old, thick oak table in the centre of the room while I raked the ashes from the stove to brighten up a good, red fire for the cremation.

Then, as it was to do so often during my life, luck ran out. Not expected back for at least another couple of hours, my father walked into the kitchen.

We all froze and stood motionless while in a glance he took in the scene. He exploded with rage, the words erupting from him with volcanic fury.

'Whose gun is that?' he roared.

We all looked at one another, and the other boys all ended up by looking at me, and he was answered.

He grabbed the airgun by the barrel, swinging the shoulder piece up in the air like a club, and turning, poised himself to attack me. I knew his capabilities and dodged, throwing myself just in time to safety under the table.

The gun crashed down on the table top, the barrel breaking off from the stock with the force of impact and the stock making a dent in the table that must be still there to this day if the table still exists.

All his rages had their violent moment of orgasm and then, becoming abruptly spent, were followed by surprising calm.

He stared at what he had done, then said firmly:

'Come out boy. Come out. I want to know exactly what happened.'

I knew from experience that it was now safe to obey. He questioned us, and got the whole story out of us, right back to the theft of the coin and the name of the jeweller to whom I had sold it.

'Go!' he told the other boys. 'Never come back into this house. Never speak of what has happened.'

He never spoke of it himself. I know that he went immediately to the jewellers, but what happened there, and in what circumstances the coin came to be returned to the museum I never knew. The thing that mattered to me at the time was that he did not report my theft to the police.

And I knew exactly why he did not do so. If he had, it would have come out how close he had come to killing me, and there were too many witnesses to his maniacal attack for anything less than the whole truth to have been uncovered.

Of course the other boys talked about what had happened – among themselves, and to other boys. From having been looked upon as a weakling, a coward, someone to be bullied, I now commanded respect and was looked upon with awe.

Only I knew that my battle wasn't won. I had to be able to respect myself, too. I was still terrified of the dark, of shadows where unseen and imagined terrors could lurk. I still whistled in the dark to keep my courage up. I still looked under the bed. I still pulled the blankets over my head.

One night, when I wakened and lay tense with terror at a sound that had disturbed me, I steeled myself to try and conquer my weakness. It was half past one in the morning, the night was still and tense with silence. There was no moon.

I got up and dressed in the dark, let myself out of the house and made my way down the deserted streets to a nearby graveyard. The gates were locked for the night but I scaled the wall.

I remember, sitting on the top of that wall, my hands ready to give me my launching push, looking down into the dark pit where all terror lay. No moment in my life had been so filled with indecision. It is probable that no decision I ever took required more courage or was more important.

'I've got to do it!' I whispered to myself. 'I've got to. If I turn back *now*, I'll always run away.'

I gave myself a push, and landed on long, soft wet grass, and lay there for a minute, wishing desperately for the safety of blankets which could be drawn up over my head. This time there weren't any and far more awful, even if imagined, terrors to face than my father lurking somewhere with his fiendish motor horn. Eventually I got up and began creeping through the graveyard.

The high walls acted as curtains against the light from the street, and at first, until my eyes adjusted themselves to the thick darkness of the moonless night, I stumbled from gravestone to gravestone.

God, I have never been, before or since, so frightened as I was that night with the fantasy of open, yawning graves in my mind, of undead corpses waiting to embrace me with their rotting flesh. We speak casually of 'the fear of death', but it had its reality to me then.

I could see again that half human face of my dead two day old sister, the origin and the reality of my terror, and I sweated until I could smell the stink of my own fear, malodorous as the dark, dank graveyard itself with its putrefying flowers, their stems rotting in the slimy water of vases and jam jars.

But I stayed to walk, straight back instead of creeping. I stayed to walk, not run, without looking back. I stayed the lifetime of maybe half an hour, until I had terror under control, until my sense of fear was mastered, not just that night but for the rest of my life.

And after I had reclimbed the wall, I walked back home, without fear. I now knew that the unknown terrors which had haunted my life belonged not to the graveyard, not to the night or its darkness, but to my own mind. I had learnt how to deal with my cowardice, but I was still a long way from conquering it and finding it, as I do now, a strange, childish thing to remember, exaggerated out of all importance.

At this time of my life it was a dominant obsession and anyone who finds this hard to understand must have had a much happier childhood than I had.

The graveyard was my self discovered therapy for the fear I wanted to rid myself of. I subjected myself to the treatment again and again, secretly, when I reached that 'lowest ebb of night when mind and body fail'. And when it became a familiar place and ceased to be a real test of my courage I looked for the challenge of other places where night and darkness were a dreadful thing.

I began breaking into and wandering through the old empty houses, defying their unknown ghosts as I trod on their squeaking boards, opened the doors with their groaning hinges; my body rigid with abject fear, turning cold at the sound of the scampering of an unseen rat or the movement of a tree against the window pane.

My training for the profession of housebreaking and burglary had started in earnest and at this very moment my father unwittingly contributed to it. Louis had become a good swimmer and something of a gymnast and my father subscribed to an idea widely believed at that time. A boy made healthily tired by strenuous physical exercise was not tempted to the sinfulness of what was evasively called self-abuse, with all its supposedly debilitating consequences and dangers.

So I was thrown, and I mean this literally, into the deep end of the nearest swimming bath. He took me there, and having made me put on a costume, picked me up and threw me in. Then as I floundered in panic, he dived in after me, unceremoniously got me out of the water and gave his instructions to the pool's professional 'that's the biggest part of the job, now teach him to swim like a fish'.

He also arranged for me to have gymnastic training. Bars, rings and a rope ladder were put up in the garden for the three of us, and we were made to work hard at our physical training.

To everybody else's surprise I quickly outshone my brothers. Nobody suspected that I was already scaling walls, clinging to and climbing up drainpipes to enter empty houses. Gymnastics had a purpose and value to me and I was enthusiastic.

What I didn't understand was my father's enthusiasm, or why my hard work seemed to give him great satisfaction.

'Why is he so keen?' I asked Louis.

Louis, pubescent, and with an understanding I could not have at the age of ten, laughed and winked.

'He thinks that if we get fagged out, we'll be too tired to play with ourselves,' he said.

No direct reference to masturbation was ever made in our home but the quite extraordinary beliefs of the period – that it was injurious to health, caused a boy to become a weakling, reduced the span of his life expectancy and led to early impotence because he had squandered a limited supply of what had to be eked out to last him throughout his life – were nevertheless put across to us in such a way that any and every succumbing to irresistible temptation was a matter of guilt and fear.

Even my mother, if she visited our rooms after we were in bed, would tell us strictly: 'Hands outside the bed.'

We were told to sleep like that, with the blankets tucked up under our armpits, so that our shoulders were uncovered, and our arms and hands lay above the bedclothes.

Our father went further, on occasions when he found us in bed with the blankets snug about our shoulders, he would insist that our arms be withdrawn. He would say in ominous warning, leaving it to be understood exactly what he meant: 'If you give way to temptation you will harm yourself for the rest of your life. Discipline yourself, boy, if you want to grow up to be a strong man and have a long life.'

I don't pretend to know the answers to how parental guidance can best be applied to the problems of adolescent curiosity and experimentation in sexual matters. That my parents certainly did not know the answers there can be no doubt. They told us old wives' tales when they should have told us true facts and were remote when they should have shown understanding.

I was beginning to get the measure of my father.

I had an illness when I was eight and my baptism, nearly one year later, was intended to be an acknowledgement of gratitude for my recovery. Rather more important to me has been the promise that when I got better I should have a Red Indian outfit.

The promise was kept, but I had to have formal permission to wear it. Finding me wearing it without his authority one day, my father ordered me to take it off. In a fit of rage when I was alone in my room, I ripped it to pieces.

Afterwards, realizing the consequences of what I had done, I destroyed the evidence and, after an interval of a few days, approached my father and asked if I might wear it.

'Yes, all right,' he agreed.

'Then may I have it father?' I asked innocently.

'*I* haven't got it, boy,' he said.

'But it's gone. I can't find it. I thought you must have taken it,' I said.

'Well, I didn't,' he replied. 'You must look for it. Now go away. Don't bother me.'

He never referred to it again. I had established that it was lost and convinced him that I was not to blame. I had learnt how to evade punishment by using cunning, and I put the lesson to immediate good use.

The cupboard where he kept the motor horn, his cigars, private papers and the dreaded dog-lead whip, had never been as safe as he supposed. I had already discovered that its lock could be opened by the key of our toy box, but I had never thought of a way in which to use this knowledge to any advantage.

The next time I got a whipping I decided grimly that it would be the last. At the first opportunity I took one of his cut-throat razors, opened the cupboard and cut the whip up into small pieces – and defiantly left them there for him to find.

He found them all right – and soon enough, for that whip was in constant use. I've forgotten now which of my brothers was to have been the victim when he went for the whip and discovered what had happened.

There was a furious scene and we were cross examined thoroughly, but there was absolutely no evidence as to the identity of the culprit, and at least he was a just man so nobody was punished. Neither was the whip ever replaced. I think that secretly he was frightened of the habit that had developed of using the whip more and more frequently and of his own increasing lack of self control when he was using it. I think he was beginning to have a haunting fear that one day he might go too far and cause serious injury. I think that he was as relieved as we were to see the end of it.

Not that this stopped his outbursts of rage, or softened his manner or changed him in any way. But he began to find other ways of punishing us.

For example it was the year after I had destroyed the whip that Louis and I pooled the money we had saved to buy a second hand gramophone and some jazz records that were popular around 1930.

It was music of a kind that had never been heard in our home before, and my father heard it coming from Louis' room where we were playing our small selection of those old 78's one afternoon.

He burst into the room, demanded to know all about this 'devil's machine' and the 'profane' music. We admitted to joint ownership. He took the records, and broke them, one by one, over his knee. Then he confiscated the gramophone.

Apparently he changed his mind about it being 'the devil's machine' when he discovered that records of sacred music and of psalms were obtainable. We never got it back, but subsequently we were to hear it playing 'The Lord's music' when he had visitors.

Gradually, as I grew older, Louis began taking over the role of being the dominant influence in my life. He was four years older than myself and at fourteen, going on fifteen, he had begun going out with and petting with girls.

I realize now that my big brother was pretty vague about his exploits, but at the time his boastful stories about girls who let him feel their breasts and encouraged him to put his hand up under their clothes and feel them under their knickers, and all kinds of other things I was too young to know about, excited, not so much stirrings of any premature personal desire, but the natural curiosity adolescent boys and girls inevitably develop about sex and each other's bodies. The subject was the great mystery, the ultimate taboo about which in our house, there was a challenging conspiracy to conceal every single fact.

I was about eleven when I began trying to peep when my sisters were undressing, but I never learnt anything of interest this way. Next I tried finding excuses to be playing on the floor when female visitors came to the house, positioning myself so that they had to step over me, giving me the opportunity to look up under their skirts.

Louis was the one who caught me at this game. He called me a 'dirty little devil', but not in a disapproving way. He took me to his bedroom window.

'If you want to see a girl showing the lot, that's where you need to be,' he said, pointing out obliquely across the road. 'From there you can see right into the maid's room next door but one. She strips off and washes right by the window every night when she goes to bed. Because she's up in the attic she thinks she can't be seen, so she never draws the curtains. You never saw such big tits in all your life.'

I had never seen any at all, and the prospect of the peep show and the forbidden excited me.

'What time?' I asked eagerly.

'You young devil,' said Louis, laughing. 'At your age, too! But it's too late for you, my lad. After *your* bedtime. Not till about ten o'clock at night.'

I had my secrets from even Louis. Our home life was not one that inspired any of us to ever confide anything we could refrain from boasting about. Nobody knew about my night prowlings or my climbing escapades.

That night I climbed out of my window over the neighbouring roofs until I reached the vantage point from which I knew I would get a view far better than anything Louis could have seen from across the road. I was about to discover what all the exciting mystery was about.

For about fifteen minutes nothing happened, except that my sense of excited anticipation grew more and more intense. Near-by and distant public chiming clocks, out of synchronization with one another, finally told me that the magic moment of discovery must surely be near.

Another ten minutes went by, but I was now prepared to stay there all night until she came.

Then the light went on, and with joy I realized that from where I was I would have a complete view of most of the room and a full view of the washstand with its flower patterned basin and ewer. If the window had been opened, I could have reached forward and touched it.

She must have been about eighteen, a well built, healthy country girl in the full ripeness of her physical beauty – the type of girl, although I didn't appreciate it at the time, who would too soon lose her voluptuousness and would soon become like most of the womenfolk of her kind – squat, stocky and grossly overweight. She had a plump, rather vaccuous, apple-shining face, but it was not her face I had come to look at.

She walked across the room and disappeared from my view, but I disciplined myself to keep exactly where I was, relying on Louis' information that she would come to the washbasin. If I had moved now, I might have lost my best vantage point to study her naked body.

At last I was rewarded. She came to the window and the washbasin and now she was wearing only a pair of serviceable, unattractive knickers. My fascinated eyes, however were obsessed by the sight of her breasts.

I still believe that I have never seen any woman with more beautiful breasts than this girl, although of course I realize that every first experience has an importance of impact that both makes it unforgettable and in some strange way incomparable.

But certainly it is true that she had very large, and very beautiful breasts. And their weight had not yet strained the pectoralis muscles so that they stood proud and firm from her young body, yet soft enough to change shape and form, with that fluid geometry of the female body which is always delightful and beautiful to see. Her nipples had the pinkness of youth, and stood out proud and high.

I lay there feasting my eyes as she poured water into the basin, then bent over it and soaped and washed each breast in turn, cupping it in her hands like a ripe fruit. I was so near I could have reached out and touched that lovely, forbidden fruit.

Then, turned towards me, she dried each breast separately, taking her time over the procedure, almost as if she intended to show it off for my close inspection.

Finally, with her back now to me, she pulled her knickers off.

My view was of a large, pear shaped bottom, its deep cleft ending in an intriguing vortex where the firmness of her thighs tapered away underneath her body like a natural entrance to the greatest and still unimagined reality of the greatest mystery of all.

While I could see that she was washing this intriguing part of her body, my position was now such that I merely had a view of her bottom. When she took the towel and began to dry underneath herself I began to be possessed by the dismaying thought that she would soon walk away, and I would not see what she looked like from in front.

In desperation, reckless in my determination to discover the truth about girls, I reached out and quickly tapped on the window pane with a finger nail.

She heard the sound without understanding it, and turned. She actually moved right up to the window and looked out so that what I had wanted to see was literally presented in closeup hardly more than a foot away from my face.

I was terribly disappointed. I had expected something utterly different from my own penis and balls, but I had expected the difference to be dramatic. Instead there was an absence of anything – just a thick growth of dark, coarse hair, with a slight but natural parting by a barely recognizable cleft that disappeared underneath her.

That was all there was to it. Girls didn't have anything. They just had nothing but a growth of rather disfiguring hair.

She turned slowly away, and I began silently and cautiously to make my return across the rooftops to my own home.

Yet disappointing though the climax to the adventure had been I must have awakened half a dozen times during that night with the picture of her breasts in my mind, each time recklessly reducing my expectancy of longevity. The fantasies that accompanied these experiences of pre-pubescent sensuality, inspired though they were by the girl, did not in any way involve any participation on her part. They were completely unconnected with copulation, the possibilities of which I did not consciously recognize.

The next evening I was called to my father's study. With him was a middle aged man who lived across the street from us, two doors down!

He had come to my father with the story of having seen me on the roof, peering into the uncurtained window of a neighbouring attic where a servant girl was undressing. The light from the window had made me clearly visible and on glancing out of his own windows he had chanced to see me.

I denied the accusation with the air of complete innocence that I was now able to do most convincingly. And my father, who probably did not want to admit to the possibility that any son of his could have behaved in such a way, found arguments to support my denials. There were a number of boys of my age and build in the terrace. It could have been any one of them, and of them all I was the least likely to have been involved in such disgraceful conduct.

'The boy is only twelve,' he said. 'And, anyway, I glanced into his room at about the time you say this happened and with my own eyes saw him in bed, fast asleep.'

He convinced the neighbour, but I doubt if I completely convinced him, for after a period of several days, during which time he must have given the matter deep consideration, he compelled himself to give me a forthright lecture on the perils of masturbation, and of the evils attendant upon premature carnal interest in the female.

He wrapped it up in a way that was ridiculous and, in retrospect, quite funny. He referred to a middle aged bachelor we knew, and saying that it was not God's will that a man should live alone like that without a woman to look after him, but that the time for such a relationship did not come until one had a home of one's own and needed a wife to attend to the needs which he hinted were primarily those of cooking, mending, washing and producing a family. It was to this end that the Lord had created man in his own image, to emulate him in his behaviour. And to this end, and no other, had he created woman.

And then he gave me a moment of unexpected insight into his own understanding of human nature – and thereby immeasurably increased my own.

'But there is a wickedness in us all to be purged,' he said. 'The man who came here, do you suppose I believe he saw what he saw by chance? He was there at his window to watch the girl himself. The evil he was accusing you of was an evil he knows himself to be guilty of. As for the girl – a Jezebel. Understand, my boy, that women are like this. They flaunt their nakedness to arouse wicked desires in men. It is God's testing of a man that this should be woman's nature, so that he may learn to resist lust. You may be sure that it was no chance that the window was uncurtained, but it was not to a boy on the roof that she was flaunting herself but to a man she knew to be watching her.'

This possibility had never occurred to me although later I was to realize how true it probably was and that many young women do, in fact, indulge an instinct for sexual exhibitionism in this way, well aware that they have an audience they can pretend not to know about.

Although I had been disappointed in what I had seen of the focal point of female attraction, my interest was far from abated.

I knew the simple facts about fucking. Although I had led an urban life, and had not had the country boy's matter of fact introduction to the sex act through watching farmyard animals, I had seen the occasional dog and bitch mating in the street, but that was all.

Throughout the next summer holidays I accompanied my father on what Louis irreligiously called 'the God circus' travelling from town to village and village to town on my father's missionary circuit.

This was the summer when I discovered that the weekly baptismal service was an opportunity for voyeurism, a game of prurient curiosity rather than one of secret eroticism. My father would have undoubtedly resurrected the whip if he had caught his three sons, and the young friends they brought to the peep show, at this game. But the simple fact was that it was the challenge of getting away with doing the forbidden that tempted us, and the whole business was really comparable with knocking on doors and running away into the night.

Much more exciting were the opportunities the travelling mission offered for actual contacts with girls.

My father's congregations were drawn from the local people, and his mission usually had the support of a local church which provided a choir. Sometimes the choirs were mixed, but occasionally they were made up of girls and young women.

It is true that the devil not only gets the best tunes, but the best looking girls, too. On the other hand it can also be true that the rather plain girl will allow petting to go much further than the pretty girl who doesn't have to rely on giving a boy license to attract him and hold his attraction.

Certainly these village and small town choir girls, if not ravishing beauties, were not only surprisingly uninhibited, but they were great fun to be with, had plenty of personality and were good natured with a lively sense of fun.

I was nearly thirteen, and it was spring and the exploratory adventures I had with these girls were simply a phase belonging to opportunity, only vaguely disturbing memories. About this time an incident occurred which commanded Louis's surprised admiration.

A group of us had been playing with catapults in the street and one of the catapults had itself shot up into the air and landed on the roof of a four-storey house.

Without thinking I immediately volunteered to retrieve it.

There was a convenient drainpipe and by now I was quite familiar with shinning up drainpipes. I reached the roof easily and without any difficulty, got hold of the catapult and then glanced down at the street. To my surprise quite a large crowd had gathered to watch me.

I began to think I had probably made a mistake by this public performance, and was sure of the fact when, reaching the level of the fourth floor windows on my way down, a window opened abruptly and a very large and powerful policeman reached out and insisted on 'rescuing' me.

I was taken off to the police station where, shortly afterwards my father arrived. To my surprise, however, I only got a mild rebuke from him for the escapade. Indeed, whilst he agreed with the police that what I had done could not be condoned, he was almost a little boastful of the agility and courage I had shown.

'Used misguidedly for a wrong purpose,' he told the police inspector. 'Urged on, no doubt by older boys. But one must admit that the lad has courage. As to his ability – well, all my sons have been taught gymnastics!

'A healthy mind requires a healthy body, Inspector,' he said.

The Inspector found himself agreeing, and my father walked me home, merely lecturing me quite mildly on my daring.

'What you don't realize, boy,' he said, 'is that you were using your gymnastic abilities in the way of housebreakers, burglars and thieves – common criminals.'

He was not telling me anything that had not already begun to occur to me, although at this point of my life I only had the same kind of recognition of the possibilities as I had about the possibilities of sexual experience with girls.

Later during the summer, I was now thirteen, I had my first real sexual adventure.

My younger sister, Ann, had a friend whose name was Ankie. My parents disapproved of this friendship. There was some social snobbery behind the disapproval, and there was also a religious aspect to it. Ankie wore her hair cut short and the Darbist sect believed that a woman's hair should be worn long. There was probably also some fear that Ankie might be a bad influence upon Ann. Even at ten she had developed quite pronounced breasts and any such evidence of sexuality was bound to make my father suspect that it would be accompanied by undisciplined desires.

My own interest in Ankie was, I realize now, sexually motivated. Because of my rooftop adventure, the female breast was established for the rest of my life as the major cause of erotic feeling and Ankie's little breasts intrigued and fascinated me. I wanted to see them, to touch them, and while I would never, at the age of thirteen, have dared to have asked an older girl to show me her bare breasts, no such inhibitions existed with a girl younger than myself.

I was further attracted by Ankie because I heard my parents discussing how unsuitable she was as a friend for Ann. This at once put her further into the category of what my father would have called 'the forbidden fruit', a fact which immediately stimulated my interest in her.

Ann at this time had an adolescent 'schoolgirl crush' on a friend of mine called Wimpie. I took him into my confidence, telling him that I wanted an opportunity to be alone with Ankie, and suggesting that we made up a foursome to visit some nearby woods.

It was summer again. My other sister Carol collected wild flowers which she would then press, and I proposed that Ann, Ankie, Wimpie and myself could say that we were going to the woods for the same purpose.

Rather to my surprise, probably because I was filled with a guilty sense of anticipation, no objections were raised. And so four innocent little children set off to the woods, laughing as they ran through the trees, and I do not think that even the most worldly cynic could have guessed what their playthings would be or what games they were intent upon playing.

We hurriedly gathered some flowers, all the time penetrating deeper and deeper into the woods, until we reached a high, open area which was free from paths and had plenty of hollows with the protection of bushes, briars and other undergrowth – an ideal spot that would ensure solitude with no danger of the approach of other woodland wanderers without plenty of warning.

'We've picked enough,' I said. 'Shall we stop here for a bit.'

Ankie and Ann exchanged glances, and giggled, then both of them agreed.

'You and Ann can stay here, in this hollow,' I told Wimpie. 'Ankie and I will find somewhere beyond those bushes just over there.'

Nobody raised any objections to the proposed arrangement, although Ankie and Ann looked at one another again, and began giggling.

It was Ankie, running ahead of me, who chose the spot that was to be the scene of my first real sexual experience with a girl. Because the experience was to remain memorable throughout my life, I could describe it even now in photographic detail – the sloping bank of short, sun-warmed grass on which she lowered herself; the bright sunlight high above, the little hollow that was completely surrounded by high, impenetrable bushes except for the small gap, like a tunnel, through which she had led me.

'Isn't it hot?' she said, and began unbuttoning the front of her blouse.

I was so taken aback that I could only stare at her without answering. I couldn't have dreamed of anything more exciting, but I expected to have had to persuade her to bare her little breasts and to be met with at least a token resistance of modesty. I was a little shocked.

The blouse was tucked into her skirt and buttoned right down to the bottom. She pulled it out from her waistband, unbuttoned it completely, and threw it back. Then she leaned back on her elbows, drew her shoulders back, so that her breasts were pushed forward and upwards for my inspection.

'Do you like them?' she said. 'You can feel them, if you want to. They're going to get much bigger, of course. *Much bigger!*'

I went down on my knees beside her. My pulse was racing and I was conscious of my penis trying to lift against the containing restraint of my clothing. I touched the soft but firm swell of flawless flesh with my finger tips.

'How do you know that?' I asked, needing to say something – anything.

'I've been told.'

'Who told you?'

'*Someone!*' she said, and giggled. Then she added: 'I'm going to have really big tits in a year or two, and all the other girls will be jealous.'

Her free and uninhibited use of the vulgar vernacular bewildered me.

'Where did you learn to call them that?' I asked, for I had never imagined that girls knew such words, or used them.

'From – *someone!*' she said innocently.

Apparently she did not regard our purpose of being alone in the hollow to be for cross examination and conversation.

'Aren't you going to take it out?' she asked, almost ordinarily, looking at my trouser front. 'Do you want me to take my knickers off to show you my cunni?'

Without being able to answer I begun fumbling with my buttons, not very successfully, because I seemed to have lost control over my fingers, and because I could not take my eyes off her as she threw her skirt up to her waist and then pulled her knickers off so that I had the full, almost unbelievable sight of everything I had wondered about.

There was just the faintest down of hair beginning to grow around the tiny pink mouth.

'You'd better let me do that for you,' she said unconcernedly, and reached forward, undid my buttons, then carefully pulled my underpants down my legs inside my trousers.

Freed of constraint, my penis rose up and out into full erection. I was filled with a sense of deep embarrassment, partly at showing this sight which had always been associated with private guilt, and partly because I felt ridiculous, kneeling upright like that with all my clothes on and just my trousers opened.

She looked at it critically.

'It's not very big, is it?' she said, then smiled at me sympathetically. 'Never mind, I'm sure it'll grow bigger, like my tits.'

'It *is* big,' I said, defensively, feeling humiliated.

'Well I'm used to a really big one. An enormous one. Though yours is much nicer looking.'

'Whose?' I said.

'*Someone's!*' she said vaguely.

'I want to know who this someone is!' I said. 'Ankie – tell me. *Please* tell me!'

I was sure that all along she had been referring to another boy, and that he was probably a friend of mine. Nothing else seemed possible, and I had to know with whom I made such an unfavourable comparison.

'Oh, well, if you must know – my uncle.' She pouted impatiently. This was not a time for talking, and she knew it. 'You want me to do it to you, don't you?'

Without waiting for my answer to a question I didn't understand anyway, she bent forward and took my penis in her hand and began stroking it up and down in lightly clasping little fingers. It was, after all, only the forbidden thing I was quite familiar to doing to myself, but it was unbelievably more exciting to be having it done to me by a girl sitting in the sun with her breasts bare and her legs wide open for me to kneel between them.

As one sensuality becomes more acute, all the others become subdued to it. I know what it must have looked like, looking down at her like that and at what she was doing. But I have no accurate photographic memory of the actual experience with Ankie, and even immediately afterwards I was unable to capture it, but could only remember with a sense of awe what had happened. I remember vaguely that I began to cry out, and that suddenly I had the violent spasms of familiar relief from tension.

'You don't have any!' she said with surprise, taking her hand away and immediately reaching for her knickers and beginning to put them on.

'Any what?'

'Any come,' she said. 'Any spunk. My uncle has lots. It's messy, too. I suppose you'll get it when you get older. You're funny . . .' she giggled, 'but nice. It's nicer doing it to you. You really ought to give me two guilders, but I don't suppose you have it, and it doesn't matter. It was fun – wasn't it?'

I buttoned myself up, and she tucked her blouse back into her skirt waistband and did up her buttons, too. Now that it was over, all my desires had ebbed, and I felt a sense of guilt and shame. The reality of ten year old Ankie confirmed everything my father had told me about the female being a creature of temptation to a man. At the same time I was intensely curious about her.

I lay down in the grass beside her and after a little silence, I said:

'Tell me about your uncle, Ankie.'

'Well,' she said thoughtfully, 'his is twice as long as yours and three or four times as thick.'

'I don't mean that. I mean when you do it to him. When you started doing it. How often. And about the two guilders.'

'Oh, that!' she said. 'Well, you see, he comes to baby sit when my mother and father go out – about once a week. My brothers and sisters are little and have to be in bed when he comes. I used to have to be in bed, but since last year I've been allowed to stay up later – ready for bed, in my nightdress. Sometimes I used to sit on his knee and he'd read to me. Then one night I felt him like that, and I asked him what it was, and he took it out and showed me it. He said men got like that, and when they did they needed it rubbing. He showed me how to do it. I know you're not supposed to do it to a man if you're a girl, unless you're grown up and married to him, then he puts it inside your cunni and you get babies from his come – did *you* know that? *That's* why you don't have it inside you until you are grown up and married and want babies from doing it.' She shrugged. It appeared to seem so ordinary to her. 'I don't know what's wrong about doing it when a man needs it. But, that first time, he made me promise never to tell anybody I'd done it to him. He said he'd get into terrible trouble. And – and when he put me to bed he gave me two guilders for pocket money. Two whole guilders.'

'After that?' I prompted her.

'Oh, after that I've done it to him every time he comes to baby sit – every week. And he always gives me two guilders – mind you, he used to give me pocket money before then, but not so much. He likes it. And *you* liked it too, didn't you? And I like it, too. It makes me feel all funny. I think I'll like being married and being given babies.' She giggled again. 'When you get older and have some come, maybe you'll be the one who gives me them with yours. 'Cause my uncle'll be too old to be married to.'

As nearly, and as accurately as I can, I've reported on this conversation just as it took place.

I can only hope, for the adventure was outrageously extraordinary, that I've drawn a true picture of a couple of children innocently caught up by the consequences of experience and instincts beyond their control.

I hope I have shown Ankie, not as a wicked and immoral girl, but a child as natural and as innocent in her behaviour as she really was, simply lacking understanding not so much of conventional morality but the reasons for it.

Poor, delightful, little Ankie. I wonder what became of her. Within a week or two of this adventure her parents moved to another part of the country and I never heard of her again.

In later years, recalling this episode I often wondered, too, about the uncle, and the torment of a temptation he had probably never expected to face and, even in giving in to it, must have made compromises that should be taken into account in any judgement of him.

As things turned out the experience with Ankie had immediate effects on my life rather different to those one might have expected.

As much as I had enjoyed the experience with Ankie, she had made me feel ashamed because I had been unable to give her a present.

It wasn't that my father was mean about our pocket money. On the contrary, we were entrusted with all kinds of minor day-

to-day expenditures, and it was regarded as a part of our training.
But we had to account for 'every penny' we were given. The
balance of actual 'pocket money' which we could spend in any
way we saw fit was negligible.

Suddenly I had a need for some money of my own, money
that I could spend as I wanted to. I wanted an independent income and the only way I could acquire this was through stealing,
the possibilities of which hadn't as yet occurred to me. But they
would before long.

One morning only a week or so after the adventure with Ankie,
my father went out and almost immediately there was a sudden
squall of heavy, driving rain. I was on the landing, next to his
study. The landing window was open and the wind blew the
curtains inwards and the rain began driving in.

Quite naturally, I shut the window. Then, quite naturally, I
remembered that my father's study desk sat under his window,
and that he had probably left that window open. So I went into
his room and, finding that I had been right, shut the window.

I was about to leave when I noticed that a desk drawer which
was normally closed and locked was slightly open. I never
thought of resisting the temptation to open the drawer and to
rifle through its contents. Under some draft notes for a sermon I
discovered about sixty guilders in a wad of banknotes – worth
around about five pounds in those days. It was quite a considerable amount of money at that time, not much less than a working
man would have earned in a month and, to me, a fortune.

I took it and stuffed it in my pocket without thinking of the
consequences, and shut the drawer quickly.

I feel very sure that if I had got back to my room and thought
about the nature of my theft, I would probably have extracted
one note and returned the rest, realizing that I might get away
with the theft of, say, ten guilders and that my father, when he
came to miss it might blame himself either for a loss or a mis-
calculation.

I didn't get back to my room. I had just reached the study
door when it opened and there he was, glowering at me with
immediate suspicion.

'What are you doing in my room, boy?' he demanded to know.

I told the truth, which is always a convincing thing to be able
to do.

'I came in to shut your window, father, because of the storm,'
I said.

'Oh, yes. I see,' he said, looking at the window and the limp wet curtains. 'Good boy. As a matter of fact, I remembered it myself and came back.'

But he had remembered more than that. He had remembered the unlocked drawer, and must have come back to lock it, for he walked across the room, fitted his key into the lock and turned it.

'Well?' he said, looking back at me. 'What are you waiting for.'

I ran off to my own room.

Now I was in trouble, and I knew it. As soon as the money was missed, its disappearance would inevitably be connected with myself and my visit to his room during the very brief time when it could have been stolen. If I could have opened his drawer and put the whole lot back I would have done so.

Indeed, I tried, with every key I could find, and also trying to force the lock with my pen knife.

I thought of other solutions to what was the most serious situation I had ever been in. I thought of ransacking the whole room so that it might be supposed that a burglar had broken in, but when I couldn't even open the desk drawer, I had to rule that idea out.

Eventually I decided that there was only one thing for it. Now was when I must leave home, never returning. This seemed feasible. I had what seemed to be a great deal of money and by pretending that I was fourteen I would be able to find work. Added to the fear of my father's wrath was the attractiveness of any escape from my home.

I had acted on impulse when taking all the money, but now I thought my actions out carefully, and in consequence acted much more intelligently. I took nothing at all from my room to suggest that I had left the house with the intention of running away. My plan, which I realize now to have been thoughtlessly cruel, involved a change of clothing. But nobody had to suspect this, so I left the house wearing only what I stood up in, and carrying nothing in my pockets but the stolen money.

I went to the other side of the town and bought myself a cheap pair of trousers, a sweater, jacket and raincoat. At another second hand shop I bought shoes and a pair of socks.

Then I went down to the beach, stripped off all the clothes I was wearing except my underpants, letting them lie where they fell, just above high water mark. Nobody was about, nobody saw me. I put on the new clothing and set off on the Rotterdam road, heading towards Belgium. The frontier, only fifty miles away, seemed like a frontier to freedom to me.

I had been a small boy of six when I had run away before, with no money. This time it was quite different, and as far as I was concerned I had finished with my family for life.

I knew that Ann would cry her eyes out, and I felt badly about that. I knew Louis would be very upset when my clothes were found and it would be assumed that I had been drowned, and I regretted that. But they would get over it and maybe one day, when I was as wealthy and successful as I intended to be, I would reappear into their lives – and very impressed and awed they would be with the man their long-lost brother had turned out to be.

I slept in a barn that night, bought bread and cheese and milk from a village grocery shop the next morning for my breakfast and reached Rotterdam, which I knew quite well, early in the morning. I spent some time in the town, savouring my new found freedom and had a good meal at a cafe.

I ate cheaply, though. I was shrewd enough to realize that my sixty guilders, already considerably depleted by the second hand clothing, would not last forever. As long as I had a reserve of money, I was all right. Since everything depended upon it, every penny I spent had to be replaced as quickly as possible by money earned. This meant that the sooner I was over the frontier the better, but an unanticipated problem had arisen. The new shoes were pinching and I knew that if I undertook the long walk, and still almost all of it lay ahead, I would be crippled before I reached Belgium.

By instinct I had wandered down to the busy dockside area. Here, sitting resting, with my shoes off, on the stone steps of a disused building on De Boomjes, which is a long quay on the right bank of the Maas, I considered my plight. In that busy, bustling background nobody gave a second glance to the young boy except the strutting pigeons.

Just above me, two bridges crossed the river to North Island, beyond the island spanning the Konings Haven water to connect up with the suburb of Feijenoord. The nearer bridge was a road bridge, the farther one carried a railway line to Beurs Station, just round the corner in the city centre.

I sat there watching the ships going down to the Nieuwe Watereg and out to the Hook and the open sea, and felt tempted to change my plans, and be a stowaway. It would have meant no more walking.

And then I found myself watching the trains crossing the railway bridge, and suddenly I saw the whole of my adventure in new perspective. I wasn't a child running away from home this time. I was a boy, leaving home, so why did I have to walk – at least, why walk any farther than the railway station?

I bought myself a ticket to Bergen-op-Zoom, about seven miles from the Belgian frontier and twenty miles north of Antwerp, and arrived there early in the evening. Bergen is a small town, an old town, a barracks town, its main businesses being oyster culture and an export trade in fish.

I had packed a lot into my day and I wanted, so to speak, to take a deep breath before I tackled the adventure of crossing a frontier illegally, so I went down to the waterfront area and found a cheap lodging house that called itself an hotel. The dining room of the hotel also served as a public cafe and was obviously used by the quayside workers; pretty rough and not particularly clean.

The 'hotel' lobby was not much more than a corridor leading to the stairs and the rooms above, with a 'reception desk' built back into the cafe where it also served as the cash desk.

The 'hotelier', who was also the cafe waiter, was in his shirt sleeves. He was around thirty and, confronted by him, I immediately regretted my choice of lodgings. I didn't like the look of him at all, and he didn't much seem to like the look of me when I said, as boldly as I could, that I wanted a room for the night.

'Pretty young, aren't you?' he said.

Strange how what had happened with Ankie had changed me. I wasn't a child any more, and all my fears now were not of situations but of their consequences.

'No law about only being sixteen, is there?' I said.

'*You* – sixteen?' he said. 'Where's your luggage?'

'I'm joining my uncle in Antwerp, but I'm not due there until tomorrow,' I said. 'My things went on ahead. I decided to spend the night here; I thought I'd like to travel on the steam tramway.'

'Pull the other one!' he said.

A buxom, sluttish red-head had joined him behind the counter and had listened to all this. She winked at me.

'Shut up!' she told him, and it was an order given by someone who was used to giving the orders. 'He'll pay his four guilders for his room for the night, won't you – sir?' she said looking at me as she said the final words. 'In advance?' she added, and her eyes asked a question to which I nodded my answer.

It was an outrageous charge of course, and I knew it. But in a way I didn't mind paying over the odds. My reference to Antwerp had been quite deliberate. They guessed about me, and I knew it didn't matter. They were going to help me in another way they didn't know about yet.

'I want a meal, too,' I said.

'Certainly sir,' the red-head said. She looked at the man and laughed, nudging him with her shoulder. 'Give the gentleman a menu.'

I was grossly overcharged for the meal, too. But she could cook, and I went to bed with a solid meal in my stomach, locking my door and wedging the back of a chair under the door knob.

In the morning only the woman was about.

'Look after yourself,' she said as I surrendered my room key. 'And if there's anything else . . .'

I hadn't even had to ask.

'I've got to change some guilders into belga,' I said. 'Might as well do it now, that is if you can do it for me.'

She knew perfectly well that I wanted to avoid going into a bank or exchange bureau.

'How much –' she asked.

'Forty guilders,' I said.

She did a hasty mental calculation, or maybe it wasn't a calculation but an assessment of the situation.

'Twenty belga,' she said.

'That's not much!' I protested.

'Take it or leave it. Think I don't know I'm taking a chance?'

I gave her the guilders.

I did not, of course, take the steam tramway that linked the Dutch town of Bergen-op-Zoom with the Belgian city of Antwerp. I walked, following the course of the Schelde southwards towards the frontier, keeping just off the roads, in the fields, a boy aimlessly out for a walk. I wanted to get the lie of the land, study the actual frontier, consider how I might attempt to get past the frontier guards, and then wait for nightfall to make a daring attempt.

I seemed to have come a long way and, in spite of my sense of direction began to wonder if I could have strayed off the route, when I saw an old man working, clearing a drainage ditch in an adjoining field.

I went over to him and asked how far off and where the frontier was. To my surprise he answered me in Flemish. I was about four kilometres from the frontier, he said.

Then he pointed in the direction from which I had come.

I had crossed the frontier without even knowing it.

It didn't go well after that. Flemish and Dutch are languages so similar that I had no problems on that score, but I could not find anyone who would give me a job, and of course I could only look for casual work of a kind where no questions would be asked. In my mind I had worked out a reasonable story but I got the same kind of jolt that naive holiday makers get who look at the glossy holiday tour brochures, and expect the reality to be like the pictures.

The truth is that I looked only thirteen. The truth is that my manners and speech betrayed me as a runaway from a respectable middle class Dutch family. The truth is that this was 1934.

Just across Belgium's other frontiers, in Germany, the Jew bating had begun; in France King Alexander and Louis Barthou were assassinated. It was the year in which Dollfuss was murdered and Roehm dragged from his bed and shot. There was a sense of unease and unrest, although the armies of Europe were not yet in uniform.

Armies they already were – of unemployed.

And that was the sharp, harsh fact. There weren't jobs to be had, not even if you had the skills, the qualifications and the right cards.

People were kind on the farms and in the villages where I asked if there was any kind of job I could do. They never asked awkward questions, whatever their suspicions. People who are finding life difficult find no entertainment in making life difficult for others.

So while I was not given work it was not unusual to be given a mug of tea, perhaps a hunk of bread and some cheese, even a nip of home-made beer. Occasionally I got a few small coins to 'help me on my way'. Once I got a sudden hug and a kiss from a, by no means too old, farm labourer's wife, responding in a way only I was aware of and she obviously didn't intend as she hugged me impulsively against the soft cushions of her quite enormous breasts. Yet afterwards, when the farmhouse was well behind me and reality had become memory, I started to blubber like a child, not missing something I had recently sacrificed but something I had never really had in all the years of my life and which I had now left behind.

I had no great adventures as I worked my way southwards towards the forests, travelling aimlessly and quite slowly, sleeping in barns or isolated outhouses. I had no memorable moments of danger, and I managed to keep my remaining money more or less intact.

What wore me down, crushed my spirit and made me slowly come to terms with the hopelessness of this kind of independence and freedom, was the little things. The practical realities nobody would think of unless they actually experienced it.

Never to have a toilet seat to sit on, and to get used to using grass instead of paper to clean myself, sometimes, to later discomfort, inadequately. Never to have a bath, never to have hot water for a wash. To constantly have dirty feet, and to have to wash my socks in cold water and wait for them, sometimes interminably, to dry again. My trousers lost their shape, the bottoms became stained. The raincoat became torn and soiled. The neck of my sweater became greasy. I began to be able to smell myself. It began to get colder at night. More and more often it rained, and I was caught in it, and my clothes did not dry out properly.

My transformation from the cocky, self confident boy who had bought a railway ticket at Rotterdam to the unkempt, frightened child who was ferretted out of the undergrowth of a wood near Ramilles by an alert young policeman, took seven weeks.

My tail was between my legs. I was what I looked and was recognized to be; a frightened child on the run, like a lost young animal unable to fend for itself.

They gave me a bath first. They found me some clean clothes that more or less fitted – I think they belonged to the son of the desk sergeant at the police station to which I was taken. And they gave me a meal, the best meal I've ever had in my life – hot food, meat, steaming gravy. I wolfed it down with little regard for table manners.

And then I talked. I answered all the questions. I wanted to go back home. I wanted Louis, Ann, my bedroom, even the predictable sternnesses and angers of my father and the prim aloofness of my mother. I wanted Jaantze with her apple-crinkled face and her indecisiveness about whose side to take when there was trouble.

I had been caught in the morning and early in the afternoon someone had cut through a lot of red tape, I was on my way home. There were brief and no doubt waivered formalities at the frontier station where one plain clothes man handed me over to another, and when we reached the Hague there was a police car waiting to drive me home.

'You're quite a lad, aren't you,' said the young plain clothes man with friendly reassurance. 'You know, it was pretty cruel on your family, but, by God, you fooled us all with that fake suicide a couple of months ago. Nobody questioned it. You were written off.'

My spirits began to rise, but alas, the Darbists apparently disregarded the story of the fatted calf.

My father was waiting for us, and he was in no mood to greet a repentant lamb into the fold.

'Well, here he is,' said the young plain clothes man cheerfully. 'And a merry dance he's led us all, eh? What do we do with him, I wonder?'

'Reform school,' said my father coldly. 'It's the only measure left.'

I don't remember what else he said. I think my mother kissed me. I remember that Louis and John, Carol and Ann all hugged me. I remember that there were tears in Jaantze's cow-like eyes. But the moment and the opportunity had gone.

Oh, my father, if only you could have kissed me then!

II

An Afternoon When Childhood Ended

I have known two bottle-a-day men.

One of them drank whisky. He started his drinking at the end of the day, took it straight and usually slept where and as he was when the bottle was empty. It was a way of committing suicide and he died, in due course, of cirrhosis of the liver.

The other man was a gin drinker, and he started before breakfast, spread it out over the day, diluting it five to one with tonic. The last time I met him he was in his sixties, had recently remarried – and not just for companionship – and was laughing his head off because an insurance company doctor had given him a clean bill of health.

Dilute what is potentially dangerous, don't concentrate it! I don't have any other suggestions to make in this respect and I think the same principle can be applied to young boys and reformatory schools.

I was thirteen when, backed by my own father's recommendation, they put me into a reform school.

I don't want to say a thing against the people who ran that Reformatory, except that there were bars on the dormitory windows and broken glass embedded in the cement capping of the high walls. I don't suppose the conditions were less tolerable than in some boarding schools of only a few years ago to which wealthy parents paid high fees for the privilege of sending their sons.

It was spartan.

We used to fill the tin water bowls in the washroom before we went to bed. There was only one slow running tap, and filling all the basins took a long time. It was now winter and we had to get up, in the dark, at six in the morning. The washrooms were bitterly cold and by filling the bowls overnight we could scramble through our ablutions quickly. In his soap dish each boy kept a stone of his own choosing. When the water in the bowl had frozen over during the night, the stone was used to break the ice.

But the food, though plain, was good. The classroom tuition, although it catered for a below average level of literacy, was sound. The workshops, in which we spent much of our days in being taught trade crafts, were well equipped and the training was practical.

What was hopelessly wrong was the concentration of all the embryonic elements of a criminal society in circumstances of infection.

We learnt far more from one another than ever we learnt in the classrooms or workshops. Above all, we learnt the distinction there was between 'them' and 'us'. We learnt to recognize that each one of us, in our different ways, did not belong to ordered society.

Most of the boys were thieves; and burglary, robbery and violence was the currency of most of our conversation.

It was here, in the reformatory, that I first began to realize and consider my own potential as a burglar.

I came up against, for the first time in my life, the knowledge and the realities of homosexuality. With one possible exception, that I only appreciated much later, I don't think we had any boys there who had inherent homosexual characteristics. It wasn't an emotional thing. It wasn't even a substitute for heterosexuality. It was simply an inevitability that arose through the crowding of pubescent boys, mostly coming from backgrounds where moral standards were low, into packed dormitories. Constantly erecting penises could not always be concealed, were the subject of ribald jokes, and there were inevitably boys who showed them off proudly. We had one boy the far end of my dormitory who waited to gather an audience before he performed his nightly masturbation – not as sexual exhibitionism, but to take bets on how far up his body, on which ink lines were drawn, he would ejaculate his semen.

I knew that homosexual acts, ranging from mutual masturbation to sodomy, took place in some of the dormitory beds after the lights went off by a time switch, but I was one of the majority of the boys who never became involved in it.

It wasn't a sense of right or wrong, of censure or disgust even. It may have been something to do with my father's total lack of physical affection towards me, or I may have the experience with Ankie to thank. Whatever the cause I could fantasize about the flesh of women, but I had an antipathy towards contact with the flesh of the male so strong that throughout my life I have, almost instinctively, avoided even shaking hands with a man when it has been possible to do so without being discourteous.

Anyway my interest in sex was unexpectedly diverted into at

least a healthier path by a boy called Jan who occupied the next bed to me.

Jan was an orphan and his only relative was his sister with whom he lived in Amsterdam. He was fourteen and she was seven years older than him, and a prostitute.

Jan worked as a tout for his sister, and he was also an outlet for the sale of pornographic photographs of her, and of her taken with men. He had managed to smuggle a collection of these photographs into the reformatory with him, and they had become very well thumbed by the time I came to see them.

For the first time in my life I saw descriptively detailed pictures of the union between a man and woman and even though the positions of Jan's sister with the men in the pictures were contrived exhibitionism, she was a beautiful girl.

I found myself filled with an impatient eagerness to have such an experience with a woman. It tormented me. My ambition to be out of the reformatory was inspired by it.

I made my first escape quite easily. During an exercise period in the main yard, there was an unattended tradesman's supply van. I simply got into the back when nobody was looking, crouched down behind some empty cardboard containers, and was driven out to freedom. After a mile or two I dropped off the back of the van and began the ten mile walk home. There was nowhere else to go, but I felt that I could rely on my brothers and sisters to help me and hide me.

I was picked up by the police about an hour later, and taken straight back to the reformatory. The only punishment I got was a lecture and isolation from the other boys in a cellar area for a couple of days.

I went back to my companions something of a hero, several of whom wanted to know if I intended to try it again, suggesting that, if so, they would accompany me.

The idea was exciting and gave us something to think about and talk about. The 'Big Break Out' was a great adventure, and we made the most of it. I was aware, however, that I would have to be devious if I were to retain my leadership of the exploit. The idea had centred around me, in the first place, because of the cheeky way in which I had made an escape, but the truth was that any boy who had really wanted to could always have got out in exactly the same way.

Until then, nobody had ever thought about escaping. Nobody was serving a long sentence, and for many of the boys life in the

reformatory was probably preferable to the life they had had
outside.

My leadership was likely to be soon challenged because the
idea attracted the hard core of the most criminal element in the
reformatory, among whom I was the amateur. Indeed, had I
not inspired the idea, I would have been the last boy the others
would have invited to join them in the adventure.

The natural leader would have been a boy we called Danno.
He was fifteen, nearly sixteen and this was the second reform
school he had been in. Both Danno's father and one of his older
brothers were serving prison sentences. He was the youngest of
three sons, and they had all had reformatory school experience
and were all criminals.

Danno would inevitably have taken over the leadership of the
adventure and treated me as a protégé with good promise, had I
not been determined that it was *my* exploit.

In the dormitory where the affair was first discussed Danno
said that the exploit must be limited to twelve boys. It must take
place at night so that several hours would elapse before it was
discovered that we were missing. One of his brothers was a
'driver' – that is, he specialized in selecting and stealing cars for
get-away purposes. When we had decided on a date, he would
make contact with his brother. Something would be arranged –
a van, a lorry, or even, audaciously, a coach or bus – to meet us at
an arranged pick-up point and time. The problem was how to
get out at night, for the dormitories were locked before lights-out.

At that point in the preliminary discussion I was able to assert
my claim to leadership. 'No trouble,' I said. 'There's a bar in
the window beside my bed that is loose. It is easy to remove it –
I've already tried. There's a drainpipe I can reach, to the right of
it. The rest is simple. We know where the dormitory keys are – in
the housemaster's bedroom. I borrow them and let you all out.'

Danno shook his head. 'You're crazy, young Hoff,' he said. 'It
would take a bloody spider to get down that wall.'

'Want to bet that I'm not a bloody spider?' I asked.

Danno managed to be rich in our currency, and had been
winning well recently in the tossing-off betting.

'You're on, Hoff,' he said. 'Five fags says he'll break his fucking neck. Any takers?'

There were, hesitantly, several. They were all familiar with
that wall, but suddenly this had become a much more serious
thing than the vulgar fun of watching a frigging.

I removed the bar, squeezed through the aperture and by holding on to the adjoining bar, I was able to stand upright on the narrow window ledge. Then with tremendous concentration, I swung myself outwards towards the right, at the same time balancing my body weight inwards towards the wall. With my right hand I found and held the drainpipe, let myself become like a pendulum, then steadying myself, got a firm hold and quickly shinned down the drainpipe. I then quickly made my way to the housemaster's bedroom, took the keys and returned to the dormitory through the corridor door.

'Jesus!' said Danno, 'you *are* a fucking spider. You bloody knew you could do it, too, didn't you?'

'If it can be climbed,' I said, 'I can climb it. I'll put the keys back, and be with you again in a few minutes. Tie a sheet to the head of my bed and swing it out to me when I'm up the drainpipe. No point in making it more difficult than it need be.'

I was back within ten minutes, and after that it was *my* escape with Danno in charge of the detailed organizing.

Someone said: 'But how do we get out of the yard?'

'I'll climb the wall,' I said. 'I take with me a rope made of sheets tied together for the rest of you to come up. We put a blanket over the glass.'

There were no arguments this time about my abilities.

The escape took place three weeks later and went off well. It was an adventure, a challenge to authority rather than escape from interminable and intolerable incarceration. Despite arguments, when everybody was safely over the wall, I insisted on going back to return the sheets and blankets to the dormitory, to lock the dormitory door behind me and return the keys to the housemaster's room before making my third climb of the night to rejoin the escapers.

'God, I can just see their faces when they discover we've gone,' said Danno. We were crowded in the stolen van his brother had borrowed. 'They'll never know how we got out.'

But, of course, they did. It is a myth that there is honour among thieves. There is always a sneak, and there was one this time.

I was dropped off at a point that I said would suit me, which was, of course quite near my home, and I spent the rest of the night in the garden toolshed. In the morning, when I thought it might be safe to do so, I crept up to the house and, seeing Jaantze alone in the kitchen when I looked through the window, let myself in.

Everything had to depend on Jaantze on whose sympathy I felt sure I could rely. All I needed was just a little money and I was beginning to have strong faith in my powers of persuasion.

Jaantze did not look in the least surprised to see me.

'They were right!' she said, and looked at me pityingly. 'They said you'd make straight back here, for all your cleverness.'

'They?' I said, taken aback. 'Cleverness?'

'*I* don't call it cleverness,' said Jaantze. 'They say it's a miracle you weren't killed. And then to come back with the sheets and to climb the outside wall a second time! Showing off, that's what you were doing, Armand.'

I turned back to the kitchen door, deciding to rely on Jaantze for nothing more than an uncompromising silence about my visit.

'It's no use, you know!' she said. 'You may as well stay and face the music – and it mightn't be as bad as you think. If you go, well you can trust me to say nothing, but you won't get far. This time they're really looking for you, and you aren't going to make fools of them again.'

The trouble was that I could only get as far as I could walk. All undercapitalized ventures fail. I nodded miserably and closed the door on my avenue of escape.

'That's a good lad,' she said, and added with a surprising note of authority. 'They can wait a bit longer, I reckon – your father for you, and your mother for what was to be her breakfast. Sit you down, and get that into you.'

There were eggs and bacon and hot coffee and when I was coming to an end of them, Jaantze went out. It was not she who returned when the door reopened, but my father who came into the kitchen.

There wasn't going to be a fatted calf. There wasn't even going to be a forgiving welcome. But neither, it seemed, was there going to be an unholy row from my earthly representative of the Holy Father!

'I've been having some discussions . . .' he began.

I have to make my own deductions about their true nature and with whom they were. But it seemed that as far as the authorities were concerned, and that meant both the police and the reformatory officials, I was regarded as a spirited and courageous youngster who had suffered from a harsh home background and who had had the courage, when the limits of toleration had been passed, to try to be independent a little too soon. Taking the money from my father's desk had been wrong, but it was a family matter, like a wife, who was kept short of housekeeping, helping herself to her husband's loose change. It had been a mistake ever to put me in a reformatory. But when I had been there, I had been one of their best behaved boys – apart from the fact I seemed to be a born escapologist. The companionship compelled upon me at the school had not been in my best interests. Nor, on the other hand, did they really want a boy of my talents and remarkable skills among them. They were running a school for bad boys, not a maximum security jail for the most hardened of criminals.

The upshot of it was that I made, with my father, a formal appearance at a juvenile court session later that morning and I was discharged into his care, he being given private counsel while I awaited him in an outer room. I never knew what was said to him, but he obviously found it disconcerting.

So now I was back home, with my father obviously a little nervous about disciplining me.

Boys are young devils, believe me. Treat a kid the right way and maybe he'll give you blind loyalty and obedience through thick and thin – I'm only guessing about that. Treat him the wrong way and you can expect no mercy whatsoever. I know the truth about that.

I'd got my father just where it suited me. Anything wrong I was caught doing now, he'd get the blame. Maybe there was a rough justice in that – I only saw my advantage at the time.

My fourteenth birthday came close after the death of my grandmother. Great Aunt Martha, who was very deaf, came to the funeral and remained with us. I transferred to High School and found I could take it all in my stride, especially the languages.

In short, for a few weeks I took a breather and let things settle down, but underneath the surface I was poised on a springboard, tense, excited, full of secret intentions and determinations. I wasn't the adolescent who only a few months ago had stolen some money from his father's desk and run away from home.

How does one measure age? I wasn't much older in time. I wasn't much older in experience; not really, not yet. But in knowledge and in character I had already irrevocably crossed the enormous gulf between the child I had been and the man I was to be.

I was on the springboard, poised to dive into *my* chosen life – into the deep end! From the high board!

I was going to burgle. Not perhaps, not sometime in the

future – but for sure, and now, as soon as possible. Just let them all stop being aware of me and keeping their eyes on me. The dormitory talks with Danno and the other experienced young thieves in the reformatory were responsible for this decision.

I was going to have women too. Not one day, but now and as soon as possible. Just let me commit one robbery and I'd buy that first experience the same night. The photographs of Jan's sister showing exactly what the experience was were responsible for that.

And then one evening it all began to happen, though not in the way I had planned or with the results I had anticipated. Great Aunt Martha had a visitor, and left her room to go downstairs and entertain the caller.

It was my first chance to look around the old woman's room, and she had money hidden everywhere. A few banknotes in a drawer. More at the bottom of a trinket box. Some stuffed under the mattress. Yet more under a corner of the carpet.

It seemed obvious that she was a bit queer in her mind. It was equally obvious that she couldn't possibly remember all her hiding places, or know how much was in any of them.

I helped myself to one note from this place, one note from another, milking every hoard I could find, not counting how much I was taking but knowing that it would be enough.

Then I went downstairs and out by the kitchen door and headed for the city's red-light district.

I was just fourteen and to tell the truth I more wanted to have *had* my first experience than to actually have it. I was nervous and self conscious because I was doing this deliberately, and it wasn't going to happen naturally and unexpectedly. That is not a good thing, and age has nothing to do with the fact. I was conscious of the fact that I couldn't command an erection and frightened lest when the time came either awe or anxiety would dominate my mind and I'd just make a fool of myself.

However, I went to the street of prostitutes, to the established place where they practised their profession, a boy just turned fourteen determined to discover what it was like to fuck a woman.

I walked the length of the street, looking at the girls surreptitiously and my fears, that anxiety might prove a reason for being incapable of achieving my purpose, soon left me. For although none of the girls took the slightest notice of the fourteen year old boy walking past, the window display of breasts had such an increasingly erotic effect on me that I began to realize that if I walked up and down the street enough times I would eventually experience orgasm without even having spoken to one of the girls.

Actually I did walk the length of that street three times, for usually, even in the business of prostitution, it is the woman who makes the opening approach and invitation. Even in a 'red lamp' street selection is still, instinctively, the woman's privilege. There is more rape in marital beds than in brothels!

If I had passed apparently unnoticed by the girls the first time I walked the length of the street not regarded as a potential client because I was a child, the second time I was aware that I was being seen and looked at, although ignored.

The third time, they all knew and understood. I *was* there for business, a young boy lacking the courage or experience to make the approach that nobody was making to me – not just because I was an improbable client, but because the police clamped down on them for corruption if they did business with children.

I had hardly begun my third tour of the window shopping than a buxom young blonde leaned so far out of the window that her breasts nearly came out of her dress, and called to me: 'Hey, kid! Go on home, there's a good boy. You're too young. Nothing for you here.'

The girl at the next window laughed; added with vulgar frankness: 'Come back when you're a bit bigger and it's a bit longer, sonny.' I hurried out of earshot of them, then slowed down a little. I wasn't coming so far and then going back home without having the experience I had been dreaming of, and had stolen money to have.

The girl at the window at which I finally braved myself into actually stopping at was a little older than the other two who had spoken to me.

'So?' she said.

'I . . . I want . . .' I said awkwardly.

'Yes, I know what you want,' she said, rather wearily I thought.

'I have money,' I told her quickly.

'You all have that, too!' she told me wryly.

'Then, will you . . .'

'Go away,' she said, turning from the window. Then she looked over her shoulder at me. 'I've a kid of my own, older than you. For Christ sake, go away will you!'

'I'm sorry,' I said awkwardly.

She gave me one last look.

'You won't get what you want here, anyway. We've all got our livings to think of, and anybody who gave it to you would be out of business if the police knew. And the police know. Believe me, they know.'

She withdrew from the window, shut it, and the curtains closed on her, on her life as I had glimpsed it without having then any perceptive understanding. But that woman is one of the women I've thought about many times during my life – with increasing compassion as I have grown older.

At the time she might well have caused my resolve to weaken. As I neared the end of the street, however, I was, at last, solicited. She had red hair, and as little as there was of the upper part of the dress she was wearing was a vivid green. Her skin was extraordinarily white, almost translucent and she was resting her almost naked breasts in her hands, cupping them upwards.

'You want to enjoy yourself?' she called down softly.

The uncertainties, the humiliations, the sense of something like shame that had all belonged in turn to my mind since I had first entered the street were swept away in the surge of excitement as everything suddenly resolved itself in this one girl and myself – she who could and would give what I could and would pay to be given. I ached for the unknown.

'Five guilders?' she said.

I couldn't speak. I could only nod.

'Then don't hang about out there. Come in quickly. Door on your right,' she said, and drew the curtains to.

By the time I got into the room, the green dress had already been discarded, and she was wearing a white slip. She held her hand out without a word, and I took some of Aunt Martha's money out of my pocket, without counting it, and gave it to her. There was at least as much as she had asked for, probably more. She looked at it quickly, and put it into a drawer, then let the slip fall over her shoulders, to slide down her body so that in the dim light she seemed to be standing in a pool of whiteness.

She was not completely naked. She was wearing tiny green lace panties with a cut-away crotch which made their removal unnecessary and through which strong black, and not red, hair stood out in a bush neatly trimmed, like a hedge.

It was, of course, her job to know the male in all his moods and at all his ages. I realized later that she summed me up very quickly when she realized that it was her breasts, and not the erotic genital exhibition, that compelled my attention.

There was a big, red plush settee in the room; indeed, I remember no other furnishings. She went over to it, and sat down, and beckoned me to her side. I remember being vaguely relieved that I was not being told to undress while she sat and watched me. As I reached her she took the heaviness of her breasts in her hands and offered them to me.

'Go on!' she said. 'With your hands. With your mouth. No nibbling, though. No biting.'

The immediate temptation was irresistible to me and, the moment her hands were free, I felt them at the buttons of my trousers, opening them. The next moment my penis was in her hand and I had a quick glimpse of the utterly disinterested expression of her face as she pulled down on the stiff shaft, at the same time delicately touching the frontal part of the glans with her extended finger tips. It was for all the world like a milkmaid milking a cow. The whole experience was over with about half a dozen caressive strokes and as I came she held my penis to direct the ejaculate between her breasts to prevent any soiling of the settee.

As soon as it was over, she pushed me away, walked across the room, and came back unselfconsciously drying her body. She began putting the slip on again.

'I thought . . .' I managed to say.

'I've given you what you needed,' she said. 'You can have anything you want, of course. You name it, I'll tell you what it costs. But *that* was five guilders' worth and, by the look of it, from now on you're wasting a working girl's time, so button up and piss off.'

I got out. When I left the house, she was already back at the window. She didn't even look at me as I went by.

Like nurses, like wives, like any categorization of women you care to think of, prostitutes are all kinds of women. The job's always the same; the women are always different. What a bitch that girl would have been if circumstances and experience had made her, say, a schoolteacher instead of a whore.

My mouth was dry. I felt sick. I found a peppermint in my pocket. It had a filthy taste and I spat it out.

That night I swore to myself I'd never have anything to do with a woman again. My father was right when he said it was woman's nature to corrupt and debase men. Then I gave myself the escape clause. *If* I did, it certainly wouldn't be with prostitutes.

*

Inconclusive though the experience had been, I had got something out of my system and my thoughts now concentrated on the other of my goals in which I would not be relying on anyone else for the excitement and the thrill.

Great Aunt Martha never missed her money, but what I had left of it soon slipped through my fingers.

The focus of attention had now gone off me and about a week after the adventure in the street of prostitutes I was walking home from school one evening when I passed a house that was apparently being vacated for a period of several days.

There was a car at the roadside and the family – a man, his wife, a young girl who was obviously their daughter, and a dog – were leaving the house, the man carrying two suitcases. A woman from the adjoining house was out on her doorstep, saying goodbye to them.

'We'll be away about three days, Grethe,' the man said. 'There's been no time to organize anything. Would you take in the milk, and see that the papers are pushed through the letter box – no point in advertising that the place is empty.'

I bent down as if to tie a loosened shoe lace, and listened to the conversation. It seemed that there had been a sudden family death and the family were going away, at short notice, to attend the funeral. I doubt if any of them even noticed the schoolboy on his way home. I loitered at the end of the street until the car had driven off and the neighbouring woman had gone back into her own house. Then I went back and had a good look at the house.

It was a substantial town house, recently re-painted and with heavy, expensive curtains at all the windows of its four floors. The window glass shone in the late afternoon light. The owners were obviously as well off as their two year old foreign car, their clothes and their luggage had suggested.

I made my way round to the back of the properties, for I had learnt from Danno and the other boys at the reformatory that this was usually the safest way to make an entry. It was unpromising.

I had another look at the front facade. On the third floor a sash window had been left very slightly open, and right next to it was a drainpipe leading down to the ground. There were no problems at all about getting into the house, but there was the problem of a street lamp right opposite the house. Not being seen by some casual passer-by, in what would obviously be a little used street at night, was a sheer gamble. I had not, and never have had the slightest desire to be a gambler. It is a disastrous weakness that no criminal can afford and I assure you that the movies which suggest that all criminals haunt the race tracks and the gaming rooms as reckless gamblers have it all wrong – not the successful ones, anyway.

The successful professional doesn't drink much, doesn't gamble much, doesn't talk much and trusts nobody, women least of all. It is a business in which there are too many inherent risks to add to them needlessly.

I had to have darkness. It was as simple as that. Well, I thought, that wouldn't be difficult.

I said goodnight to the family early, telling them I was tired. Since my return home, I had taken to locking my bedroom door at night, wanting the new habit to be challenged. Of course it had been. From the temporary position of strength, I had got away with it when I had called out that I wasn't a child any more, to be tucked in at night, and to have people looking in to see if I was asleep.

I was completely prepared for the adventure that now lay ahead. I locked my room door, changed my shoes for plimsols, slipped the rubber bands round my ankles that were to be used like bicycle clips round my trouser legs, took the length of prepared knotted rope I had bought and concealed under a loosened floorboard, and went out through the window.

The rope, tucked in behind a drainpipe, would never be seen at night, and had been prepared as my way in and out of the house at night when I was supposedly in bed.

It was still quite early in the evening.

Danno had once said: 'The best time is when people are still up and about, with the radio on, talking, having a drink, making noises. As long as the night's full of noises, you're pretty safe if you happen to knock something over. The worst time is when everybody's gone to bed and there are no noises. That's when you can't afford to make a sound.'

This adventure went exactly as I had planned it.

I dealt with the street lamp by shinning up the lampost and removing the bulb. There were lit windows in both the adjoining houses, and I could hear a radio playing loudly. I found my drainpipe and it felt secure. I went up it easily, and getting in the window gave me no trouble.

I had brought a small torch, and I took my time, exploring

the rooms, floor by floor. In the main bedroom I found a trinket box in a drawer. There were rings, brooches, necklaces and a watch. I couldn't value them, but they were by no means rubbish. In a drawer at *his* side of the bed I found a gold cigarette case and a packet of french letters. I took both.

The real find was unexpected, on the ground floor, in the kitchen. *She* kept an old chocolate box in the knife drawer. I nearly ignored it, but something made me look into it. It was divided up into sections and, oh, she was a good, methodical housewife, that woman. She budgeted for everything, and put the money aside, in that box, week by week – so much for the milk, so much for the window cleaners, so much for the quarterly gas and electricity bills.

And the quarterly bills must have been just about due. Altogether there was about six hundred guilders, that was about £50.

The front door had an ordinary tumbler lock, and needed no key from the outside. I let myself out, and walked away.

What a way to make money, I thought. And somewhere in the city, every night, there had to be a score of houses practically asking to be entered and robbed. It was just a matter of keeping one's eyes and ears open, not being impatient, never gambling but always taking an opportunity when it was recognized.

During that year I did about a dozen robberies. I never found quite so much cash again but soon, by chance and cunning, I found an outlet for the watches and jewellery I stole.

The chance was that one evening, in a busy shopping street, I recognized Danno's brother who had driven the truck in which we had made our getaway after breaking out of the reform school. I had given none of the boys my address, nor taken any of theirs. At the time that had seemed wise. I hadn't wanted to be involved with them once I got away. But the trinkets and watches I had now accumulated from three burglaries were becoming a problem to me. Not only did I want to turn them into whatever money I could get for them, but they represented danger. I had a safe hiding place for them, of course – a cache in the eves of the house, reached from the attic, but I wanted rid of this evidence of the secret side of my life. And it occurred to me that Danno's brother might help, so I followed him.

The chase involved a bus ride into a poorer quarter of the town. He was a young man who stood out in a crowd and that made him easy to shadow because he could be picked out a street away. His walk was an impudent swagger. He had broad shoulders, and a head of short, unruly, curling blonde hair. He was continuously looking back over his shoulder, but not because he suspected that he was being followed. He eyed every attractive girl up and down with open, frank admiration, usually speaking to them with a laughing grin as his head turned and they went by.

I wished I had known what it was that he said, because it certainly worked, and he got away with it. For every one of those girls, when she passed me a moment or two later, showed by the expression on her face that she had just had something quite outrageous said to her and that she had loved it.

I followed him to the street where he lived and the house where he lived and then I went home. That night I got, from my cache, just the gold cigarette case. Danno's brother was the only known contact I had with the criminal underworld, and since I was now in business as a burglar I couldn't risk trying to find a fence by picking on a likely jewellers as I had done four years before when I had stolen the coin from the museum. I saw now that that had been taking the kind of chance I could no longer afford.

I decided to try to dispose of just the gold cigarette case first. It was the one thing I had been able to value in jewellers' shop windows, where similar cases were priced around eight hundred guilders. I knew I would have to take very, very much less than even the second hand value, but I wanted to know what sort of depreciation of value there was on goods that were known to be stolen.

I mustn't pretend that I was clever enough to plan what happened. I simply knew that I was taking no risks by going to Danno's brother and saying that I wanted to sell a stolen cigarette case, and believing that somehow a sale would result.

My luck was in when I went round to his home the next afternoon. It was he who answered the door, obviously on his way out when I had rung the bell. He did not recognize me immediately.

'Danno gave me this address,' I said.

'Danno?' Then he knew me, and grinned. 'I've got you. You're the kid Danno called a spider. So they didn't pick you up?'

'That's right.'

'That's *smart*! What do you want?'

'I need to raise some money – in a hurry.'

Danno's brother was only open-faced some of the time. Now he looked very cautious indeed.

'You did say *raise*?'

'That's right. I've got a gold cigarette case. . . .'

'Stolen?'

'That's right.'

He started to laugh. It went from the back of his mouth going, spasm by spasm, down his throat, until he was almost hysterical with it and his eyes began to water. He rocked with it.

'All bloody mighty!' he said as the laughter began to die down. 'Well, that's cool.'

'I've got it here,' I said, patting my pocket.

Then we did business. He drew me into the hall passage, and examined the case. He weighed it appreciatively in his hand. He said he would have done a deal with me himself, make me an offer, but he had no money. He could, however, sell it for me, taking a percentage for his trouble. I'd have to leave him free to make the deal and get what he could. I could come back in the evening.

I said that suited me.

He let me out and I walked away alone.

I began to make my way back to the town centre, but a few minutes later I saw a cafe across the road and realized I was thirsty. I went in and bought myself a pastry and a glass of coke, and sat at a table near the window consuming them. I was half way through the drink when who should walk by but Danno's brother.

The opportunity was an obvious one and this time I was much more cautious in following him. The shop he took me to was a shoe repairers, but he wasn't carrying any shoes for repair and when he came out about five minutes later he wasn't carrying any repaired shoes. On the other hand, as he came out, he was still putting his wallet away into an inner pocket.

I picked up a hundred guilders from Danno's brother that night, and when he said that he'd always be glad to help me in the same way at any time in the future I thanked him and said that I would keep in touch.

The next day I visited the shoemaker myself and got myself a fence.

I took in a pair of shoes for repair and when he handled them, his hand encountered the best of my collection of stolen rings. I had felt fairly certain that the three stones set in it were real diamonds and as he looked at the ring I knew I was right.

'What's this?' he said.

'For sale, if you are interested,' I said.

He stared at me, uncertain and hesitating.

'I can tell you the house it was stolen from and the date,' I said. 'There's quite a lot more stuff of the same kind – watches, brooches, necklaces . . .'

We went into the back of the shop, and I disposed of all the proceeds of my first two robberies, and thereafter, for more than a year I did regular business with the old man. He only handled things that could be worn or carried as accessories by travellers going into Belgium or Germany. He was a handling agent, really, nothing more, in an established international network that dealt with nothing big and didn't have to because the volume of their business was enormous.

It was not the most rewarding way of disposing of stolen property, but it suited me and must have suited a lot of petty thieves in the countries where the network operated. There were no risks. If anyone was picked up, even if they talked, the trail could only lead to one contact up the chain, one contact down.

I was glad to have got rid of all my stolen property – all, that was, except the stolen packet of french letters. Those I had taken to carrying around with me, not with an immediate intention of usage but with a premonition that sooner or later they would be needed and that when the occasion did arise, this time it wouldn't be planned.

And of course, when it did I forgot all about them!

I was fifteen by this time. I had been asked to deliver a parcel to an elderly, sick member of the church at Delft, about five miles from the Hague. It was summertime. I was on holiday from school and now had a bicycle.

When I got to Delft I had difficulty in finding the address. Several people had given me directions and eventually I knew that I was in the right area, a rather shabby, working class district, but I still could not find the back street where the old man lived.

A pretty girl, coming out of a shop with a carrier bag, obviously belonged to the district, so I asked her for directions. She smiled, said she was going that way, that it was difficult to explain how to get there, but she would show me.

I walked beside her, pushing the bike and she gratefully let me hang the heavy carrier bag on the handlebars. We talked as we walked. Her name was Hennie, and she was sixteen. She was the kind of nice girl a boy would not have hesitated about taking home to meet his parents, and she was easy to talk to.

I didn't flirt with her, or even think of doing so. Because of my experiences, right from the maid I had watched through her bedroom window to the street of the prostitutes, I associated sex with large, full breasted girls; and Hennie was immaturely flat. There might have been a boy's body under the open necked shirt she was wearing.

When she had shown me the house I was looking for we lingered for a moment or two longer, talking. We talked about classes, the teachers we had and our favourite subjects.

It was interesting, stimulating talk and we both, obviously, had a lot more to say to one another, but she told me that she had to go because she was expected home with the shopping she had gone out for.

I told her I could cycle back to Delft the next day, and I asked if we might meet. She said that she would like that. She had a bicycle, and she suggested that we might go for a ride in the country. She gave me her address.

When I arrived there the next day I found that she lived in a very poor house. She must have been watching for me, because she came out to meet me in the street, and I was not invited into the home.

She said that she was sorry, but the bicycle ride was impossible. She had been left to look after her seven year old sister and a neighbour's little boy of about the same age. But since I had come all the way to Delft, if I liked we could go for a walk and take the children with us.

We walked out of the town on the Rotterdam road. The countryside was close and it still *was* countryside in those days. We strayed off the road down a sloping, grassy embankment, overgrown with bushes.

Soon the bushes screened the sight of the road and the sound of the traffic from us, and we might have been miles away from towns and people. Even the landscape below us, the fields, the cows in them and the distant windmill, seemed like a painting in which we did not belong.

The air was warm and still, and yet it had dimensions of its own – the dimension of sound given to it by a droning bee coming towards us, weaving its sound backwards and forwards as it moved from clover to clover, then gradually going away; the dimension of perfume, the perfume nobody ever captures and imprisons in an expensive bottle, that of millions of living blades of grass, of uncountable tiny leaves of little plants, of the petals of a galaxy of minute flowers, bruised by our feet and bleeding their sweetness into the atmosphere.

The children had become tired and wanted to rest, so we lay stretched out on the sloping grass, Hennie and I together, still talking, the children straying a little further away, then curling up and falling asleep.

I was arguing with her that it was a waste of time to learn dead languages like Latin when there were so many living languages to learn, and she was arguing with serious determination that the discovery of language meant going back to the beginnings of meanings when suddenly, on momentary impulse I stopped her next, half spoken word by leaning over her and kissing her mouth.

Her mouth opened under mine, her opening lips opening my lips. My hand stole down to find a way under her skirt, and found her skirt already lifted, and it encountered, unexpectedly, one of her hands drawing her knickers off.

We kept our mouths together and I tore the front of my trousers open and rolled over on to her. Her legs parted for me to come between them and I felt her knees being drawn up, and when I put my hand down between them I could feel that beneath the soft hair that she was swollen and wet and warm. My penis found the inner orifice that I did not even know about and it seemed as if all of me, my whole body, my mind, everything was sinking into a velvet caress that belonged by comparison to nothing of known experience of my physical senses.

And I fucked her, while she lay still under me, with a sense of happiness indescribable in words. And almost at once I wanted it never to end, and it *was* ending in an eruption that was an explosion within me. And when it was over our mouths were still together in the kiss with which it had begun.

We lay still like that together for a few moments, and when I knew that the kiss had to come to an end I withdrew from the depths of her body before taking my lips away from her mouth, some strange wisdom making me understand that what had happened had been that we had kissed, and everything had been simply part of the kiss, a natural extension of it, at no moment from beginning to end something outside it.

Some times the end of experience is so vague that it is difficult to recognize just where and when it was over. At other times it is abrupt and sudden, as it was now. As I lifted myself from between her legs, wanting to now see what my mind had been too preoccupied to even visualize in imagination, she cried out sharply:

'Armand! Oh, no!'

I saw her looking towards where the children were. They had moved close to us, and were only about a yard away. The little girl had her knickers down to her ankles, and the little boy was astride her moving up and down vigorously above her.

Then Hennie began to laugh. Then I joined in. Then the children joined in. They seemed to think they had taken part in a new game.

And we laughed all through the rest of that wonderfully remembered afternoon when childhood ended for me. We chased the children up and down the grassy embankment slope. Hennie caught a butterfly, plucking it from the air in her hand; and the tears came into her eyes when she thought she had destroyed it; and I kissed her, not on the mouth, but on the cheek where the tear was, and on the closed lidded eye from where it had come.

'I want you, Hennie.'

'I know. I *know*.'

But the moment had flown, as the butterfly was fluttering away from her hand, and she was laughing with relieved delight to see it go.

How long is one summer afternoon?

How long is life to a butterfly?

Our afternoon died slowly with the cooling day. We walked with laggard steps into its tomb of brick and mortar, and it was dead; and I wanted to rush away from the flat chested girl in her faded and cheap little dress standing by the paint blistered door of the hovel where she lived, two unkempt little brats by her side, lest I remembered my deed.

'I'll come again, Hennie,' I said.

But she knew, too, and only nodded.

I wanted to give her something. And I knew now that when a man owes *this* gratitude to a woman, what he must give her is something that can never be bought.

'It was my first time, Hennie.'

'I knew. I *knew*', she whispered. 'Thank you for telling me

Nobody else will ever give you that. I'm ... I'm ...' – she struggled for a word – 'proud.'

She was sixteen, and I was fifteen. And in one moment we had all wisdom and all understanding. But all there was between us now belongs now in our minds.

'Goodbye, Hennie.' I got my bike from where it had been resting against the wall. 'Goodbye, kids.'

They screamed their excited goodbyes at me as I pedalled away without looking back, knowing I would never return lest I destroyed a dream by trying to capture its reality.

I never saw Hennie again, except in my mind, as a girl standing in the sunlight with a tear on her cheek and a butterfly escaping from her hand.

I suppose I have only ever really loved two women.

Hennie was one of them.

Not that night, but the next night, I could not sleep because of the tormenting memories of what it had been like going into Hennie.

I slept and wakened half a dozen times, tormented by the strength in my penis. Masturbation, I knew, this time would not satisfy – I wanted, I needed again to experience the real thing.

Finally I knew that there was only one escape for me, and I rose and dressed, put on the plimsoles, got out the rope ladder and went out into the night, substituting one excitement for another.

And it worked, like magic.

Tonight I was taking chances – real chances. I walked until I found myself a likely house, one in the wealthier outskirts of the town, standing in its own grounds with climbing ivy against the wall and a part opened window.

I went in. The window was that of a bedroom, and I could hear the breathing of two sleeping people in the darkness of the room. I challenged myself, challenging the memory of Hennie with another distracting demand, felt my way with cautious feet and reaching hands, across the room until I found a door.

I made my way down a solidly built staircase.

Downstairs I explored a well furnished dining room, a lounge and the kitchen. There was nothing to take that I could have carried or disposed of. I went back into the bedroom and the heavy breathing of two sleeping people, determined not to leave empty handed. Light now came from windows in front of me and my eyes had accustomed themselves to the darkness so that

I could just about identify shapes and forms.

The man was lying on his side, facing the window and the woman was turned towards him, one of her arms over his shoulder, one of her legs over his. I had no idea how old they were; they were just shapes of bodies and limbs under a light drapery of bedclothes, but even before my foot encountered the discarded towel on the floor at her side of the bed I now knew that they would be sleeping the deep, recuperative sleep of lovers, as I myself had slept with peace because of Hennie the night before.

My hand reached out for and found the bedside table at her side of the bed. My fingers began exploring the darkness. This was the first time I had stolen anything with my fingers having to see for me. It was something new I had to learn and had never consciously thought about before. I identified a ring, felt the claws about the stone, and transferred it to my pocket. There were two bracelets. In one my finger tips felt the engraved design and I decided that it was either silver or gold; I took it. The other was a bangle; beads, not pearls, I told myself and rejected it, quite enjoying the new game.

I went to his side of the bed. There was loose change, a watch, a lighter, a small wad of paper money, a wallet, a comb, a pen, a cheque book.

If he kept paper money outside the wallet, he would keep none in it, I told myself, leaving him that, his comb, his cheque book and the pen.

I left them sleeping and wondered what they would make of their losses when they woke up. I felt, with pride, that I had been highly professional. And actually, when I got back into my own bedroom at home, I found I had done quite well. The ring had a quite fine diamond, and the lighter was gold.

More important, now I slept, my appetite for excitement assuaged.

III

Parisienne Variety

In the spring of '37 there was a World Exhibition in Paris.

I was just sixteen and I had real money at my command and the proved ability to get more when I needed it. Because of the Exhibition, passport formalities had been waived and all one needed was a form of identity card which I already possessed.

I decided to leave home again.

This time I did not think of it as running away. I left a carefully considered note for my parents in which I said that I felt that, at sixteen, I now had the right to have an independent life of my own choice. With the advantage of a good education, for which I thanked them, I was now capable of standing on my own feet and proposed to do so. I was aware of having been a disappointment to them, and I regretted that. But since this would always be the case, it was only sensible for me to resolve the situation in this way, and I was sure that they would ultimately agree. They were not to worry about me. I would ask for help if I needed it.

My tongue was in my cheek as I wrote this letter. It was like a prisoner escaping from jail leaving a letter to the Governor of the prison, thanking him for his cell, for his solitary confinements and asking him not to raise the alarm.

And that was, of course, the sole purpose of it. When they found this letter they could not report me either as a runaway or a 'missing person'. I knew my father. He would not take this letter to the police and report me to be missing again. Nor, because of his principles, would he be capable of reporting my disappearance by concealing either the fact or the contents of my letter.

They say Paris is a woman's town, but Paris is herself a courtesan. Oh, there are a thousand Parises, one for every citizen and one for every visitor, but there are no whores like the whores of Paris, no brothels like the brothels of Montmartre, and no city in the world where, whatever a woman may be, she is more of a woman for being in Paris.

I loved Paris from the moment I arrived there. I found myself a cheap hotel near the Place Blanche. I couldn't wait to get myself a girl. I dumped my case in my room, and went out to get the feel of the place.

But because of the Exhibition, Montmartre was in its own festival mood, with the stalls, and the sideshows, and the fire-swallowers down the centre of the boulevard, and the sex shops and the nude shows along the pavements, and the girls in the tired old side streets with their eyes only on the deeply breathing, palm sweating tourists. And at sixteen I could *never* look like a fat-walleted middle aged American or an unleashed English suburbanite.

The only girl I took back to my room that night was about five inches high, and she sat, naked, on opened and crossed legs, like a Yogi devotee. She was made of rubber, and realistically coloured. No little detail of her anatomy had been neglected, and you could make her do her exercises by turning a wire handle underneath the base board upon which she was squatting. A very observant genius in his own way had shaped the wire and inserted it into the moulded rubber.

As I amused myself with this fascinating toy, bought at the corner of one of the streets just along from the Moulin Rouge, I heard voices from the adjoining room; a woman's, then a man's. Then there was the sound from the corridor of a door being opened.

I went to my own room door and, when I opened it cautiously, I saw a man going hurriedly down the stairs. He had that furtive manner so many men have immediately after an illicit adventure.

I opened my door a little wider, and presently the girl came out. She was young and attractive and there was no doubt in my mind about her profession. I spoke as she was going by.

'Is it necessary to go out again?' I asked quietly.

She turned and looked at me.

'You?' she said. 'You're very young.'

'You prefer men like that?' I asked, nodding towards the well of the staircase.

'One doesn't have preferences,' she said.

'All right, no preferences. But this is my first night in Paris, and the place excites me. But I don't know my way around yet.'

She glanced at a watch on her wrist. She told me her fee.

'It'll have to be straightforward and quick,' she said. 'My protector will be expecting me. I can't spend time teasing you.'

As she came into the room I kicked off my shoes and dropped

my trousers. My penis sprang up from underneath my shirt. She hesitated.

'You're clean? It's foolish to take a chance.'

'Are *you*?'

'That's a foolish question.'

She pulled a zipper and her dress opened on utter nakedness which she completed by shrugging her shoulders so that the sleeves slid down her arms. She hurried to the bed.

'How do you want to do it? How about this way? Then you can watch yourself doing it, and it'll be quick.'

She bent over the edge of the bed, drawing one knee up and outwards, getting her shoulders down and holding her bottom up high so that her cunt was held right back to me, completely shaven, the moist pink orifice agape for my entry.

All my self control went, and:

'Jesus!' she cried, as I went into her. 'Take it easy! You don't have to try to get your balls in, too.'

'I'm sorry,' I said, but I was only half aware of saying it as I watched the sight of myself, wet from her, strong for her, going in and out of her. And it was the seeing more than the feeling that finished me almost immediately so that I collapsed on her, trying to hold her, almost sobbing in my relief.

She wriggled her way from underneath me, squatted briefly astride the bidet by the bedside. I lay on the bed, only half seeing her as I began slowly to recover from the strange post coital feeling of sadness there always is when there has not been a woman's need and a woman's love. She struggled back into the frock and zippered it up, then looked at me.

My coat was over the back of the chair.

'The hundred francs?' she said.

'In my wallet.'

She found it, opened it. She waved a hundred franc note at me.

'*I've* never rolled a man yet, but you watch it. There's plenty who will.' She glanced at her watch and tossed my coat to the floor. 'Jesus he'll kill me.'

Although I took her advice and didn't make myself ever again so vulnerable to being 'rolled', I have to admit that it happened once or twice in Paris. And what with the girls, who were there right on the doorstep to give almost every day its satisfactory conclusion, the hotel bills, the restaurant meals, the sightseeing and one thing and another, my money drained away far more quickly than I had anticipated.

I had not begun burglaring again and I didn't know when I would begin again.

I find the reason for this easy to understand myself but difficult to explain. I had been born and had grown up in the Hague, and knew the streets round where I lived like the back of my hand. I could never have found myself trapped in a cul-de-sac for instance, and I knew where all the railway lines ran and which streets led down to them, but not across them.

But now I had to learn something new. I wasn't a pickpocket, I wasn't a bag snatcher, I wasn't a shoplifter; I was a housebreaker. When the time came I would go back to my chosen profession. But at the moment there was no compelling incentive to take chances of a kind and I was having much too good a time to let the future worry me.

I spent a lot of time at the Exhibition. The first visit was simply the curiosity that attracts people to highly publicized exhibitions. I enjoyed it enormously and struck up a conversational friendship with a young Polish woman who was running a doughnut stall at which I had paused for a snack.

Her name was Polja, and the truth was that I was lonely and needed someone to talk to. My only human contacts were with the prostitutes I fucked at night. They had no time for conversation with clients like myself.

Polja was about twelve years older than myself, a very frank, uninhibited young woman, and, like myself, lonely in Paris. I soon found myself making for the Exhibition most days of the week, simply for the opportunity of talking to Polja.

It was stimulating, exciting conversation, because I soon found myself able to talk to Polja, seriously and thoughtfully about things I had never discussed with anyone before, and would have thought it impossible for a man to talk about in such a way with a woman.

I would meet her for her lunch break and we would have a snack together and then find somewhere fairly quiet and sit in the sun and talk. I told her all about myself, keeping nothing back. Nothing seemed to surprise her, much less shock her.

She thought I was foolish having sex with prostitutes.

'You mean the risks of VD?' I asked.

'No. You're much more likely to get that from an enthusiastic amateur.

'But prostitutes aren't good for you, Armand. They'll make you come to think about sex the way they have had to come to think about it. You'll miss what they miss.'

'You mean love, Polja.'

'That's a big word,' she said. 'It's got a lot of meanings. A different meaning, maybe, for every one of us. I think you'll find it difficult to fall in love – the whole way, so that you couldn't even want any woman except the one woman. Love is made up from many ingredients – liking, affection, respect, understanding, sympathy and the genuine desire to please. These are the things you should be looking for.

'With regard to sex it is an experience to be shared. From your previous experiences you will teach her, and she will teach you from hers. Through this you will acquire understanding of each other and learn much more – this is the best way.'

Finally, inevitably, the day came when I realized that my holiday in Paris had come to an end. After I had paid my hotel bill, there was not much money left. I told Polja this that day.

'So I won't be seeing you again,' I said, and gave her the gift of perfume I had bought that morning, recklessly overspending.

'What are you going to do?' she asked.

'I don't know yet. I'm not going back home, of course. I'll be all right. The devil looks after his own. I wouldn't have wanted it to go on like this anyway. I'll think of something.'

'You can come to my place,' she said abruptly – so abruptly that I knew that the idea and the offer had been uncontemplated.

'You mean – go to bed with you, Polja.'

'Well, I only have one bed. And we both need our sleep.'

'We wouldn't just sleep, Polja.'

'I hope not!' she said. 'When is your hotel room up?'

'Not till the end of the week. But I'll go back and pack my things now, and clear out.'

'You really want me then?' she asked.

'Suddenly – yes. In the same way, of course, yet somehow different.'

'I can't teach you love, Armand,' she said seriously.

'Why not?' I asked, teasing a little.

I was very, very fond of Polja, and lived with her for about three months. Even now I don't think of her as a woman I fucked. I made love with Polja. Mind you, ultimately it was the same thing – it was just our understanding and feelings for each other that made it different.

She taught me how to control myself and how to give her the orgasms she so desperately needed. But nice though the prolongation of lovemaking with Polja was, it was hard work and needed a lot of skill. And in the end it was only her basic sexual needs I satisfied and I never really found the woman Polja really was.

One day there might be a man who could satisfy all her needs and would recognize her for the person she was. He'd be a lucky man, and she'd be a happy woman.

There were, of course, a happy three months. For me they were three of the most valuable months of my life. Through Polja I discovered that one must give to be given.

I learnt to anticipate her moods, and not to try to impose my own upon her. I learnt that the relationship between a man and woman is developed by little attentivenesses on both parts. I learnt not just to be kind, but to be conscious of being kind.

And I was faithful to her during those three months not, mind you, that she gave me any reason, need or opportunity to be otherwise.

We didn't go out, although on Saturdays she would leave me to clean the flat while she went shopping. It was a routine that carefully avoided any spending of money on my part except for fares to and from the Exhibition, where I still met her for lunch.

For of course, I was living off her.

I could have gone on doing it indefinitely the fact, tactfully, never being brought to the surface. I was giving her something she wanted and which I think had been missing for probably quite a long time. But it could not go on indefinitely, and we both of us knew that, although it was a thing we didn't talk about.

I began thinking about the immediate future and becoming restless. A recruiting poster put the idea of joining the Foreign Legion into my head. The enlisting age was eighteen and I was still only sixteen, both in fact and on my identity papers. The next day I was still sixteen in fact but eighteen on my identity papers.

I told Polja of my decision, and then she surprised me.

'It's been a happy time, Armand. You'll never know how nearly I have loved you. How I've deliberately made myself remember some other things – things that made me believe I could never let another man have me, until that day when you came to the Exhibition to say goodbye and I realized, suddenly, that you were just a boy and that this was the moment in your life when *I* could give you something you needed – the warmth there is in it, the closeness. And I felt – does this sound silly to you? I felt that if I could do that, then there would have been some purpose in being a woman, after all.'

'You did that,' I told her, not understanding as well at the time as I was to do when I became older, and thought about her.

'I couldn't let myself go all the way with you,' she said. 'You're sixteen, I'm nearly twenty-nine. But, if I've given you something you'll be grateful for, you've done the same for me.'

'Do you want to talk about it?'

'No! Let's go to bed.'

I took her to the Exhibition the next morning and we said goodbye there. Then I went down to the recruiting office to sign on. That night I was on the Marseille train with instructions to report to Fort St Jean.

I had romantic ideas about the French Foreign Legion, but my ideas had all come from the wrong sources – fiction.

IV

Cote D'Amour

I wore the uniform of the French Foreign Legion for exactly three weeks, and that was long enough.

It was long enough to discover that being a Legionaire is most tolerable if you are a Frenchman. The N.C.O.'s give the toughest time to the English. They concede a cautious respect to the Germans and most other nationals are just pushed around as misfits rather than professional mercenaries.

All life in uniform is tough when one first gets into it, whichever army you get into. A fighting man is no damn good to anybody, and a dangerous liability if he won't obey the orders, never questioning them even if they mean his certain death.

The indoctrination starts the moment you walk through the gates of your first training centre. You will no longer be treated like a human being, because victorious armies aren't made up of human beings; they are made up of machines – machines of steel, but also machines of flesh and blood; both equally expendable. There is no other way. Ask any old sweat and he'll give you the same answer in any one of a hundred different languages.

They knocked hell out of me those three weeks at Fort St Jean. I was shamed, humiliated, degraded, de-humanized in the process of reducing my personality to a malleable pulp from which, with any luck, a Legionaire could be shaped. For those whose souls are smelted, for those who emerge at the end of the process with steel forged into their characters, it is a fine thing to be that kind of fighting man.

But my blood has never stirred to martial music, my chest has never tightened with pride at the sight of a national flag. My menities are of my own choosing, my hostilities of my own timing.

Those three weeks at Fort St Jean did me good, but that small dose of the discipline was quite enough.

We were being marched at the double in the blazing sun, endlessly round a square when suddenly I felt as if one of those naked bayonets had been plunged into my guts, and I collapsed, rolling over in screaming agony.

Unless you die, right there before his eyes, you get no sympathy, as a Foreign Legion recruit under initial training, from your squad sergeant. He's had men fake lunacy to get out of it all. He is familiar with minor self inflicted amputations on the part of men to whom the hell of it has become too much to take. The collapses, the simulated evidence of agony of those who maybe need only just a little bit more pressure to come through as good material, are very familiar to him.

The responsibility of judging whether you are faking or really in some serious trouble is his. If he proves to be wrong, too bad; he will be backed, up to the hilt.

I got a boot in my backside and the promise of extra latrine duties at the end of the day if I didn't get up, at the double, and rejoin that senseless merry-go-round of sweating men.

I got up. I stumbled forward, my eyes stinging with the salt of the sweat running from my scalp, and the bayonet went into my guts again. I remember seeing the cobbles coming up towards my face, and nothing more.

When I came to, I was in the hospital ward, I ached all over, but that was the exercise. Otherwise I was fine, but worried about what had happened to me and what it meant.

The orderly came over, and asked how I felt. I said I was okay and asked what had happened. He said he did not know. He did not seem to be very interested. He had a rotten job and he resented those who filled the bedpans he had to empty.

He went away to report my return to consciousness and presently two Army doctors came back with him and the bedclothes were thrown back. I had been put into bed naked, and the senior of the doctors pointed to an abdominal scar I had. It was red and inflamed in a way I never remembered having seen it.

'How did you get that?' he asked. 'What was the operation for?'

'It was when I was eight,' I said. 'They said I had an abscess inside me.'

He prodded my carcass with the end of a pencil, asking me to tell him when it hurt and asking questions about the operation.

I let the doctor know when it hurt, dramatizing it a bit to convince him.

Then the two of them discussed it, but not with me, of course. It seemed that there were adhesions behind the scar, that there were probable internal weaknesses. I was waste material. They went away and left me.

I stayed in the ward a couple of days, having it entirely to myself. Nobody told me anything, except the orderly.

'You lucky bastard,' he said. 'They'll sling you out for sure, and that'll teach you to ever volunteer for anything again.'

When he found out that I was completely mobile, wasn't going to need a bed pan and didn't have any dirty habits or any disgusting wounds for him to clean up, he became quite human and friendly. We spent the time playing a two handed card game which I suspected he had invented himself, since its rules always seemed to be in his favour. I think he marked the cards, too, and knew most of them by gravy stains and patterns of wear and dirt. Anyway, in those two days he had taken every franc I had.

On the third day I was told to dress and was given my own clothes. An NCO came up to the ward and took me to the administrative block where I was given a short interview by a captain.

I was told that in consequence of an old abdominal wound I had been found to be medically unfit for further service with the Legion and was being discharged. I had to sign a document which said that I agreed that the cause of my unfitness had existed before enlistment, that I had not disclosed the fact of my unsuitability and that I accepted full responsibility for any aggravation of my condition that might have been consequential to my period of training.

It was all quite reasonable, I thought, although at that moment I would have signed anything for, from the moment I had put on civilian clothes again, I began to be treated once more as something at least approximating to a human being.

I was told I would be given a rail warrant back to Paris, returning me to the place of my enlistment. There would also be a discharge gratuity, enough to tide me over while I found employment.

In the orderly room, where I had to wait for my discharge papers, the warrant and the gratuity, I found myself sharing the bench seat with a young Englishman whom I had last seen in uniform but who, like myself, was now in civilian clothes – very good, well tailored clothes.

He told me that he, too, was waiting for his discharge papers. I asked him if, like myself, he was getting out on medical grounds.

'Not exactly, old boy,' he said. 'But there are always ways and means, you know.'

He asked me where I came from, and I told him I was Dutch.

'You speak jolly good English,' he said.

I told him that I had a command of several languages and a smattering of one or two others.

'You speak this lingo – French?' he asked.

'I was living in Paris when I enlisted,' I said.

I could see that he was turning an idea over in his mind.

'What are you going to do now?'

'I don't know. They're giving me a rail warrant back to Paris and the girl I was living with there would be glad to have me back with her. But I never like going back and I don't much like the idea of being kept by a woman.'

'You're broke?' he asked.

'I'll have exactly what they give me as a gratuity,' I said. 'And as I've only been in for three weeks, that won't last long.'

'Just about pay for one decent meal!' he said cheerfully. 'Look, I'll tell you what – I've a notion to go to Nice. I can get by with the language, but it's much better if there's someone else to do the talking. Why not come along with me?'

'My warrant's to Paris,' I reminded him.

'Oh, don't give that a thought. I'll pay all the expenses and pay you a salary to be the interpreter. I don't have money problems.'

I did; so I accepted the offer, and we left Fort St Jean together – in a taxi!

So I departed from the Foreign Legion in style. The taxi driver took us to a good restaurant, where we had an excellent meal with a bottle of wine.

Nice is a hundred miles from Marseille, but the hotel on Boulevard Dubouchage was a million miles from Fort St Jean. By now I knew that my companion had not been exaggerating when he had said that he did not have money problems and at dinner that evening I was summoning the maître and ordering judiciously from the wine list with all the aplomb of someone to the manner born.

I was told as much by George as he saw fit. He came from a wealthy, aristocratic family. He was an old Etonian, and he had been 'sent down' from his university. He was the 'black sheep' of his family.

'The guv'nor got pretty cheesed eventually so I cast off. Had some friends who had a villa at Cannes and decided to ride things out with them. But you know how it is. I fetched up in Marseille instead. Met some chaps and got pissed one night, and the next thing I knew I was in the jolly Legion. Didn't like it awfully; did you? Anyway the old wheel of fortune did me a bit of a favour and I was able to pull a few strings, and here I am.'

I told him no more about myself than he had told me about himself, but said I had one problem that had to be resolved right away. I needed a proper passport.

My identity card said I was eighteen, but a little careful doctoring of my discharge papers pushed the year of my birth back another three years and made me twenty-one.

The next morning I visited the Dutch Consulate. The Consul proved absent and his substitute, an old man, did not have much experience with the kind of problem I presented to him. I said that my passport had been destroyed during a fire in the barracks. I now only had this discharge paper to establish my identity and I needed a passport for a new job as an interpreter.

Although it is my principle to stick to the truth, there are always some occasions when it is necessary to lie. Then it is wise to make it a good, big one, something nobody could possibly believe to be a complete invention from beginning to end.

I got my passport without trouble.

We moved on to Monte Carlo. George was strangely restless. It wasn't simply that he was itching for excitement; he was all on edge.

The first night in Monte we went, naturally, to the Casino. It was my idea, but George was obviously very much at home at the tables. He was a real gambler – no systems, no superstitions; just hunches. He made all his bets *en plein*, playing for the high odds. The only pattern in his gambling was that when he stayed on a number for a series of coups, he doubled the stake each time.

He had very occasional luck, but that is all the gambler who never bets on rouge, noir, pair or impair, passe or manque requires. He cleaned up about ten thousand francs without getting the least excited.

We went on to the balcony where the big losers are supposed to commit suicide.

I said, perhaps recklessly, 'The way you play, it beats burglary.'

'Ever tried that, Armand?' he asked. 'Burglary I mean?'

'Now, why should you ask me that?' I said.

'I don't know. Call it a hunch. I've always thought that if I'd had the incentive it might have been an exciting thing to do – going for the big stuff, of course.'

I had no incentive, however, to be his initiator. He had just picked up ten thousand francs, he was picking up all the tabs and, while it lasted, I was having the time of my life.

We didn't go back to the Casino. Having slept through most of the day at our hotel, George now said that he fancied what he called 'a bit of the other'. I didn't know what he meant at first.

'A tart, old son,' he said. 'Nothing but the best, of course. Lay it on, will you?'

The best guides in these matters, in any town, are the taxi drivers, so I picked my taxi driver and let him pick the brothel. He took us to a high class place called Villa de Paradis.

The door was opened by a maid who welcomed us in as if we were expected guests. She took us through to a lounge and said that Madame would join us in a moment.

'I say,' said George, 'this is a bit of all right.'

'It's going to be expensive,' I said, looking around. It was very plush, all velvet, gilt, crystal and silver.

'So what?' said George. 'We're only young once. And who wants a knocking-shop anyway? I bet the visiting millionaires do their screwing here. By jove, I like it. I really like it.'

Madame had the manners of a grande dame, and welcomed us with the single word:

'Gentlemen?'

'A friend suggested our visit,' I told her.

'Of course. I have many friends. But,' she added, 'my friendship, which involves the companionship of my young ladies, is expensive.'

'That was to be anticipated, madame,' I told her.

Then the fencing was over, and she laid it right down on the table. The tariff – the bill of fare.

And yet, when one worked it out, it wasn't all that unreasonable. The upkeep of the place had to be pretty high, and no doubt she had a lot of sweeteners to pay off. She had eight girls in the place and they were available for afternoon, evening or night time appointments. Each of the three sessions for which a girl could be booked included appropriate refreshment – afternoon tea, dinner and, in the case of the final appointment period, not only supper but *petit dejeuner*, which meant that she was yours for the night. And there was an all-in engagement rate of 4,500 francs a day.

I remembered the frantic five minutes in the hotel bedroom just off the Place Blanche that had cost me a hundred francs. That girl had been earning at the rate of very nearly 29,000 francs a day!

Three of the eight girls were already engaged. Of the others, two had night time appointments.

'That gives us a choice of three,' said George when I explained the situation to him, 'because we might as well make double session bookings. I do hate having to turn out of bed afterwards and go home. It just isn't done, unless the lady is married and expecting her husband back.'

'A choice of three for you,' I said. 'I'll take my pick of the other two.'

So the photographs were produced, and they were not at all the kind of photographs with which Jan had initiated me into the world of pornography at the reformatory. They were artistic poses of extremely attractive young women, discretely draped and very professionally taken.

George made his choice, and then I picked one of the other two girls – a pert black haired girl called Nadia. He paid Madame her fees and then she took him away and returned for me a few minutes later.

She took me upstairs, knocked at the door of a room, and then opened it and led me inside.

'Nadia,' she said. 'This gentleman has asked for your companionship until tomorrow morning.'

I was in a well furnished sitting room, at one end of which was a large double bed.

'Hello,' said Nadia, getting up from her chair and coming towards me as Madame departed, holding out her hand.

She was wearing a short, white towelling bathrobe and as she held out her hand, the bathrobe fell open – she was naked underneath it. She was also flawless, perfectly beautiful.

'You'll find a robe in the bathroom,' she said. 'Through there, the door by the bed. How nice that you don't have to rush away. Do you want me to order dinner to be brought up, or shall we just have a bottle of wine and a meal later, when we feel like it?'

'As you wish,' I said.

'Then – wine and love now, and supper later, before we go to bed.'

I had a terrific time with Nadia. She was the only prostitute I ever knew who was a prostitute from choice, because it was what she wanted to be, the way another girl may want to be a singer, a dancer, an actress or an artist.

Sex was an art to her. The Villa de Paradis was exclusive and its clientele were wealthy, cultured men. Madame was selective, too. If her recommenders, like the taxi driver, did happen to bring or send any man she disapproved of, she would express her regrets saying that all her girls were engaged, and get rid of him.

Nadia's art was to give ecstasy, and she excelled at it. She took pride in her skills, in her ability to inflame the mind, in her knowledge of men's sensuality.

From Nadia I learnt a truth that I think many men never appreciate – that the big difference between a man and woman is that the man is always a performer and can never be an actor, whereas every woman's performance may sometimes be that of an actress. Nadia was an actress, all the time, and delighted if opportunity gave her the chance to go through her whole repertoire with a man.

She had that opportunity with me, for George was apparently as equally delighted with his choice of girl and, the next morning, booked both girls for all three of their sessions the next day, and then did the same thing on the following day.

So I had three nights and two days with Nadia and learnt more from her about the sensual pleasures of sex than I had learnt even from Polja in three months.

'The trouble with men,' she told me seriously, 'is that either they are over excited when they enter a girl, and almost immediately lose all self control and so rob themselves of pleasure, or they discipline themselves to self control and boast how long they can last, but they are only lasting by denying themselves pleasure. We have it all wrong. It is the woman who should make love to the man's sensuality, not the other way round. I'll teach you.'

And she did, and whether I mounted her, or she me, or I took her from behind, she controlled the depth of my penetration either by her position or by holding me away from her so that she could use the controlled relaxing and tightening of her muscular vaginal orifice sometimes on the root, and sometimes on the glands of my penis while I was powerless to move in her. She knew just how to bring me to the edge of the precipice and hold me there, draw me back to temporary safety, then take me back to the threshold of a climax of relief that she allowed and gave when she, not I, thought fit.

George bought gifts for both girls on what was our final visit to the Villa de Paradis, identical expensive wrist watches. I also took roses for Nadia, and she understood that these were the personal thing.

She took them from me as a leading lady on the stage takes her bouquet as a tribute to a fine performance.

'I'm so glad I've pleased you, Armand,' she said.

I felt strangely sad for her, remembering how Polja had told me that I would find it difficult to discover love. I knew that Nadia was probably incapable of ever finding it.

George was thoughtfully silent, too, as we returned to our hotel. Eventually he said:

'I'm afraid it's got to be over, old boy. I really must get back home.'

Then it came out. His father had died. George had inherited quite considerable wealth. That was how the strings had been pulled to get him out of the Foreign Legion – strings pulled, I gathered, from quite high places.

His father's funeral had already taken place before his release could be arranged, and George had decided on one last fling before he went home to undertake responsibilities he did not discuss.

'It's been a hell of a good last fling, Armand,' he said.

He insisted that I should take half the money he had won at the Casino.

'Can't leave you on your uppers, old boy. And since we've shared everything since we got out of Fort St Jean it's fair enough that we should share the winnings, too.'

It wasn't a very good argument, but who was I to disagree? But it reminded me of the fact that I was, in a sense, George's employee, and he probably looked upon me as a paid companion-interpreter. Among his own kind, if ever he referred to me, he would probably describe me as: '. . . an interpreter I engaged. Dutch chappie. Can't remember his name. Think he was a crook. Must say, though, the blighter didn't crook me.' And he would touch the side of his nose with his finger. 'Eyes too wide open, what?'

How else do newspaper political cartoonists make the subjects identifiable except by caricature? This caricatures the way George talked and the way he probably regarded me. Yet – he doesn't come back to life as a reality even to me now unless I draw my word-picture of him in this way.

Remembering, now he was going, that I was an employee, I helped him pack, settled the hotel bill for the two of us up to date, got the taxi, took him to the station, stood in the queue to buy him his first class ticket, carried his luggage, got him his corner seat, bought him a copy of the previous day's *Times*, and: 'Cheerio, old son,' he said. 'See you around some time.'

I went back to the hotel and picked up my own luggage.

George had given Monte Carlo the meanings of a first class hotel, good living, gambling at the Casino, the Villa de Paradis, and the *sexpertise* of Nadia. Here I had lived, briefly, in a world where money was 'no problem' and 'only the best' was acceptable.

He had also given me the experience of living with someone who took all this for granted, someone who thought that everything had been created especially for them and that everybody else was there to cater to their needs.

While I was being thrashed as a child into subjugation, George was being given a 'superiority' complex. And now just as I would always expect hostility and take brutality for granted, George would always take servility on the part of others for granted.

He *was* superior.

And while I secretly resented this, knowing that the assumptions of aristocracy are the biggest confidence trick in the world, I also envied it.

I also knew that I didn't want to stay on in Monte Carlo without George. It was like leaving Hennie had been. I had to get out with the illusion intact and not allow myself to be confronted with my own reality of the place.

So I went straight back to Marseille.

Carrying my suitcase, I walked past the big hotels and found myself a rented room in a side street just off Rue de Rome, near the docks. This was much more my mark.

I picked the place because it called itself Hotel de Clichy. No other reason; but during the short time I was there I wondered what qualifications were necessary before a rooming-house keeper could call his establishment an hotel. They had to be pretty low. The Hotel de Clichy must have just scraped in.

The first night I was there I went out late, not looking for any kind of adventure, not having any other purpose than to quieten my sense of restlessness and to make myself tired. It was still a bit unbelievable to realize that only last night there had been Nadia, and Nadia's room in the Villa de Paradis. The transition from that to the cold, empty room in the Hotel de Clichy had been very abrupt and I needed to reacclimatize myself to reality.

As I came out of my room the door of the room opposite mine opened and a girl came out. She was wearing a candlewick dressing gown and carrying a towel and other things that suggested that she was going to take a bath in the bathroom shared by the occupants of the rooms on that floor.

She was a pretty girl, and the way the gown fell suggested that she had a nice, slim body and full, attractive breasts. As our eyes met, she gave me a little smile, and of course I looked round after her as she made her way to the bathroom.

Then I saw that the poor girl had a bad limp, that she was a cripple and that one foot was turned inward. When she walked, she had to use one hand against the wall to steady herself.

Watching her brought me down to earth. This girl represented the reality of life, while Nadia had represented simply an illusion. Yet there was no getting away from it – the illusion excited and attracted and the reality repelled.

I knew the truth, and I didn't like it.

The truth was that when I had seen the girl in the doorway across from my room I had immediately and instinctively felt excited at the idea of a pretty girl with a bedroom just across the corridor from mine. I had been ready to say 'hello' to her, and to begin making conversation with her. It was no use pretending to myself that I hadn't actually contemplated beyond that first step. The hard fact was that I had recognized her as a girl I could very probably, and certainly very conveniently, enjoy fucking.

But the moment I had seen that she was a cripple, even though I had felt an immediate sense of compassion for her, my whole attitude had changed. I'd probably get to know her as 'the girl across the corridor', but there was no hurry about it because there was no purpose behind it.

Frankly I didn't much like myself, but there was nothing I could do about it. I was what I was.

On the next couple of days, during which I wandered about Marseille, exploring the city and getting to know it, the only way there is, which is on foot, I encountered her two or three more times in the corridor outside my room and we simply exchanged the time of day. She worried me because she embarrassed me.

Then, on the third day, I went into a cafe for a midday meal and when I came to pay my bill, there she was behind the cashier's desk.

'So *this* is where you work!' I said.

'Now, don't tell me you've been wondering!' she laughed. 'You make it sound as if you've satisfied your curiosity about a great secret.'

'I suppose we all say some stupid things,' I admitted.

'But *I* have been wondering about you!' she said, intent on counting my money from the till.

'Oh!' I felt, foolishly, a bit alarmed.

'Yes. For the last twenty minutes. I've never known a customer to take so long over his lunch. I wondered if you were *ever* going to finish.'

I looked around the restaurant, and then realized that it was empty.

'You mean you've been waiting? Couldn't go until I left?'

'Oh, don't let it bother you,' she told me, laughing. 'There's always one last customer, and Jeanette and I – Jeanette's the last-one-on waitress – have bets about when they'll leave. Then we're free until four o'clock.'

I felt that I couldn't just pick up my change and walk out.

'You don't get your lunch until then?'

'Oh, no. We have ours early.'

'Then, what do you do?'

'Well, first I always go down to the waterfront and feed the gulls. There's always a lot of broken bread, half eaten rolls, you see. . . .'

'That's where you're going now?'

She nodded. I couldn't just say: 'How interesting' – and walk out.

'May I wait for you, then?'

She looked embarrassed.

'That's kind. But I'm sure you've other things to do . . .'

'No, really!'

'Besides, I walk so slowly, so badly. Ever since my accident. . . .'

'It was an accident, then?'

'Would you believe I was on the stage? In the chorus line! Only three years ago.'

'Oh, that's terrible for you. What happened?'

'A car. It didn't stop. I'm just beginning to get used to it. As used to it as I'll ever be. It's funny though, people are much kinder when you're a – when you're a cripple. A kind of compensation.'

She did walk badly. It was terrible the way she walked. After a bit, when she was with you, she couldn't keep up trying to make it look not as bad as it really was. Then you wanted to take her hand and squeeze it and say: 'For God's sake it's all right. It's not you. It's only a leg.'

But of course it *was* her.

Her name was Anne-Marie. She'd had the lot. Both her parents had been burnt to death in a fire when she had been a kid. There was nobody else, no other family, and she'd been in an orphanage. Then she'd gone on the stage.

'Well, that's the nice way of saying it. I was one of the g-string girls. Would you believe that – *now*.'

'Yes, I'd believe it.'

'I'd got good legs. Good everything. I've pictures in my room. I can't throw them away, and I can't look at them either. Mind you it's only the one leg that makes any difference, even now. Ugly. Twisted.'

What the hell could you say to her? Oh, yes, I know now. I didn't then.

There was a fascination about the not wanting her that was like a magnet to me. I wanted to like her, and I did because she was sweet. I wanted to feel love for her, and knew that if I just felt that once I would get an erection for her.

Then I'd do for her something similar to what Polja had done for me. But a man cannot do it out of sympathy and kindness the way a woman can, and I couldn't feel the love.

Poor little crippled Anne-Marie.

She wasn't asking for the love, although she was someone to love with tenderness. She wasn't even craving for the sensual thrill of it, though I was sure she'd have been far from frigid. She just wanted to see a man looking at her naked body and having an erection for her despite that terribly twisted, misshapen leg which she showed me, almost challenging me.

I wish I could have done it, just once for her. It would have been a kindness. I like to think that there was eventually a man who could, and did, giving her back something the doctors could never have given with any miracle. I was too young.

I don't really think that I would have teamed up with Charles if it had not been for Anne-Marie.

I met him in the cafe where Anne-Marie worked, although she had nothing to do with the introduction. He was a Frenchman from Alsace. The cafe had a bar, and Charles started coming in each morning for a cafe noir and a cognac. We got talking, the way one does. He said he had just deserted from the Army. I told him I had just got out of the Foreign Legion. It gave us common ground for the beginnings of conversation.

I told him, simply as a good story, about George, and Nice and Monte Carlo. He said it sounded a lot better than Marseille, and what was I doing back in Marseille? I said it was cheaper to live here, and my funds were running low.

As with Anne-Marie, these conversations took place over a course of days.

He wanted to know what I proposed to do to get back into funds. I knew exactly what he wanted to know. He had me taped, just as I had him summed up.

Charles was lean, and tall and one could see the shape of the bones behind the sallow skin. He had restless, suspicious eyes. I knew that we had some things in common, but he wasn't, like me, a loner. And when he looked at a woman, it was at her hands that he looked – at the rings she was wearing and the handbag she was carrying.

I saw his usefulness to me, though. Just as my knowledge of the French language had been useful to George, Charles being French had a similar usefulness to me. For the time was coming when I had to start acquiring money again.

Eventually he invited me back to his room for, he said, 'a talk'. As we walked down the road together, he suddenly said, producing a scrap of paper:

'Here's my address. I've missed out the number – you'll remember that. It's twenty-two. Can you run?'

'Of course.'

'Take a wall in your stride?'

'Of course.'

'You'll know when to run. We'll split. You take the alleyway first left. There's a wall. It leads to a derelict site. If you are interested, come and have that talk I suggested. We'll know what we're talking about, and you'll already be in on the deal.'

There was a fairly well dressed middle aged woman approaching us. It happened suddenly.

'*Now*,' said Charles as she reached us.

I hardly saw him snatch the bag. I was already running, and I was in the alleyway when the woman began to scream. The wall was child's play. I made my way to the street written on the scrap of paper. Once I found it, I tore the paper up. The safest memory notes are in the head where nobody else can read them.

When I reached the right number, a window on the second floor opened and Charles looked out.

'Just come on up,' he said.

'Ever done this before?' he asked with a grin.

The woman's bag was on the bed, still unopened.

'No,' I said. 'It's not my line.'

'What *is* your line?' he asked.

I had already made my decisions.

'Housebreaking,' I told him. 'I'm good at climbing. I'm *really* good at climbing. But I haven't done any jobs since I left my home town. I knew my way around there. I knew how to get rid of things.'

'We could make a good team,' said Charles. 'I know my way around here. I can get rid of anything. I'm an all rounder. But I gave you the escape with the wall to climb because that's where I come unstuck. What do you say?'

I already knew my answer, but there was no point in seeming too keen.

'I've this,' he said, and put his hand under the mattress and produced a small automatic pistol.

'That's dangerous,' I said, and this time my hesitation was genuine.

He snapped the barrel open and showed me the unloaded chamber.

'It's for effect, that's all. And it's effective.'

I took a deep breath.

'All right. When do we start?'

'We've already started,' said Charles, and opened and tipped the contents of the woman's handbag on the bedcover. 'Down the middle. All right?'

Although I justified my decision to accept this partnership because Charles could make contact with fences, was on familiar territory and I was not and had the advantage of being native to the country, it was out of character for me to work in partnership. I was a loner. I did not believe in relying in any way upon someone else because I could never trust anyone else to behave and react exactly as I would myself. In partnership one is always vulnerable to someone else's mistakes.

The real truth was that the partnership would compel breaking the association with Anne-Marie, and I was incapable of doing that without an outside, compelling reason.

The way things were, I saw myself becoming more and more

deeply involved with Anne-Marie and I knew that my compassion for her must not become a reason for changing the course of my life.

'All right,' I said.

'We'd better stay in the same place,' said Charles. 'I don't know about where you are staying, but this place is okay. They don't ask questions. Ricco, who runs the place, has a police record himself. He knows the score. What do you think?'

'I think I move in here,' I said.

'Right! Let's go and fix it with him.'

I moved from the Hotel de Clichy that afternoon, but first I fed the seagulls with Anne-Marie. I couldn't just disappear out of her life. I couldn't just leave a note for her.

It was another occasion for lying, basing the lies upon the truth.

I told her I was on the run, both from the police in my own country, but also from the Foreign Legion from which I had deserted. I said that I had been recognized and that the time had come to get out – and fast.

She did not believe me.

I showed her Charles' pistol, and then she believed.

I said that even this last meeting was a risk I shouldn't really be taking.

'But I couldn't just disappear.'

'It's *not* me then?' she said.

I kissed her for the first and only time.

'It's not you, Anne-Marie. I've felt guilty about our friendship all along. It wasn't fair to you. And so many things have been unfair for you.'

'It could have been more than a friendship,' she said.

'I know. That would have been beautiful. But it would have made this worse, for both of us. And this had to come, eventually.'

'You couldn't give it all up?'

'Too late. I've had one taste of prison. I'm on the run for the rest of my life. And a man on the run has to be alone. Some things can't be changed.'

'And I can never run,' she said looking down at the twisted foot.

'No, you can't run – but *not* for that reason.'

We walked back to the restaurant where she was due back on duty. The last thing she said was:

'Do you need money, Armand? I have some, saved. You can have it all.'

I knew it was the moment for the *coup de grâce*.

'I'm all right for money. I made a good hit with a bag snatch this morning.'

'Oh, Armand!'

'That's me,' I said. 'That's *my* crippled leg, Anne-Marie.'

I'm sure she wept. I did not look back to see.

That same night Charles and I did our first break-in, an export warehouse down by the docks. He had had his eye on it for some time, but his problem had been getting in. It was no problem for me – a drainpipe climb to the roof, and a skylight entry. Then I let Charles in by the time-keeper's door.

He had two hikers' rucksacks with him. What we were principally after was a consignment of Swiss watches for which he had a market, and anything else portable we might lay our hands on to fill up the rucksacks.

It was a good start to the partnership and Charles was tremendously impressed by my skill as a spider-man.

'A pity I haven't more jobs like this laid on,' he said. 'The next one we do, we'll do in a big way. We need two or three others we can trust, and a lorry.'

I would have been very content to let the warehouse robbery, which commanded rather disappointing reportage in the next day's evening newspaper, keep us in funds until we actually needed to 'do another job'.

But Charles looked upon crime as an occupation. There might be no regular, predictable weekly pay packet, but he thought that there should be a weekly income. Both the hours and the days off were irregular, but it was a job. You might do day shifts, or night shifts, but you went out to work every day.

One of the most profitable jobs we pulled was at a first class hotel. Charles had got hold of an impression of the pass key from the hotel chambermaid whose sexual needs he was satisfying. From her he also knew the routine of the hotel cleaning staff and the time when there would be no chambermaids, housekeepers or other hotel staff on what promised to be the most profitable floor for our operation.

We had dressed so as to appear as telephone engineers and we went unhurriedly from room to room, dealing only with those rooms where the 'Room Service' card had been hung on the outer door knob to let the chambermaids know that the room was vacated.

Charles let himself in with the pass key. The plan was that if by any chance the resident was in the room, he would explain that a telephone fault had been reported and he had come to check it. If the room was unoccupied I would stay in the corridor and give him a signal if anyone was approaching. Then I would saunter away as if I were an hotel guest, and he would get out of the room fast and just become a room service man on his way from one job to another.

It went perfectly. Travellers in foreign countries usually have considerable sums in travellers' cheques which they do not carry around with them. They are incredibly careless, never seeming to realize that the signatures they have to put on these at the issuing bank can easily be copied by an expert forger for the endorsement. Provided they are moved swiftly from the city or resort of theft to another city, preferably in another country, they are easily turned into currency. The international network for the disposal of stolen travellers' cheques is a complex one of illegal currency dealing with innumerable corrupt links with the official exchange system. It is virtually impossible for the police, or the banks, or bureaux de change to put a finger on the infiltration of stolen travellers' cheques into their systems.

We had a real clean up that morning and Charles collected a toolbox full of rings, watches, necklaces and other small valuables besides a worthwhile haul of travellers' cheques, for which we collected twenty per cent of face value.

It was child's play, with no anxious moments. But, of course, it was not an operation that could be repeated.

One way and another we had now accumulated considerable funds, and Charles suggested that we should move on to Nice.

I was not enthusiastic at returning so soon and so close to the scene of my adventure with Nadia, but Charles was insistent and finally I agreed. We were in funds, and he suggested that we should live well. Since I knew Nice, even though slightly, he left the arrangements to me. So we went to the hotel on Boulevard Dubouchage, where I was known and remembered and impressively welcomed back.

It was all as unfamiliar to Charles as it had been to me when George had so very recently initiated me into this manner of living, and Charles was more than impressed – he gloried in it.

'This is the bloody life, isn't it!' he said as we wandered around the streets of Nice, drank in the smart bars, rubbed shoulders with the wealthy expatriates of other countries. 'Merde! I could go on living like this for ever.'

There was no more bag snatching, no more luggage lifting, no more housebreaking. Charles was having the first holiday of his life, and he was not going to endanger it.

It took him a couple of days to acclimatize himself to his new surroundings. By then he was a couple of new suits to the good, together with new shirts, shoes, ties and other accessories that made him passably a 'gentleman' provided he kept his mouth shut and, if he did open it, disciplined himself to drop those familiar words of his vocabulary which completely betrayed his background.

Naturally, during those two days, our capital became recognizably reduced. Then he came up with the inevitable suggestion that I should have foreseen – not that foreseeing it might have altered the course of events.

To prolong this manner of living would only too soon require replenishment of our funds. While we still had enough capital to finance a legitimate means of doing this, he wanted to try his hand at the Casino at Monte Carlo.

I argued that the Casino did not exist to enrich visitors, but itself by them.

'Your pal George cleaned up, didn't he?' said Charles.

'Yes, but George was a hardened gambler – and he had luck.'

'Do you think I'm not a gambler. Every job I do is a gamble. And I'm on a fucking lucky streak. I *know* it. If you won't come, I'm going alone.'

I went with him, hoping to keep him out of trouble.

This time it was I who knew the ropes. I explained the table to him, and the odds. He lost consistently and steadily. Since *we* were not fools enough to leave money in hotel bedrooms, I had been fool enough to bring all my money with me – and only too soon, mine was in the pool.

It melted on that green baize table. The white chips could have been snowflakes, the way they melted. The colours of the other chips simply dissolved.

He shifted around from *en plein* bets to *transversale*, to *bas à cheval*, to *millieu* to *rouge*, to *manque*, to zero. The little white ball mocked him. He was constantly just one throw ahead of a win. When he bet horizontal, vertical won. Evens came up consistently when he chose odds. The ball found a high compartment when Charles had staked on low numbers. When he made an *en plein* bet, the winning number was tantalizingly one up or down on his choice.

He got nothing back, not even once. The croupiers rake took away and never gave.

Yet right until the very end Charles believed that the luck had to change. And finally we were cleaned out – really cleaned out. There was no more money to buy any more chips, and there were no chips to cash in.

We walked out into the night.

'Merde!' said Charles. 'What do we do now?'

'Walk,' I said glumly.

'I'm sorry, Armand,' he said.

I began to laugh.

'What the hell. It wasn't our money, anyway.'

He began to laugh with me, and we started on the walk which I reckoned was going to be all of twenty miles. It was some consolation to know that we had paid for our hotel for the next few nights, that we had luggage there and, if the worst came to the worst, one or two things we could sell. Clearly we were going to have to do a little thieving and Nice was as good a place as any and probably better than most.

We were well out of the principality when a police patrol car, whose occupants probably had nothing better to do, pulled up alongside us and asked us for our papers.

I showed them mine, and they were satisfied. Then they asked for Charles's, and I realized from the way he just stood there, assessing the situation, that he was wondering if he could make a run for it.

I knew then that Charles hadn't got any identification papers, and that we were in trouble.

I got behind him, and said in a whisper: 'For Christ sake don't tell them our hotel.'

He would understand. Half the things amongst our possessions were stolen, and by now some of the descriptions might have been circulated. He went forward to the car.

We hadn't left the revolver behind and, since he had been going to do the gambling, I had insisted on carrying it. While the two policemen were giving their attention to him, I got rid of it quickly, flinging it into the shrubbery by the roadside.

The manners of the policemen were changing rapidly from civility to abruptness. They were beginning to get us taped. We were driven into Nice and taken to a police station.

The questioning was now less cursory. The examination was more penetrating. We were separated and questioned separately, the one about the other. The discrepancies revealed areas of investigation to be concentrated upon. We were in the hands of experts to whom this was everyday stuff.

They apparently found out that Charles was a deserter. I never saw him again. My passport had been issued locally by the Dutch Consul and the police were a good deal more observant than he had been.

They did not accept it that I was twenty-one. They disbelieved the story of the fire at the barracks and I was stuck with the lie of having been an interpreter. I was destitute, I had obviously been living by thieving and on my wits in the company of an Army deserter. I was unimportant scum and, fortunately, they were not going to bother to investigate whatever petty thieving I must have been doing when they already had all the evidence they needed to deal with me and get rid of me.

I spent the rest of the night in a cell and the next morning I was in the dock. I was charged with being a vagrant and for having a passport displaying a false age. The sentence was three months imprisonment.

The nation of the guillotine and of Devil's Isle is not notable for any gentleness in its handling of convicted criminals. Any notion I had that a French prison would be in any way similar to a Dutch reformatory was savagely and brutally knocked out of my head within a few hours of the prison gates closing on me.

I had added a little more than four years to my age.

And I had indeed sacrificed those years.

By the time I really was twenty-one I had lost the greater part of them to a life spent behind the bars of three successive prisons.

The period of toughening up now lay ahead.

V

The Night I Nearly Murdered Heidi

The way riot police carry truncheons, the guards carried short iron bars.

The iron bars were an official issue and their official purpose was for testing the firmness and soundness of the cell window bars. I often wondered who the sadistic bastard was who conceived this validity for arming the guards with a weapon that could be used for jabbing a prisoner's muscle when an order was misunderstood or not obeyed quickly enough.

Neither at the provincial prison at Grasse where I had my first experience of the French penal system, nor at the notorious Sante where I was later to spend ten horrific months, did I ever see those iron bars used for their issued purpose only.

But, by God, I can still cringe at the memory of their other, everyday use. The last few weeks before release, mind you, are one of the best times in a man's life – they give the evidence of bruising time to disappear.

Man is a thinking animal, and that is his superiority. I did a good deal of thinking during the three months I was in the little man-made hell of Grasse. And I came out with a conclusion that may seem rather an odd one.

Poetry is nonsense. A poet can never express a reality, because he does not command words; they command him.

> 'I never saw a man who looked
> With such a wistful eye
> Upon that little tent of blue
> Which prisoners call the sky,
> And at every wandering cloud that trailed
> Its ravelled fleeces by.'

So wrote Oscar Wilde in the 'Ballad of Reading Jail'. It is lovely stuff to read, music in words, this picture of a soldier waiting to be hanged for knifing a naked whore in some sleazy bedroom.

But it is bunk! I've been there when men have been guillotined. I've waited in that breathless silence that exists, waiting for the sound of the blade falling, when the lifers, who hear it slicing down through a man's neck, begin the panic sound of pandemonium that follows.

'Little tent of blue!' Forgive my derision. 'Wistful eyes!' What crap!

Men in jail stink. They itch. They spend their time catching bugs. They lie, they cheat, they are full of hatred and fear. They masturbate, they sodomize. They are degraded by the smells of sweat, urine and excreta. They are brutalized by the guards they infect with their own brutality. They are beasts, they are animals in cages.

They do not look with poetry in their souls at the sky. The highest they ever lift their eyes is to the level of the prison wall over which lie the taunting realities of women with soft breasts and spread thighs and the tempting bush of pubic hair parted by its cleft; over which lie bottles for the drinker, tobacco, drugs; all addictions of one kind or another.

Believe me! The poet cannot communicate the reality of prison life.

I hated every moment of Grasse. I knew I was descending rung by rung into a recognition of degradation that erodes the innocence with which every child is born. Now I could recognize it and trace my own path downwards – the indignity of the thrashings by my father, the learning to know the smell of my own uncleanliness when I had run away from home, the un-romantic recognition of sexual realities in the reform school dormitory, the humiliation of maleness in my first encounter with a prostitute, the brutality of that brief period in the Foreign Legion – and now Grasse.

The putrescence was still a pit, but I was down into it and its stench was coming up to meet me.

'Tent of blue' be damned. There is no looking up when you are going down.

The eyes betray fear. They betray cunning. They betray hatred. There is no wistfulness.

They picked on me, the guards, during my first three weeks.

'That's how it is,' said Jean, one of the two men in their early twenties with whom I shared a cell. 'They know the ones to pick on, the bastards, and anyway, they give a going over to newcomers, especially young ones doing a first stretch – and a short stretch. They're making sure you'll remember. After a bit, don't worry, it'll be someone else.'

He was in for pimping. They'd run him out of his business because two of his girls had become unclean and he'd gone on working them.

He was right, for after three weeks I got some respite and the target for brutality became a snivelling, middle aged clerk who had been caught cooking company books, poor devil, to pay off a blackmailer who was threatening to tell his wife about a lapse into homosexuality.

I counted the days. It is strange that a short sentence may seem longer than a long one. With a longer sentence, you reconcile yourself to what has happened, start looking for ways to make it tolerable. When it is comparatively short, you live out the full length of every day, counting them off, then recounting them in case you've made a mistake.

The three months in Grasse did not toughen me. They nearly broke me. They drained and exhausted me. Despite my experience, I was too young for the savage realities of an adult male prison and when the morning of my release came the freedom that lay beyond the gates terrified me.

My self confidence had gone. I had nowhere to turn, unless I went back to the crippled Anne-Marie. I had no friends, I had no money, I was in a foreign country.

There was no place to creep away and lick my wounds, and have someone give me shelter and rest while I recovered and healed from the kind of bruising that never shows.

I had no belongings, just the clothing I had been wearing when Charles and I had been picked up on the coast road from Monte Carlo to Nice.

Grasse is a mountain slope town about nineteen miles from Nice, a town where they manufacture perfume. A hundred miles separated me from Anne-Marie, even if I found her still at the Hotel de Clichy.

And I was frightened of going back to Anne-Marie. If I returned she would expect – and with every right – to be taken as a woman again. And it would be impossible for me. I would be impotent with her. I knew it.

A guard opened a small gate in one of the two larger ones, and I walked out into the blazing sunlight, as frightened of my freedom as I was relieved to be free.

'Armand!'

It *sounded* like my mother's voice.

'Well?'

It *was* my father's voice.

I stared at them in disbelief, and then in relief. It had never even occurred to me that there was a solution in going back home. It would have been impossible because however beaten I might be in this moment, I was not defeated. But to be taken back without acknowledging my need of help, was quite a different matter.

There was a hired car waiting at the other side of the road.

'How did you know?' I asked, concealing relief, pretending resentfulness.

'What are Consulates for?' said my father. 'I knew where you were within days of your sentence.'

'You didn't try to get me out?'

'When will you learn that you must purge yourself of your guilt?'

'Yet you have come for me.'

'My responsibility for you is a cross I still have to bear.'

'It *is* going to be nice going back home,' I said, pleased to be able to conceal my relief with bitterness and resentment.

'*Armand!*' said my mother, disapprovingly, reprovingly, yet appealingly.

My father's face was stern. He said nothing. I allowed myself to lapse into a mood for them to interpret as sullen, resentful silence. But, oh, I was relieved at the manner in which my immediate problems were being solved for me.

We drove down into Cannes, where we had a meal – the first good meal I had had since the night of my arrest. Then we began the long train journey back home.

It was an uncomfortable journey, made so by uncomfortable conversation. The Damoclean sword of my father's wrath hung over my head, but I knew he would not smite me with it yet – not on a train journey, not in public. not until he had me on his own territory, not until I was home and he could get me alone.

Things had changed when I got home. The most important change was that Louis, who was now nineteen, had left home. He had heard about my return and he came round to see me the first day I was back.

The storm had still to burst. The double journey to the South of France and back, on which my mother had insisted on accompanying him, had tired my father and he was not ready for his encounter with me. Louis came round when he knew that our father would be out.

'Well, you've really invited the wrath of God this time, haven't you?' he said with a grin.

'I don't know. I'm not sure. So far I've been treated as if nothing has happened.'

'It's to come!' he said cheerfully. 'And when it comes, expect to be the scapegoat for the lot of us – John, Ann and myself. It was my turn when you cleared out. My God, but you've no idea what you let loose. I really thought he was going round the bend. But it was okay for me. I was eighteen, so I walked out and got myself a job, and there was no way he could bring me back.'

'I can understand him taking it out on me for you,' I said. 'But not John and Ann. . . .'

'Ah, but you don't know what I learnt when he blew his top after you scarpered. Carol, who is a frigid bitch if ever there was one, is the only one of us, it seems, who hasn't been a bitter disappointment to him. He always took it out on you, when you were here, but he wasn't as blind as we thought him. He'd known all along about the girls I was screwing; suspected anyway.'

'But John?' I said.

'You never knew about John, did you? Neither did I until that day when it all came out, all the things he and mother kept from the rest of us. You know the way you and I always looked on John as being a holier-than-thou and a sneak. It seems that he'd been pinching money from mother's purse for years. Remember how, because he was the eldest, he used to be sent sometimes with money to pay tradesmen's bills? Then that practice was stopped. *We* never knew why. It never occurred to us to wonder why. But the reason was that John had pocketed the money meant to pay a coal bill.'

I found it hard to believe it, although I knew, of course, that Louis had to be telling the truth.

'And you said Ann,' I reminded him.

'Oh, Ann!' he said. 'You're not going to believe this, but it's true. Do you remember Dick?'

Dick had been at school with me, was a year older than myself. He was the son of a devout member of my father's church, a very diligent and promising student, and my parents had approved of and encouraged my friendship with him. I hadn't disliked him, but I had been cautious about friendship with him. Neither his home background nor my father's approval of him had been any recommendation in my eyes.

Soon after I came out of reform school the friendship ended.

Dick stopped coming round to our house – which struck me as a bit strange because he seemed to be beginning to have a bit of a crush on Ann. Of course he had only been fifteen and Ann was only eleven at the time.

I'd assumed that Dick's parents had put a ban on his association with me because I had become a reformatory school boy.

'And you got it all wrong,' said Louis when I told him this. 'And this isn't gossip or guess work, it's fact. A policeman actually caught Dick on the job with our little sister down among the sand dunes one afternoon, and she *wasn't* being raped. Lucky for him they couldn't persuade her to say that's how it had been, or he'd really have copped it – a girl of only twelve. As it was the juvenile court gave him a suspended sentence and put him on probation.'

I cannot say I was shocked. I'd got over being shocked by people, but one never gets over sometimes being surprised. And what surprised me wasn't Ann, whose sexual precociousness I'd become aware of when she had been only ten and I had had my adventure with her friend Ankie.

I was surprised about Dick. I was surprised that all this had remained hidden from the rest of us. I was puzzled by Louis' suggestion that I had in some way been made the scapegoat by my father. I told him this.

'Oh you bet they kept it quiet. And of course you were the whipping boy. Could you imagine him talking about a thing like that to Ann? I bet you he never ever really discussed it with mother. He wouldn't know how. But you – all you did was a bit of lying, a bit of thieving, and a bit of running away. He could face up to that. He could cope with that. He could take it all out on you. And don't expect to find him changed – except for the worst.'

Louis was right. My father had not changed. I had just two days' respite, and then he was ready to deal with me.

In his own time he summoned me to his study, and the interrogation began. Do not imagine that I broke down easily, or that my confession came quickly.

The interrogation went on all through that day, and through most of the next. When I had run away from home the first time I had financed my adventure by stealing from him. Now, the thing he wanted to know was where I had obtained the money for this escapade.

He was devious and clever. He knew, without my telling him,

that I had enlisted in the Foreign Legion in Paris. He knew I had been discharged from the Legion in Marseille. He knew I had been picked up as a vagrant, penniless but well dressed, in the early hours of the morning on the road from Monaco to Nice. He knew the dates.

His questions moved from time to time and from place to place without seeming to have relevance to one another or to the thing he really wanted to know.

Who was the man who had been arrested with me?

How long had I been in Paris?

How had I got from Marseille to the other side of Nice?

Each question was followed by long silence. He used these silences as a weapon. I would remain tight lipped at each question, refusing to answer. Then he would sit staring at me, and it would go on and on for a minute, for five, for ten.

It is a terrible technique. I could not terminate the interrogation by getting up and walking out. I had to sit there in that silence knowing that eventually one of us would have to speak again. And when I knew that it would never be him, even if we sat there hour after hour, I would say something – anything to end the silence.

And back immediately would come the next question, one either leading from what I had said, or one that seemed completely unrelated, or the original and unanswered question rephrased in the light of what I had just said.

He had all the time in the world, and I was a physically and mentally exhausted boy who had been dominated by him all my life.

He took my answers, the little scraps of information it seemed unbetraying to give him, like pieces of a jig-saw puzzle, and fitted them together.

Every now and then he would show me the growing, but incomplete picture he was wringing out of me.

'No, no . . . it wasn't like that,' I would find myself protesting at some challenging assumption.

'Then how *was* it?'

Silence.

'All right. Let's go back to this man Charles, the army deserter who you've admitted was a thief. Where were you coming from, where were you going?'

He punched me with questions. He tortured me with silences. My determination disintegrated. I forgot what I had and had not told him. I began to attack him. I lost self control. I tried to wound him. I told him what I knew about John.

He knew he was winning, and maintained complete, impassive self control. I knew I was losing, and could not stop myself.

I told him I knew all about Ann. What sort of father was he to let his children be what we had become? Did he dare to blame a little twelve year old girl for letting boys screw her! That was his fault, nobody else's and if nobody else knew it his bloody God would know it. How dare he take it out on me?

Incredibly, unbelievably, I heard myself calling him a fucking bastard, and shouting it out at him.

And he never blanched.

'All right. You want to know. I stole the money to get to Paris. To get away from you. Two thousand guilders, from a house I burgled.'

And *that* was what he had wanted to know. The long interrogation was over.

The police arrived an hour later.

He had done the spade work for them. I was broken. I no longer cared. I answered all the questions. It did not matter what happened now. I was even glad to realize that I would certainly be sent to prison. There was, after all, something to be said in favour of a short iron bar being jabbed against a flexed bicep. Only the body is bruised, not the mind.

Not that the Dutch prisons use this instrument of torture.

I was sentenced to six months in jail to be followed by six months probation. I had already proved that the security of a reform school was inadequate, and as I had already served a sentence in a French adult jail, in spite of my age, it was decided to treat me as an adult criminal. My record justified it. I was beyond reforming. I had to be punished.

I was the youngest prisoner they had ever had in the State prison at Scheveningen and, in consequence, although the treatment was harsh and there were no concessions to comfort, I tended to be treated as a special case. I did not have to share a cell, I was isolated in every way from the older, more hardened, criminals and I was given lighter work to do, with shorter working hours. A special arrangement was made that I should continue my study of languages. Volunteer teachers paid visits to the prison to give me tuition and I was allowed all the text books and recommended reading suggested by them.

Because I represented an unusual case, I suppose, my father

obtained permission for more frequent and private visits than those normally allowed.

It was a strange thing, but now that the responsibility of punishing me had passed out of his hands he sought a different kind of relationship with me. His role was not of inflicting retribution, but persuading repentance.

He prayed for me, aloud and in my presence. He addressed himself to an invisible – and quite unresponsive – omnipotence whose location, for some reason, always seemed to be about six inches and slightly to the left of my shoulder. He invited me to join in these appeals for my own salvation, and I actually found myself turning, half expecting to see a recognizable personality behind me.

I must concede to his sincerity. In this new role he did not spare himself.

I was fortunate that I could expiate my guilt. I should think with understanding of his own guilts, those of which I had justly accused him. John, Louis, myself and Ann – to him the Lord had entrusted these four souls and he had failed in his duty and allowed evil to corrupt us. If I could not pray for myself, I should pray for him.

I might have had a little sympathy if he had asked *me* to forgive him for turning me over to the police. But it wasn't my forgiveness he wanted – it was God's. I decided that *that* was none of my business.

It was the summer of 1938 when I came out of prison, my second prison sentence, my third time behind bars. I was now seventeen.

Hitler had taken over Austria. German troops were moving guns up to the Czechoslovakian frontiers. People were talking of war. Although the First World War had just ended when I was born, I had learnt at school how Holland had maintained her neutrality only by having a big army. After the fall of Antwerp British troops had fled to safety across the Dutch frontier, and there had been a big internment camp for them up at Groningen in the north. Later many German children, victims of malnutrition, had flooded into our country. Finally we had given refuge to the ex-Kaiser Wilhelm.

Now, objectively, the Dutch saw the dangers ahead probably more clearly than any other nation. With France and Britain on the one side and Germany on the other at one another's throats again, the little countries would be in the nut-crackers.

All Great Powers like to play their war games on 'away' grounds if they can. So Holland was preparing, so one heard, with alarming plans to blow up the sea walls and to flood whole areas of the country.

I was conscious of the tensing atmosphere, but it really meant little to me. I returned home to a condition of truce. It seemed accepted that my stay would be a temporary one, but that for the moment anyway I needed the refuge of the family home. There was the general hope that I might be the wiser for my experiences, find myself work and eventually settle down to a career.

First of all I got a job as a stable boy; I had some idea that I might become a jockey, but perhaps because I wasn't ready to settle down I didn't last long in this job.

It wasn't important. I didn't have to have a job, times were unsettled as all over Europe people old enough to remember 'the last time' waited for the Western Front war to erupt. All the familiar things of everyday living seemed much the same, yet there was an air of unreality.

My father was so much preoccupied with the fate of humanity that I became incidental to him. When I said that I wanted to study car mechanics and maintenance, he at once agreed. When I said I wanted to continue my study of languages, he nodded his vague approval. For a time I was going to both night school and day school.

Almost casually he arranged to give me a quite generous allowance. It was as if he wanted to buy off any trouble with me for the time being by making it unnecessary for me to steal.

And for a time I 'went straight'. I'd had my taste of prisons, and I was now known to the police in my home town. Rightly or wrongly, I felt that they had their eyes on me.

I'd also had my taste of women, too.

I had decided that every girl and woman, once she had lost her virginity and had experienced three or four different men, was always available to any man she liked. That is provided she was not emotionally committed by love to one particular man, and providing the approach was right, the opportunity and cir-cumstances were such that she could 'give in gracefully' and could afterwards deny or conceal the fact that it had ever hap-pened if she wanted to do so.

I don't, now, looking back, think that this was a cynical assessment of women.

The truth is that women are very practical and realistic about sex, but romantic about love, whereas men are romantic about sex and realistic about love. And the irony is that each pretends that it is the other way round!

One learns without necessarily being conscious of having done so until later.

During this phase of my life a political situation, about which I had no deep personal feelings, began to steer me back on to the course of life I had temporarily abandoned.

There must have been many people in Holland who assessed the war-situation and realized that the Germans would have to extend all their frontiers to the coast. Many of those with the wealth to make it possible, began, therefore, to withdraw before the Germans moved in and took things over.

Our war began around dawn on May 10, 1940. I was asleep at the time.

Looking back it seems that a lot of people had 'been asleep' for a long time, although hindsight wisdom is always easy. The Germans would have been damned fools to hit at the Maginot Line.

They flooded into Luxembourg, Belgium and Holland at four o'clock in the morning.

Our war lasted four days, of which I missed the first three hours. Then my father wakened me to tell me the news – although at that time it was not so much news as rumour.

It didn't stay rumour for long. That morning the German Air Force dropped four thousand paratroopers into Holland, nearly their entire force of trained parachutists, and they dropped them right on our doorstep – around the Hague and Rotterdam.

The invasion was soon over, and the German military administrators moved in.

There had not been much more than a hiccup to the normal way of living.

The administrators wore velvet gloves. Certainly they were arrogant, but it would be wrong to regard this as a national character trait. Their country was beating the hell out of everyone else.

Nevertheless, unless we insisted, they wanted no trouble. Armies are effective in fighting, not very good in policing. They were prepared to hold us lightly and even politely.

To be truthful, although I was now just nineteen, the new situation meant very little to me. The civilian hardships and shortages were still a long way off, and life under the occupying force was agreeably familiar.

And then slowly I began to realize that the evaluation of right and wrong had taken on a shift of character. Authority, with its policies dictated by the German military bureaucracy, was looking for saboteurs not sneak thieves. It was safer by far to have had a bad record as a burglar than a good one as a burgomaster.

And there were a lot of empty houses whose occupants had fled with nothing much more than they could carry in a couple of suitcases.

I went back to burglaring as a quite deliberate decision. I was experienced, I was on my home ground, thefts of the kind I anticipated making would not be reported and the police were otherwise occupied.

I tried to put myself into the situation of the wealthy house-owners who had shut up their homes and gone away for the duration – hopeful of finding things more or less intact when they eventually returned.

Money, rings and other jewellery they would, of course, have taken with them. But people of this class would have heavier, bulkier valuables that they couldn't carry; silverware, jade, valuable ornaments. Clearly they would hide such things away before leaving. They would have to do it in a hurry. The hiding places wouldn't be pre-planned and carefully prepared.

I picked the nearest unoccupied big house to my home to put my ideas to the test. I had little difficulty in making an entry. The downstairs windows had been shuttered, but there was a single storey lean-to at the back of the house with a skylight. The skylight was bolted on the inside. A little pressure with a tyre lever I had brought with me rooted out the screws.

I spent almost a couple of hours going over the attics, lifting carpets and looking for loose floor boards. I thought of everything – skirting boards, chimney flue recesses, quickly contrived false back walls or ceilings of cupboards. I knew I had to be right, and that what I was looking for was bulky. There were areas of wall paper in some of the rooms that betrayed the fact that framed paintings had been removed.

Under a situation of alien occupation of the country, there would have been no safety in putting valuables, like paintings, into commercial storage, nor would they be put in the grounds of the house.

I did a little calculation, finally, about the size of the missing picture frames, and then there was only one possible place, but it was so stupid that I had overlooked it.

They'd drained the water cistern in the roof, and cut off the mains supply, and just dumped everything hurriedly inside the tank. It was quite crazy, because the house, being empty, was liable to be commandeered, and then the first thing that would have been done would have been to turn on the water main stopcock.

I'd brought a bag with me and I filled it with as much of the solid silver as I could carry. Then I made an inventory of the rest of the things.

The next day I visited the old shoemaker.

At first he pretended not to know me, or remember me. Then he told me that he was no longer in business as a fence for stolen property. The international syndicate, of which he had been just one feed line, had had to suspend operations because of the war situation. The channels by which stolen goods could be moved from one country to another had all been closed.

I showed him the silver, told him what else there was, and said that this was only a beginning. He passed the tip of his tongue round his mouth. He was clearly tempted.

'There *might* be other markets,' he said.

'Our new tourist trade, looking for souvenirs to take back home?' I asked.

'There are possibilities,' he admitted. 'The selling prices may not be high, though.'

'Why not make them pay for what they'll eventually find and take anyway?' I said. 'That's patriotism, isn't it? Shall we be patriots, you and I?'

'I *am* a patriot!' he said to me. 'Believe me, I *am* a patriot. All right, leave the stuff with me. It could even be a useful thing. I have some contacts. Come and see me in a week's time.'

He was a patriot, all right, and that was my bad luck. That was why he had been tempted. He'd seen a usefulness in the business I'd made possible that he hadn't explained to me.

We did great business for about three months and then, one day, when I let myself into his shop, I found he had other visitors – and they were in uniform. They weren't the ordinary German military either, and they weren't *all* in uniform.

The old man had already been methodically and scientifically beaten up. There was quite a bit of blood around the backroom of the shop where they were questioning him, and quite a lot was still on his face.

They had ripped the place apart and when I saw the transmitting equipment I knew that I had walked right into trouble. I was invited to sit down, and then immediately helped to sit down – a warming-up for the beating up I, too, might expect.

I've often wondered about the morality of criminals, and how strong an influence upon them is the sheer sense of adventure. Although I was an exception to it, some of the most hardened criminals prove, in time of war, to be the most daring and reckless of patriots. It is as if they sharpen their teeth on a legitimate enemy.

The network to which the old man belonged did not, it was true, exist any longer for the purpose of moving stolen goods from country to country. With the coming of war it had simply adapted itself to becoming a channel of communication for espionage and for any subversive underground work that might come its way.

The old man was a patriot, all right. And he had seen that with the role of a seller of loot to the occupying forces he might create a screen for his real activities, even gain some kind of immunity from investigation. Unfortunately they had already been on to him.

I was taken down to the Binnenhof where the occupying forces had established headquarters. They kept me there for twenty-four hours, and they really put me through it.

I stuck to my story that I was nothing more than a thief with a record, and that I had used the old shoemaker as a fence long before the war.

Fortunately the records were all there to be checked and in the end they believed and handed me over to the Dutch police.

I wasn't a child any more. I wasn't a teenager any more. This time I was sentenced to a year to which was added the six months of probation.

I went back to Scherveningen, a common criminal now without any of the special privileges of family visitors or educational tuition and opportunities. And the jail was a lot tougher now.

Theoretically it was still a Dutch prison, in the hands of the Dutch. In fact, and for very good, sound reasons, the Germans ran it. A prison full of hardened and desperate criminals, staffed by their fellow countrymen during an occupation could have easily become a garrison of resistance. So the Dutch guards watched us, and the German guards watched them. And the German guards had the guns.

It was a matter of human response to a situation, that the Dutch guards tended to treat us with some degree of leniency. We were prisoners within the walls of Scherveningen, but so were they within the frontiers of Holland. Naturally these circumstances did little to help pass my eighteen months, dreary day after dreary day.

Louis was my only and very occasional family visitor. The family had become split up and my parents were living just outside Bourtange, right in the north of the country, right up against the German border. It was a sensible place to ride out the Occupation. The further north you were, the further you were from all that war meant, the closer you were to the enemy frontier, the less he feared your potential for acts of hostility. His anxious focus overlooked you, went beyond you.

Louis did not have a lot of sympathy for me. I had asked for the trouble I was in. I had to admit that this was true.

'Anyway you're not missing anything,' he said.

'That's what you think,' I told him.

'Oh, *that*'ll be there for you when you come out,' he assured me with a grin. 'I tell you, if you don't have any patriotic inhibitions against screwing frauleins, you want to get yourself inside Germany. With all their menfolk taken away, they're going crazy for it.'

Our father, he told me, had taken my backsliding into crime very much to heart.

'You really knocked him out this time,' he said.

'He had it coming to him,' I said.

'Think that, if it makes you feel better.'

'I don't really feel anything at all.'

'That's the best way of all for it to be.'

'It's *my* life.'

'Okay. But when you get out, live it, don't rot it away.'

It was good, sound advice.

I came out of Scheveningen in the March of 1942. I was now twenty-one, and there was no question at all of going home again to my father's house. I was on my own, young, healthy, fit and tough and my country was under the occupation of a foreign power. Like it or not, I was going to have to have a role in events, and I was required to report to the Labour Exchange.

I had certain immediate options for which I could volunteer. If I did not volunteer for one of these special services, or if I volunteered but was not accepted, then I would be directed into employment. With three prison sentences and one reform school sentence behind me I could only expect to be given an unpleasant, undesirable job.

The course I had taken in car mechanics and maintenance suddenly had value. One of the volunteer jobs was that of truck driving in Germany. It was classed as a hard labour job, which meant extra rations. Moreover volunteers for such work did not live in labour camps, but had private lodgings.

I volunteered immediately.

They gave me a driving test, a formal medical examination, and a short course on combustion. Within a few days I was given all my necessary documentation and sent to a village called Beierfeld to work for a small transport firm. The business belonged to a man called Max Wendler, to whom I reported after I had checked in with the local police and the committee in charge of alien labour in the province of Sachsen.

Max was about forty. He had a four-truck business which he had built up from nothing. He was short, sturdy and as strong as a bear. At the time I joined him, he was in real trouble. The army had drained off every able bodied man that could possibly be spared. The light industrial work of the district, which was pottery, was being run almost entirely by women. The only men Max could get as truck drivers either had disabilities or were army medical rejects. At best, Max was only able to keep three trucks on the road and this meant doing a driver's job himself and then tackling the maintenance and service work at night.

The work largely involved transport of the crated manufactured goods either to other towns in the region, or to the railway. But there was also a coal-haul run, and this involved shifting twenty tons of coal – a whole railway wagon load – from the goods yard to the yards of the industrial users.

The lorry used for this job was a five tonner, so four trips were required. The lorry had to be backed up to the side of the wagon, tail board down, and then the coal had to be shovelled in. The trouble was that the wagon was in the railway yard for exactly four hours, and if one hadn't shifted all the coal by that time, what was left was tipped on to the trackside, from where it then had to be lifted shoulder high, shovelful by shovelful.

This was one of my jobs, and I had to do it singlehanded.

'I'm glad to see you,' said Max Wendler, looking me over when I reported to him.

I'll bet he was, too!

Wendler lived in a house adjoining the garage where he kept and serviced the trucks. I was to lodge with him. He was married, and they had a schoolgirl daughter. Frau Wendler was around her husband's age.

She was short, sturdy and as strong as a bear!

Just like Max. They looked like brother and sister, not that they behaved in a way that brothers and sisters should behave. Max was always slapping and pinching her bottom, and she loved it in a playful way. They would even hug each other like a couple of bears whenever they met, even after a few hours' separation.

One wondered, though, what a man saw that was exciting and arousing in a woman like Frau Wendler – until one stopped to wonder what a woman saw in a man like Max Wendler.

I liked her from the start. She fed me well. I could talk to her, and without ever interfering she tried to give me a lot of sound advice much of which I should have taken instead of laughing at it.

Louis had been right. Move into a small town where all the virile young men, boyfriends and husbands, have been taken away by the army, and you find out right away what it must be like to be the solitary ram in a flock of sheep during the mating season.

I went into a barber's at lunch time on my first day in the town. I'd chatted to a girl at the despatch desk of the pottery factory where I'd made my first pick-up that morning, and when I'd cautiously suggested meeting her in the evening she had agreed so quickly that I felt pretty certain that my eighteen months enforced celibacy was going to end before the day was over.

I was the barber's only customer, and he talked as he cut my hair. Naturally I told him who I was, where I was from, and who I had come to Sachsen to work for.

I was pretty sure that it would be the same as at home and that a barber's shop would be where I could get a supply of french letters. I didn't even have to enquire. When it came to the time when barbers ask politely if there will be anything else, he assumed my requirements and simply asked how many *capote Anglaise* I required.

I said, as casually as possible:

'Oh, I'd better take a dozen.'

He looked at me with surprise.

'Only a dozen. I could give you a good reduction on a gross.'

'A gross!' I couldn't resist it. 'That'd be wishful thinking.'

'They won't last long around here,' he said, and winked.

He was right, too. The girl I met that night took it all for granted and didn't want to waste any time. We had one cup of coffee in the cafe where she had told me to meet her, and then she took me straight back to her room and I'd used up three of my stock before I left her, quite early in the evening, because we both had to be up for work early in the morning.

I felt a whole lot better for the experience and I had the pleasant feeling that I'd done the same thing for her, too.

For the first two or three weeks, I had the time of my life. I had a girl every night, usually a different one each time. I was obsessed by my own feelings of virility. Half the time I was driving Max Wendler's five tonner around, just thinking about it kept me in such a state of erection that sometimes I laughed out loud with exuberance at the crazy notion, when I came to change gear, that what did I need with that gear shift lever sticking up out of the floorboards when I had one of my own!

'You want to watch your step with the girls around here, Armand,' Frau Wendler cautioned me. 'A lot of young women, without men – oh, I'm not blaming you, or them. But it's a dangerous situation.'

'Of course it isn't,' I assured her.

'If it was always the same girl, I'd say nothing,' she said. 'For a woman, with any man there are always risks of many kinds. And for a man with any woman there are risks, too. That's life. They have to be taken. But if you take the risks with woman after woman after woman, one day your luck will be out.'

'Don't you believe it!' I said.

The day my luck ran out was a Sunday.

Ironically, I had capitulated to myself about the measure of my virility. I had a day of rest from work, and I would make it a day of rest from women.

Max had been continuously urging me to take advantage of the fact that I was working in such a beautiful province as Sachsen and to see some of the tourist attractions. There were ruins at a place called Prinzenbrunnen that he particularly recommended.

So on that Sunday morning I suddenly announced that, yes, I
would go out to Prinzenbrunnen.

'You haven't a date then?' asked Frau Wendler.

'No. Isn't it terrible? I must be losing my attractions to the
ladies.'

'Well, now!' she said, smiling and, I think, understanding.
'It's going to be a nice day. The woods will be beautiful. I will
pack you some sandwiches. And if it seems that I give you
enough for two, that is because I know that enough for two is
only enough for one of Armand!'

I had to change trains at a tiny Saxony town called Aue, and
to wait there some time for my connection. It was a hot summer
day. As I stepped out of my compartment at Aue on to the
almost deserted platform, a young German soldier and a pretty
blonde of about twenty came towards the compartment of which
I had conveniently opened the door.

He was fully kitted out, and was obviously going back to his
unit after a period of leave. He slung his equipment on to the
seat I had just vacated, and then stood chatting to the girl. I
had moved across the platform to sit on the nearest bench seat
in the sun, knowing I had about twenty minutes to wait. I
watched them from there, partly because there was nothing else
to do and partly because a slight breeze was blowing the girl's
light summer frock into a moulding of her legs. The frock was
tight across a shapely little bottom and there was no betraying
line of any undergarment so I figured she was quite naked under
the frock – below her waist, anyway. I found myself speculating
on the likelihood that they had just had a last fuck somewhere
before the poor devil went off to the Front, and that I might
well be looking at a man who had just enjoyed it for what was
going to be the last time in his life.

It was an interesting speculation because here was I, a completely objective observer, appreciating an experience he'd just
had, far more than he seemed to be appreciating it himself.

The post-coital feelings of men vary enormously. For some
men it can be the best and most appreciated part of the whole
experience right from the beginning of arousal. For others it is
a period of utter withdrawal from the woman – not just the
physical withdrawal from her body, but a complete withdrawal
from the relationship with her.

It seemed to be like that with this young man, because I
noticed that if she put a hand on his sleeve or touched him, he

appeared to find an excuse to avoid the physical contact. It was also clear that he was steering clear of any intimate, tender talk with her. He was laughing, making gestures with his hands, trying to be entertaining, and he seemed glad when the signal was given for the train to leave.

He kissed her in an abrupt, hurried manner, and withdrew far more urgently than was necessary from the arms that seemed to hold him back in a desire to keep him from ever leaving.

She was Heidi.

I watched her stand on the platform as the train went out, waving to him. She went on waving long after he had withdrawn from leaning out of the window to wave back to her.

When she finally turned away and I saw her face, I was pretty certain that I had been right and that she had just been fucked. And I felt sad for her. Even though I was sure that women wanted and needed the experience just as much as men, they are the ones who must surrender themselves to being possessed. And even if it has just been healthy sexual fun, without any deep emotional meaning, they deserve more gratitude from a man for that surrender than the young soldier had given her.

She moved to the next seat along the platform and sat down. I watched her and saw that she was sobbing. There was nobody else on the platform, the solitary porter on duty having gone to wherever he disappeared to between trains, On impulse I got up and walked over to her.

'Forgive me,' I said. 'But it's a lovely day, the sun is shining, and you're a pretty girl. You oughtn't to be weeping like that. Is there anything I can do to help?'

I, who thought myself so wise, said *that*!

'I've just been seeing off someone . . . someone I'm fond of,' she said, looking up, her face not unattractive with the tears glistening on her cheeks in the sun. 'He's gone back to the Front. I might never see him again.'

'That's true of every time two people say goodbye, however many times a day and for however many years they may do it — every time a husband goes off to work, for instance,' I told her. 'Your boy friend is just as likely to come back as if he were your husband going off to the office in the morning. He'll probably come back, and propose to you, and you'll marry him, and you'll have five children, and in a few years' time you'll be waving goodbye to him when he goes off to work, and it won't really be any different from this goodbye, will it?'

A smile came over her face at last.

'I never thought of it like that!' she said. Then she pouted. 'But – he didn't seem to mind going. He even seemed to be glad when the train went. And . . . well, that's not what I'd expected.'

I *had* been right.

'The important thing is to see something from the other person's point of view,' I told her, trying to be very wise about it, for personally I thought he'd been an unfeeling, ungrateful bastard. 'A man, going back to the Front, has got to steel himself to the realities of what that means. The last thing he can afford to do is show his emotions. I daresay he *was* glad when the train finally went, since he *had* to be on it. It ended the danger for him of you making him behave in a way he'd think of as being unmanly.'

'Really?' she asked, and made room on the seat for me to sit down.

'That's right,' I assured her.

The introduction was over, so we formally introduced ourselves to one another. And when I had told her as much as was necessary about myself, and what I was doing at Aue on that morning, I suggested that if she had nothing better to do, and if it would cheer her up, she might care to join me on the trip to Prinzenbrunnen. I showed her the sandwiches Frau Wendler had supplied.

'I can't possibly eat them all on my own,' I said.

'All right,' said Heidi.

It really was a glorious day and Frau Wendler had been right about the woods being beautiful. They were pines and they provided a soft carpet for our picnic. We chose a place well away from any paths, where the sunlight shafted down through a clearing, and it was soon very obvious that this was an area of complete privacy where nobody would intrude upon us.

This was not the way in which I had intended, expected or been prepared for my 'day of rest' to develop. But as Heidi lay there in the sun after we had finished the sandwiches, I could not help but be conscious of the utter, tempting nakedness underneath her dress. Nor did she help me to keep my mind off the inevitable thoughts of her cunt.

I tried to tell myself that it must be casual and unselfconscious on the part of a girl who had just been weeping over the departure of her lover, but the fact was that every time she moved her dress rode higher up long white legs that very definitely were not being kept modestly closed.

And then finally she drew one knee up and let it fall outwards. I knew that I had only to move a little further down the slope to be able to look right up under the dress, into the open avenue between those opened legs, where there would be no shadow except that of the bush of hair . . . if my speculation was as right as I was sure it was.

I was incapable of resisting it. My penis was finding its own way up into full erection, despite the constraints of my clothing. I took out the packet of cigarettes I had in my jacket pocket and let them slip down the slope to give myself the excuse to move to where I wanted to be.

I made the move half expecting her to close her legs, straighten them, smooth her dress down to her knees. But she didn't, and I found myself looking at a delightful, pouting and swollen little mouth surrounded by such a light growth of very fine, very blonde hair that it concealed nothing.

It was so naked, and she had such an exceptionally large clitoris that it was standing out from the top of the cleft like a pink, moist rosebud, that I knew that she was as randy as she had made me become.

I lay there looking at the lovely sight, and she lay there looking at me looking, obviously leaving the next move to me.

I had come out unprepared, and had no sheaths with me and I knew, with some strange precognition, that this was the day Frau Wendler had wisely warned me about, the risks taken once too often, when the luck ran out. But I had not spent those days and nights in Monte Carlo with Nadia without learning a great deal about the alternative sensual pleasures of sex.

I reached forward and began caressing the siken warmth of her inner thighs, slowly moving my hand further and further upwards until I was finally in a position for my fingers to open the soft lips and to enter her. Nadia had taught me where and how to touch, where and how to caress, and where and how to massage to produce sensations of torturing pleasure to the delicate and normally concealed sexual anatomy of a woman so that a man may do more with his finger and still more with his tongue than with his penis.

Although every woman's sensuality is subtly unique to herself, Nadia had taught me what no man may learn on his own and what few women either can or dare to explain to a lover about themselves. And certainly with Heidi it worked, for as I caressed with gentle pressure above and round the proud little clitoris I saw it and the soft inner lips of the nymphae begin to diffuse with colour, and as the glans of her clitoris withdrew into its hood, I slid two fingers into the vaginal vortex, spreading them apart when they reached the muscular orifice so that, without penetrating it, I could agitate it with rapid little movements.

She began to gasp and contort. When I looked at her face, her lips were drawn back and her teeth were clenched.

It was over in a few seconds, and when it was over she drew her other knee up, tightened her buttocks and thrust her cunt up and out boldly towards me.

'Now fuck me!' she ordered.

The word in German has the same dramatic and onomatopoeic hardness that it has in English, lacking the softer sounding versions of the French and original Latin descriptive language words.

I ripped desperately at the front of my trousers, kicking my shoes off, pulling my trousers and underpants off, and showing myself to her.

'Quick!' she said reaching her hand out for my penis.

'We mustn't,' I said in agony. 'I haven't a sheath. Play with it for me. For God's sake.'

She shook her head. There was a strange look in her eyes.

'I want it – inside,' she said tensely. 'You can fuck, if you *promise* to pull it out before you come. Don't you want to?'

She had it in her hand, her fingers caressively teasing.

'Yes. Yes!' I gasped. 'I want to.'

'And you promise?'

I was now utterly lost.

'Yes. I promise.'

I went into her with almost violence and as I felt the little muscular orifice opened by, and then close tightly behind, the circumcised head of my penis, her knees tightened into my sides and I felt everything I could no longer see opening to me, and there was no self control, no hope of it and my semen was spurting into her at the end of the first thrust.

She held me to her with her legs, letting me finish. Then, when my heavy breathing began to subside, she said quietly:

'You promised to come out. You *promised*!'

'I couldn't help myself,' I said miserably.

'I'm just at the worst time for being caught,' she said, drawing away from underneath me. 'It's a risk I've never taken before.' She reached for my underpants, dried me on them first and then herself. 'But probably it'll be all right. Oh, God, I hope so. My father would kill me if I had an illegitimate baby.'

'It won't come to that,' I said, trying to believe it myself.

'But it *could*,' she said.

'It won't. If . . . if you get pregnant, then I'll marry you.'

'That's an easy promise to make, *now*!' she said.

'I mean it,' I said.

I wanted nothing of the kind to even have to be considered, but I had already considered my immediate danger. Heidi had only to accuse me of raping her and I would be in real trouble. I was a foreign labourer, and if a clean, healthy young fraulein of good Aryan stock said that she had been raped by a foreign labourer, then she *had* been raped by the decadent, lustful, animal alien. And, dear God, although millions of nice ordinary Germans genuinely didn't know, or were pretending not to believe what they couldn't possibly prevent, the fiendish things that were already happening in the concentration camps were known all right.

Let this girl, in the mood of a moment, breath an unretractable word of accusation about me, and I could disappear without trace into one of those terrible cesspools of humanity.

'But it'll be all right,' I said. And then something occurred to me. 'Besides, anyway, before me today, your boy friend. . . . These things aren't always safe. So if anything happens, it could always be possible. . . .'

She got up. Her manner had changed. It was hard even to remember the desperately sensual temptress she had been only a few minutes before.

'Do you think I'm that sort of girl – that I'd let *two* men do that to me, one after the other. If that's what you Dutch are like, no wonder our Stormtroopers just walked through your country.'

I *did* think she was like that. I was suddenly having quite a revised understanding of her. And I didn't dare tell her my thoughts.

'Poor Hans,' she said and sighed. 'I wanted so much to give him one wonderful thing to remember in case he never came back. I thought it was my duty towards one of the Fatherland's sons – but *you* wouldn't understand that, would you? It was to be *my* sacrifice; my gift of myself to a brave man. That was why I was naked and ready for him.'

I wanted to tell her to stop talking like a cheap woman's novel, and to just remember that I was the man to whom only a few minutes before she'd been lying with her legs up and knees thrust out saying: 'Now – fuck me!' What sort of mug did she think I was?

Or maybe she knew the answer to that quite well.

'But Hans – *he* respected me. Not like you, crawling down there to have a dirty look up under my frock. Then taking advantage of the fact that I was too upset to realize what you were doing until you had made me defenceless.'

Then I realized that she wasn't even saying this to me, expecting me to believe a word of it. She was rehearsing what her story would be if she found herself pregnant and she needed to use it. I had to be the first to hear it because it would be entirely up to me whether it was ever told or not.

I said nothing, which was all she had wanted.

'Oh, well,' she said with an abrupt change of manner. 'What's happened can't be undone, so let's not talk about it any more. Maybe I'll be all right. If things go wrong, I'll let you know. And I know where to find you.'

'You know where to find me,' I agreed.

'That's right. I can *always* keep in touch, can't I, Armand – you being a foreign worker!'

Oh, she had me all right. I couldn't change jobs, except with my employer's sanction. And wherever I went, if I moved on, I would be traceable through the central organization for alien labour.

We walked back to the station.

Now she told me that she had a job at the station cafe at Aue. Her home was in Duisburg where her father was a miner. Her name was Kuster, and she had a brother in the Army.

It was hard to support the feeling I had by any actual evidence, but I sensed that she already had a proprietorial attitude towards me and was establishing it.

She did most of what talking there was on the way back to the station, and on the subsequent journey to Aue.

I tried hard to understand her. She was after all the first girl to whom I had made a promise of marriage, however conditional it was, however hopeful I might be, even in this moment of making the promise, that it would never be necessary.

It was absurd that something that had taken just one second could possibly dictate the whole of the rest of my life.

But then, how long does it take a bullet to hit you – and nothing is more permanent in its consequences!

So although I argued the improbability, I already had a dreadful feeling about the inevitability.

I asked her about Hans.

'*You* don't have to know about him,' she said.

'If you get caught, if we had to marry, I'd have to know,' I said.

'His name's not Hans,' she said. 'He's not German. He's a Czech. Forget him. He's no more your concern than the girls you must have had are mine.'

Miserably I realized that she really was taking things very much for granted.

I studied her carefully and overtly now, seeing her much more critically. And what I saw was not reconcilable with the pretty blonde with the breeze moulding a thin dress into the sculpture of a naked body beneath it.

The blonde hair *wasn't* the spun gold it had seemed in the sunlight, alive with movement like ripe corn in a summer field. It was strawish, and not too well cared for. The soft mouth was, after all, rather tight and thin. Her skin wasn't good. The varnish on her finger nails was chipped. All the perfumes of her presence had been provided by the scents of flowers, of summer, of pine needles. She smelt of cheap soap; antiseptic and uninviting.

What had I landed myself into?

I realized that I was a snob. Take a girl up into the woods on a summer afternoon and enjoy the fact that she is female, and it doesn't matter in the least that she's a waitress and daughter of a coal miner. But how very, very different to take that same girl back to one's parents and to have to say: 'This is my wife,' when there was nothing more to recommend her than that she could be taken up into the woods to be laid!

We got to Aue. My connecting train to Beierfeld was due in only ten minutes, but Heidi did not offer to wait to wave *me* off; nor did I want her to.

I remembered how I had criticized the Czech soldier, whatever his name really was, for the lack of ardour in his farewell to her. Now here I was only about four hours later both feeling and showing even less as I said: 'Well. Goodbye. Let's hope for the best.'

'Let's do that!' she said. 'I'll let you know.'

I didn't ask for her address.

Max wanted to talk about Prinzenbrunnen when I got back, but soon gave the subject up when all I could give him were brief, vague, unenthusiastic answers. Frau Wendler looked at me curiously, and said nothing.

I was morose and quiet for several days. I stopped going out in the evenings. I passed up the opportunities to date girls. I turned in early, and slept badly. Max seemed to notice nothing, but Frau Wendler, who said nothing, was obviously very well aware that I was in some sort of trouble; and of course, I knew she would guess that it was over a woman.

About a week later, Max and I had our first quarrel. It wouldn't have been important but for the situation about Heidi, and the use I was able to make of it. It probably wouldn't have occurred had not the anxious situation about Heidi put me into a resentful mood.

Max had been allocated another driver, a Frenchman. The new driver did not speak any German and neither Max nor, indeed, most of the people in the district spoke any French, for the border between the two countries was about two hundred and fifty miles away.

I was asked to act as an interpreter for the Frenchman, which I didn't really mind doing in the least although he was a dull, uncommunicative fellow with some private reasons for a secretiveness I was unable to penetrate in the short time I knew him. But when Max came to pay me at the end of the first week the Frenchman was with us, I had anticipated him at least slipping me something extra for my requested work of interpreting.

It hadn't just been a question of translating conversational instructions to the Frenchman. I had to go through all the leaflets of regulations and the service manuals of instruction with him.

There had not actually been any hardship in giving up an hour or so of my evening after work to labour our way through not only the translation but also the understanding, because I was no longer going out in the evenings. But Max had expected and required me to do this and I felt I should be paid for it.

And I was in the mood to say so.

I thumbed through the money he gave me.

'Cela manque la mise en marche, Herr Wendler,' I said.

'What's that?' asked Max.

'You want me to translate? Let it go. Forget I said it. It wouldn't be worth my while, would it?'

He got it, and the little German bear bristled.

'You think I should pay you for talking to the Frog?'

'I've had to do a hell of a lot of croaking to him, so why not? After all, I'm not a P.O.W. I'm a volunteer. I've got better qualifications in languages than I have in mechanics. It ought to be worth *something* extra.'

He knew I had a point, all right. He hated being in the wrong. But a German could only be in the wrong in a dispute with another German.

'You had no right to ask or to expect,' he said.

'Expectations are everybody's privilege,' I said. 'And I've noticed that if one doesn't ask one doesn't get.'

'You're telling me you won't do any interpreting unless you get extra pay?' he asked furiously.

'You're doing the interpreting now,' I said. 'I take my hat off to you. You're good at it.'

'If that's all the bloody thanks I get for giving you a good home, sod you,' he said furiously. 'Who needs to speak fucking French, anyway. Before we've finished with the bastards this time they'll all be made to learn to speak German, anyway.'

He was just angry, of course. Once in a while he could get that way, and oh, he was a delight to listen to. In no language is bad language more explosively obscene and effective than in German. It was the first time he had let fly at me. Most importantly, though I didn't realize it at the time, it created a new relationship between us. In some ways a better one. For my purposes an improved one.

Of course I went on interpreting. And of course, as a matter of principle, I got no extra pay. It was not to be for long, anyway.

The situation was precipitated two weeks later. The letter I had been fearing but expecting from Heidi arrived.

It was badly written and illiterate, but I understood quite clearly what was left unsaid.

She had to see me, and it was urgent. I was to come to Aue the next evening. She would meet me at the station. She told me which train she would meet.

I was impatient to get it over. I finished a bit earlier than usual that day and caught the train before the one Heidi had told me to catch. I expected that she would be working at the station cafe.

The cafe was about to close down when I arrived at Aue. I was the only customer and there was only the one waitress – but she wasn't Heidi.

'You'll have to hurry,' she said. 'The kitchen staff is off already, and I finish in ten minutes.'

'I don't really want anything,' I told her. 'Actually I'm looking for Heidi Kuster.'

'Then you'll be Armand!' said the girl. 'Heidi went off duty early shift, and she's not expecting you until the next train in.'

'I got off early, too,' I said.

'Well, aren't you the eager one!' she said with a smile that somehow twisted her mouth. 'Here – come on through to the back, and I'll give you a coffee – on the house. There won't be anyone else in now, so I can shut up.'

She closed the cafe down and we went through into the kitchen area. Having got rid of her apron, she poured a couple of cups of coffee. It was clear that she was interested in being involved in the situation and wanted to talk.

'You're a friend of Heidi's?' I asked her.

'I work with her, if that's what you mean. I know what's going on, if that's what you mean?'

'And what do you mean by what's going on?' I asked.

'She's got you lumbered, hasn't she?'

'I'm not sure that I know what you mean.'

'Oh yes you do; and if you don't, you very soon will. She's missed, and she's seen the doctor, and she's pregnant, and you're going to have to marry her. No way out for you because she's already dropping hints about being raped. And if she says that, who'll believe you – a foreign conscript worker? If that happened, I wouldn't wish my worst enemy in your shoes.'

She wasn't telling me anything I didn't know – but I thought she might easily be persuaded to do so.

'It wasn't rape.'

'I'll believe you.'

'It might not be my child.'

'How right you are.'

She enjoyed telling me. She must have really hated Heidi. Of course, she pointed out, my knowing would do me no good.

The young Czech was Frans Dolezal. His father ran the station cafe. Heidi had had her eyes on Frans from the day he'd first come to Aue on leave with a minor war injury.

'Not one that put him out of action as far as Heidi was concerned. He's been sleeping with her for the past three weeks.'

'Well, in that case . . .'

'In that case what? First – did you take any precautions to prevent pregnancy? She'll swear Frans did, because she knows Frans would swear he did, *if* she could ever prove that it could be his kid. And that's the second thing, and Heidi knows it. Frans certainly took full precautions to make sure she could never pin anything on him. Heidi never meant anything to him but a bit of the other. And his old man would back him up, say he slept at home every night of his leave. Old Dolezal wouldn't have Heidi as a daughter-in-law if the Fuhrer gave him back their country in return.'

'What the hell do I do?'

She looked at me scornfully. Whatever she had against Heidi didn't make her my friend.

'You're all a lot of bastards, you men. If it *could* be yours, what difference does it make whether it is or not? Take a ticket in a raffle and your number may come up. If you don't want the prize, don't enter the raffle.' She grinned at me. 'Frans had a whole book of tickets, and you only had one – but one's enough. Some prize!'

Then she kicked me out, and I hung around until Heidi arrived. Heidi took me to a cafe in the town. On the way I mentioned the times of the trains back to Sachsen that night.

'There's one just after seven in the morning,' she said. 'You may as well spend the night. The damage is done now. I'm having your child, anyway.'

It is hard to be truthful about how I felt when she said that. I didn't want to marry her. I was pretty sure she was using me, and now I had a shrewd idea that she'd gone to Prinzenbrunnen with me with the deliberate intention of getting an ejaculation of another man's semen – a man she could compel to undertake the responsibilities that Frans couldn't be forced to shoulder if there proved to be a need.

I didn't even like her, but – !

But she hadn't been acting her sexual responses, and the memory of what had happened under those fir trees, and the thought of having her completely naked in bed in a very short time suddenly excited me. In a strange way, I'd never been quite so excited by the anticipation as I now was.

For the first time in my life I didn't have to worry about the consequences. For the first time in my life I didn't have to have any consideration for the woman's feelings. I could just use her, play out all my fantasies, do anything and everything unspeakable with her that the mind wondered about. It was her bargain, not mine.

Of course it wasn't that way at all. The barriers in the mind can't just be blown away. They are the concrete of character, not the insubstantial mists of self discipline. And when, later, we went to bed together in the bedsitter where I was to spend quite a few nights over the next few weeks, I couldn't even get an erection, and it was she who had to throw away all the reservations to cause my eventual arousal.

But that was after the discussion we had in the cafe round the corner from her boarding house.

She told me about her interview with the doctor. It was, of course, early days, but he had nevertheless been positive. I could see him and confirm it, if I wished to do so. The point was that the sooner we got married, the better it would be for the child's sake.

'*Our* child, Armand!' she said.

I said that of course I wouldn't go back on my promise to marry her. But she had to realize that it couldn't be immediate. She was a German and I was a Dutch worker. I had to make an application to Berlin for permission to marry her. Then I also had to get my parents' approval.

'Your parents?' she said. 'What have they got to do with it.'

'It is Dutch law,' I told her. 'You can check on it, but you'll find that what I'm telling you is true. I'm twenty-one, but in our country one is a minor until the age of thirty.'

'I don't believe it.'

'It's fact. I've a Dutch passport and nobody will marry us without the formal agreement of my parents. I'll have to apply to the Dutch Embassy. Oh, there won't be any trouble, but there is a war on, and it will take time I imagine.'

'You're lying.'

'Find out for yourself tomorrow.'

She pulled a face.

'Well, we can be engaged.'

'Of course. I'll buy you a ring.'

'Have you the money?' she asked with sudden eagerness.

'Don't expect anything grand. I'm a truck driver, paid foreign labour rates. And we're *not* in love, Heidi.'

'But you want to come to bed with me tonight, don't you?'

'Yes,' I said. 'And *now*. Finish your coffee and let's go.'

Fine words in the light of what happened when we did get into bed. But it was not always like that with Heidi.

There is no getting away from it that events made her one of the most important women in my life. I actually fucked Heidi more times than any other one woman in my life. I disliked her. I resented her. Yet it is true that I wanted her with a trembling, undisciplined urgency and that I had more moments of heaven with her than with any other woman.

And maybe I came to understand that vicious little slut better than I have ever understood or ever will understand any other woman.

She was as much trapped in the relationship as I was. The Kusters were Catholics, and from the very moment when either one of Frans's sperms or one of mine – and it *could* have been either – had penetrated that fecund ova, Heidi had a new, God-given human life within her. To have destroyed the life would have been as much murder as to have taken a knife and plunged it into someone else's body. She was the chosen custodian of that life. The Lord had given, and the mortal man involved had only been the Lord's instrument. And it was for the Lord, and nobody else, to take away in His chosen time.

Rubbish? Nonsense? Pathetic, stupid indoctrination?

Oh, no! There are always two Truths – yours and mine. Truth is a personal thing, nothing to do with scientific fact. Whatever someone believes *is* the truth – to them!

Then she was conflictingly motivated by the other indoctrination of her upbringing. Experience of the male penis, except for the Lord's extraordinary requirement that it should be used for reproductory purposes, was always sin. But we were expected to sin. It was even all right to conceive out of wedlock – hadn't the Lord himself demonstrated this, created the example and precedent in His miraculous way, with the Virgin Mary? It was quite all right if then you married, just as Mary had done. It had not been Joseph, Mary's husband, who had actually inseminated her; yet blessed above all women was Mary.

The sperm was *always* the Lord's. The husband was always no more than the Lord's protector of the chosen woman and her child.

I am quite sure Heidi never consciously considered her philosophy in these terms, nor would have expressed it in such words. To her it was much more simple. She'd been a bad girl; she'd got herself into trouble; there was nothing to be done about that; everything would be all right, though, if she now got married.

And she could make me marry her – I was trapped by that simple fact.

But Heidi wasn't a fool. She knew quite well that threats lose their effectiveness with time. The further that sexual act beneath the firs at Prinzenbrunnen receded into the past the less its value was to her. And, since there were obstacles to the immediate marriage she would have liked to enforce, she had to keep alive the seduced German girl's right to the protection of her foreign lover's name.

She did not love me. She did not even like me. She resented my necessity in her life, but she had a strong, demanding physical sensuality, and I could satisfy that.

I think the very fact of conflict and hostility between us created a kind of primitive savageness on both our parts that even intensified the sensuality.

She knew she had only one attraction for me. She used it with incredible frankness, not as an invitation to love, but as a challenge to lust. She made me shave it for her. Once when I brought her flowers, she made me trim the stalks and use it as a vase. She used every trick in the book, and invented many that weren't, to arouse me.

But always there was a phase in our lovemaking when one or the other of us would reach out and switch off the bedside light, or when we would close our eyes. And then, because I was trying to pretend that she was someone else, I knew that she was pretending to herself that I was Frans.

I never managed to forget that she was Heidi and always, after it was over, I had moments of hatred of her and of myself for having to give in to those needs.

I'm sure it was the same for her, poor little bitch.

Sexual love may be an act of reverence. Between Heidi and I it was a black Mass.

I made my formal applications to marry Heidi to the German authorities and to the Dutch Embassy. I bought a cheap engagement ring. I told the Wendlers of my engagement. Frau Wendler, understandably, wanted to know about my fiancée. I told her the truth if not in great detail.

'She's the daughter of a Duisburg miner, a waitress in the station cafe at Aue. I was stupid enough to make love to her without taking any precautions, and she's pregnant. I don't think it's my child, but she says it is, and insists that I marry her. I don't have much choice.'

Frau Wendler shook her head sadly.

'I'm sorry. If there's anything I can do to help. . . .'

'You did all you could. You warned me. Now there's nothing.'

From then onwards I went to Aue most nights of the week, and every weekend. The nights were not so bad. We simply went to bed and when I had done what I was there to do, either I caught the next train back to Sachsen or, if I fell asleep and awakened late, caught an early train in the morning.

The weekends were terrible. We both tried hard to make concessions, to get to know one another, to make our alliance tolerable, but we quarrelled violently. We had absolutely nothing in common except the natural, structural compatibility of an erect penis and a female vagina. Her incessant chatter about the station cafe, and its customers, about the everyday trivia of her narrow little life with its touchable horizons irritated me to the point of outburst.

If she did say anything that gave me something to comment and make observations upon, she couldn't hide the fact that my conversation bored her. She disagreed with all my viewpoints and attitudes, but did not know how to express her disagreement except in monosyllabic and scornful rejection. I disagreed violently with everything she believed, but found her too unintelligent to try to argue and discuss my different point of view.

She was untidy and sluttish. The little kitchenette was always a chaos of dirty dishes, which she would even hide out of the way, unwashed, in the oven if she did make an effort to tidy up. The tiny bathroom was always festooned with discarded underwear and stockings waiting the rinsing that was all they ever got, and then only when she had nothing clean left to put on. Every cushion in the drab little living room had cheap girls' magazines or novelettes tucked under it.

Her idea of cooking was a pan of boiling water and a can.

The only respite on those weekends was on the Sunday morning when she went off to Mass. To get through the rest of the time I took to doing the cooking, the washing up, the cleaning; and she despised me for doing what she had also been indoctrinated into believing was a woman's work.

It was very clear that our marriage was going to be hell and that it would never last. I'm sure she understood this, too. I think she accepted it. I don't think she hoped that it would last. Just so long as it happened. Just so long as she had a legal father for the child – somewhere, somehow.

Even the pre-marital relationship couldn't last, despite the belief she had that it was necessary if she was to maintain her right to be made my wife. My applications for permission to marry her resulted in an impeding sequence of bureaucratic correspondence and form filling. Berlin required authentification of the facts of my application relating to herself from her. The Hague could not trace my parents immediately and requested information from me they could have more easily got themselves.

Heidi had to recognize that the delay was not my fault, but that did not prevent the rapid deterioration of the situation between us. We alternated more and more between violent quarrels, inarticulate silences and frantic male and female animalism.

There had to be a breaking point and it came when, in her bitter determination to goad me, she produced a framed photograph of Frans and put it on the table at her side of the bed.

When I saw it, my impulse was to take it and smash it, and tear the picture into pieces. Then I became cunning. If I did that, I would be doing exactly what she wanted. I thought: 'Oh, no, you little bitch. This one's going to rebound on you. You can lie there and look at him while it's me who's fucking you. You've asked for it.'

I'm certain I was right. I'm certain she never for a moment expected I would be able to leave the picture there while I was having her. Yet, in a queer, masochistic way the situation merely stimulated the only kind of desire I could feel for her.

It was there for three nights, for having put it there she would not admit defeat and remove it herself. It stayed there as we fought as sexual antagonists, naked, on the illuminated arena of the mattress of the bed, with all its clothes stripped off. Neither of us could ever be the winner in those strange physical contests, but we both sensed that in the end one of us would break over that bedside picture of another man with his smooth, artificial, photogenic smile as if, watching us, he enjoyed our performances enormously.

I was determined that it should be Heidi and, at the time, I supposed it was. Looking back, I'm not so sure.

For on that third night, mounted on her, impaling her, driven wild by the mounting conflict of sensual need and emotional rejection, I suddenly reached over with one hand, snatched the framed picture from my side, and propped it, photograph facing downwards on her rounded belly, holding it there.

'There you are, you bitch!' I said. 'If you want him to watch,

let him have a good look. See if he enjoys seeing that . . . and
that . . . and that.'

She broke, then. She began to claw at me with her nails.

Sodding, bastard fucker, she called me. I felt the blood on my
back. I needed my hands to protect my eyes from the claws of
her nails. I collapsed on top of her with all my weight, the photograph in its frame flattening between us. She sunk her teeth into
my shoulder. I began hitting her.

I think one of us would have killed the other, but suddenly
she began to moan and I felt the violence of her contractions as
she had her orgasm and that started me, and we were suddenly
clinging to one another because for a few moments of time we
had no other need except that of each other.

We were very silent when it was over. Eventually she got up
and put on the cheap worn dressing gown she wore about the
flatlet at night, throwing the one I kept there to me.

'I'll make some coffee,' she said in a whisper.

We sat each side of the low burning gas fire in the living room,
drinking. And after a bit I knew I had to speak with common
sense for both of us.

'It can't go on, Heidi.'

No answer.

'It's a terrible confession, but I could have murdered you just
then.'

No answer.

'And you wanted to kill me. If you could have done it, you
would.'

No answer. But I was getting all the answers of agreement I
needed.

'If we go on like this, it could come to that.'

No answer. I reached out and took her hand. There was, for
once, a gentleness, and some understanding seemed to flow between us.

'Heidi! You realize that, don't you? It was terrible. I'm
ashamed.'

'I'm ashamed, too,' she said at last. 'You make me say things
I can't really believe I've said. I don't know what's happening
to me. Oh, I've not been what you'd call a nice girl. But I've
never been like this before, Armand.'

I gave her a cigarette. For once, I knew, we could talk. For
once we could be what we had never been, except in the moments

of our first meeting. We would be sensible friends, discussing her problem. I being wise about it – although now it was my problem, too.

'You feel, don't you, that we've got to keep on having sex together, or the marriage will never happen. The very opposite could happen, Heidi.'

'You broke one promise, Armand – remember, on that first time! You aren't going to break this one. You mustn't break this one.'

'Be honest – you wanted me to break that first one,' I said.

'That's not true,' she said in quick denial.

'Oh, Heidi. I'm not a fool. Let's *be* honest with one another for once. We'll neither of us ever really know for certain whether it's his child or mine – well, for sure, I won't.'

'It's got to be yours,' she said tensely.

'Okay. I've agreed to that. Marrying you will make it mine. And I'm going to marry you. I've made all the applications. I've committed myself to it. You don't have to prove it's mine, now, because too many people know we've been sleeping together here, nights and weekends. You don't have to say I raped you, to force my hand. I couldn't draw back if I wanted to. But we don't have to make life hell for each other like this.'

'It could have been different.'

'Perhaps – but it isn't. Maybe it will be afterwards, if we let things cool down for a bit, and then try again later on. Doesn't that make sense?'

I suggested that I should stop coming to Aue. I would ring her every weekend. When the consents to our marriage came through, then we would just get married quietly, find somewhere else to live and try to make a fresh start.

'I can't run away, you know,' I said.

She bit her lip.

'All right, Armand. I'm sorry about the way it's been. Perhaps you're right. But you've got to know. . . .'

'No threats!' I warned her. 'That's been half the trouble. I know how determined you are. And what happened at Prinzenbrunnen happened, and I accept it that I am responsible for what is the consequence of that afternoon.'

We talked until it was time for me to leave to catch my last train.

I travelled back to Sachsen feeling I had been reprieved.

Not from bondage to Heidi.

From the sentence of guilt of having murdered her.

VI

The Role of Robin Hood

In the winter of '43, the writing was on the wall for the Germans.

It was not that the ordinary people like the Wendlers recognized defeat, but that the belief in victory had gone.

Even in the short time I had known him, Max had changed noticeably. When I had first known him, he had slapped his podgy hands on his plump thighs and said, of the future: 'When we win the war. . . .'

Now Max muttered, as we welded a fractured cross member for which no spare was available: 'When this bloody war is over. . . .'

My relationship with him had been irretrievably damaged by the quarrel over interpreting to the Frenchman. If I had not been spending all my free time with Heidi the hostile atmosphere might not have developed from the quarrel. Now it was too late for that.

As for the Frenchman, Maurice, he had remained as sullen and uncommunicative as he had been when he had first arrived at Sachsen. He, too, was lodging with the Wendlers and it was as much to escape his company as anything else, now that I was no longer making almost daily journeys to Aue, that I at once began getting out of the house in the evening.

I wasn't looking for girls. The period of my life when I had gone out hopeful of getting to know a girl, and hopeful that such a meeting might just possibly lead to a sexual adventure, had gone for ever. I now knew that the difficulty was in dodging involvements with woman and that there were no relationships that didn't eventually, and usually fairly quickly, lead to a situation in which one either fucked or the relationship finished.

Although I knew that the urge and the need would return the experiences with Heidi had left me, however temporarily, without any urgent or tormenting desires.

For the moment I would have preferred male companionship during my evenings. Unfortunately, there were hardly any young men of my own age left in the town; and those there were tended to keep clear of foreign workers. The women were different, and that was how I came to know Brunhilde and Laura.

Brunhilde was a widow, sad and lonely, and I believe at first I brought some fulfilment to her life which, since her husband's death, had seemed empty.

Our relationship, however, was doomed from the start. She did not enjoy sex, and although she said this was not my fault, I always felt inadequate. But apart from that we came from very different backgrounds. Classwise we were totally incompatible – she was an aristocrat, a 'lady' – I was a thief, a criminal more at ease in the bedroom of a whore and I could never feel at home in a 'lady's' boudoir.

About this time one of Wendler's trucks broke down beyond repair and Max found himself with a driver too many.

Brunhilde's friend, Laura, had said that she could probably get me a job at Edeka's, a big wholesale food company in Leipzig.

Her boyfriend, Fritz, worked there and so I found myself for a while living with Brunhilde and also with a new job.

After I left Brunhilde, Fritz found me a new place to live.

The Boschs to whom Fritz took me were a poor, working class family with five children. He had a crippled leg, and he worked as a night watchman. They were kindly people, and I liked them.

Wars really hit people like the Boschs. There is always a black market. It is never for them. After I had been with them for a few days and had seen the struggle they were having, it occurred to me that there was plenty of opportunity to adjust this social injustice.

I had to play it cautiously because although I believed I had Fritz weighed up I couldn't afford to be wrong.

Under the supervision of an overseer whose attention was temporarily distracted we were loading a small delivery van to take supplies round to a group of small shops. The dispatch list called for six cardboard boxes, each of which contained sixteen lumps of margarine – about a couple of hundred pounds of sugar all told. I trollied the boxes over to the van where Fritz was arranging the various bulk supplies so that we could break them up, during our round, to the requirements of the individual 'corner shops'.

As I humped the margarine boxes into the van he slid them across the floor. When he had moved six and found a seventh waiting for him, he said:

'You brought one too many.'

'So I did.' I sounded surprised – but not too surprised. Then I grinned. 'That's the worst of being educated, Fritz.'

'What do you mean.'

'You can count above five.'

Then, he stared at me. Then, I started to move the extra box back on to my trolly.

'Why's that bad?' he asked.

'Because if we'd both made the same mistake we couldn't have brought the extra box back – that would have got the overseer in bad trouble. And I know who could have used it.'

'Who?'

'Well, say the Bosch kids.'

'Like you say,' said Fritz, 'I'm an uneducated bastard.'

He swung the seventh box right to the back of the van, out of sight. We didn't say any more about it. We finished the loading, most of it under the watchful eye of the overseer who simply glanced into the van before signing the dispatch record and giving us our gate pass. After we had made our shop deliveries I detoured by way of the Bosch home. I humped the box of margarine indoors and dumped it on the kitchen table.

'What . . .?' asked Frau Bosch.

'No questions!' I told her. I ripped the cardboard box lid open so that she could see the contents. 'Get it out of sight, and burn the box.'

'But Herr Hoff . . .'

'You *need* it don't you?' I said. 'The kids need it, don't they? Well, then.'

Then I got out. I had a sense of excitement I had not known for a long time. I was sure about Fritz now.

We did not say a thing about what had happened until after the working day was over and, even then, I let Fritz make the first move. He suggested a drink, and then we talked about it.

'You did that pretty smoothly,' he said. 'Not as if it was a first time.'

'First time I've ever stolen margarine,' I said. It wasn't trusting him to tell him what could be found out on the records by anyone who cared to look. 'But I've done four stretches. In Holland. In France.'

He pushed his hand out across the beer ringed table top. Just that. Nothing more had to be said, or ever was. I never knew his record, but I was to find him a quick, cool, resourceful thief.

What we had done, he said, was risky.

'With the size of supply Edeka's keep up?' I asked. 'It's always being replenished long before it gets down to being rock bottom. By the time they make a periodic supply and stock check, one box more or less is a book keeping error somewhere along the line. Written off without inquiry.'

'That's right,' he agreed. 'But the kind of thing we did this afternoon is the kind of thing you can get away with only once or twice. Fine; when the chance comes up, I'm all for taking it. We can work together well, you and me – nothing big mind you. You don't impress me by telling me you've been in jail four times. That means you've made four mistakes. We can't afford mistakes. Pilfering food when it's on short rations. They'd cut our balls off. So, I know the town; you don't. I'm German; you're not. If we do things my way, not yours, then we're in business.'

So we did nothing that Fritz either didn't plan or didn't agree with. And we did well but, like he said, nothing big. It added up though.

It was all small-time pilfering, really, and we never made a penny out of it, simply keeping the Boschs, and other deserving friends we could trust, better supplied with the necessities they were practically having to do without.

We only pulled one job of real daring.

Just outside the town there was the Leuna Werke Foreign Workers Camp. The men in the camp were French and Russian P.O.W's. The Germans screened their P.O.W's pretty carefully. If a prisoner's family was in Occupied Territory they had a reprisal threat that could be seen to justify, in many cases, a guarantee of good behaviour.

Such screened men created small but useful labour forces, and they got a very high degree of liberty because they weren't going to run anywhere. On the other hand they got a pretty low standard of living.

One day, when we were at the station goods yard with the sixwheeler, gangs of these men were being used to unload the railway waggons and a small detail was doing the loading of our truck.

One of them told me he was the chief cook at the camp. I asked why, if this was his job, he was at work on the railway yard gang.

'You're Dutch, aren't you?' he said.

I agreed that I was.

'That makes you conscript foreign labour like us. How about your mate? He's German, isn't he?'

'Yes, but he's all right.'

'Well, it's like this,' said the Frenchman. 'I switched with one of the work gang to come down here to see for myself if there is any way of diverting some extra supplies to the camp. They're keeping us terribly short – especially sugar. Do you have any ideas? Any way you might be able to help?'

'I would if I could. I will if I can,' I told him. 'And don't worry about Fritz. He never talks war or politics, but one thing's for sure, he's not a Nazi. We do a bit of diverting of supplies ourselves, but not on these runs. There's no way we can do it. Take sugar, for instance. We'll be taking a truckload of sacks out the day after tomorrow. But they send an overseer out with us. He checks the loading. He double checks the load before we pull out. He rides back to the Edeka depot in the cab with us. We don't stop anywhere. Impossible, you see.'

He nodded and went back to work. Presently he joined me again, told me that he'd been thinking about it, and there was a way.

'Nobody keeps a close check on our numbers while we're here, or exactly where we are. One of our own men, a sergeant is in charge of us. He has a pick-up, and if a man hurts himself or feels ill, he uses it to run him back to the camp's sick quarters. No problems.'

Then he told me what he had in mind.

'If we were loading gold bullion it would be worth it!' I said.

'If you were loading gold bullion we wouldn't be interested,' he said. 'I can't cook gold, and our fellows can't eat it. Sugar is gold to us.'

'I'll talk to Fritz,' I said after a pause. 'Day after tomorrow, you be here, and if it's on I'll give you the signal. If things go wrong, we don't know you. I'll keep a steady speed, but if anything makes me brake, God help you.'

He checked the height of the tailboard of the lorry. It was important. I told him the exact weight and the approximate dimensions of a sack of sugar. That was important, too.

'We've two men who can do it. They'll practise all day tomorrow as if they were entered for the Olympics.'

Fritz agreed to the idea. We were only going to make it possible. They were going to take the risks.

It was, really, appealingly simple.

Before we left Edeka on the run to the goods yard, Fritz reported a broken nearside wing mirror, which we had managed to damage beyond repair. The maintenance section said there was no spare, and I said that, since it was the nearside mirror, I could manage without it.

At the goods yard Fritz and I kept apart from the loading operation which was carried out by the P.O.W's and supervised by the overseer. The overseer was a German Government official, not an Edeka employee.

He counted the sacks being loaded on to the lorry and checked the full load, staying round at the back of the lorry until Fritz and I were in the cab. I started the motor, and he slapped the side of the lorry. As I began to move away at a crawl he ran along, overtaking me, and swung himself up into the cab. I accelerated away.

With no nearside wing mirror, he could not see what was happening behind us. I couldn't see much myself in the offside mirror, but then I knew. The two P.O.W's who were to be shoulder hoisted into a jump over the tailboard on to the piled sacks of sugar had exactly three seconds to make it between my beginning to crawl away and the acceleration that I had to make once I had the overseer aboard. It doesn't sound long, but a lot of action can be crowded into three properly rehearsed seconds.

As I turned out of the goods yard on to the road, I did see the P.O.W. pick up moving off to tail me, so I knew I had my two extra passengers aboard.

It all had to happen along one straight stretch of deserted road on which it would be unlikely bad luck if there was any other traffic. There was nothing on the road, nobody about.

My usual speed along this stretch was 70 kilometres, about 44 miles per hour, and it would have been suspicious if I had dropped much below it. They had to take a hell of a chance, to get that sugar and rely on me keeping an absolutely steady, unvarying speed. For they were going to drive the pick up right on to my tail, not more than a foot between us, while the two men on the back of the lorry took the sacks and swung them out, with accuracy, so that they went over the bonnet of the pick-up, over the windscreen, over the occupied front driving seat and landed in the open rear of the vehicle.

Everybody had to be very, very accurate indeed and they had to know just when to fall back before I decelerated for the bend in the road at the end of the operation.

At that speed, if for any reason I had to brake or they came in too close, the slightest impact would have spun them off the road, and I would never have felt it.

The overseer wanted to talk but Fritz, between us, took care of that. I had to concentrate on my speed, and my hands were wet with sweat as I pictured what was going on behind me.

It was going nicely – as far as I was concerned – and we were half way along our straight stretch when suddenly, from some alleyway ahead of us, a child of about four or five came out and began to cross the road.

I was conscious of Fritz's hand, on the seat beside me, convulse into a tight knot. Alarm bells seemed to shrill in my mind, and I had a sick, sour taste suddenly in my mouth, but I kept my foot off, although poised over the brake pedal; and kept the other one, in spite of its trembling, with unvarying pressure on the accelerator pedal.

If I cut my speed, used my brakes, that pick-up was going to run right under us. If I didn't. . . .!

I judged my distance. I judged my speed. I judged the speed at which the child was moving. My mind shouted its prayer: 'For Christ's sake, kid, keep moving.' And with every split second of doing nothing I knew that if I had to do anything the deceleration would be sharper, more abrupt, more final and disastrous to the men in the pick up.

The overseer yelled out:

'That child. You bloody fool. . . .'

'Oh, God!' I heard Fritz say.

I kept on going and the child disappeared under my offside wing, and for a moment I didn't know. And then I saw it, still crossing the road, staring back at us in our wing mirror.

The overseer pushed Fritz back.

'You're a maniac!' he said. 'I'll report you. . . .'

I was shaking, but only inside my mind.

'You do your job, I'll do mine,' I said. 'If I'd sounded the horn, I'd have scared the child and it would have stopped. Then I'd have had to brake, hard. At 70, on this road, she'd have skidded. Whatever it looked like from where you are, from here there was no danger. We missed the kid by a mile.'

'You should have slowed. . . .'

'Who's driving – you, or me? I've a clean, accident-free record. I still have. I'll keep it that way. But I can do without back-seat drivers.'

It was no way to talk to a German Government overseer, but I needed to unwind. We were coming to the building which, when he saw it, would tell the pick-up driver to drop behind because now I had to slow down for the bend. On that bend the two men on the back of my lorry had to drop off. The overseer was giving me the excuse to make it less dangerous for them than it would have otherwise been.

'We'll talk about this when we get back to the warehouse,' he said as I dropped speed, changed down, and came into the beginning of the bend.

I dropped right down, almost to a standstill.

'You want Fritz to take over the driving for the rest of the trip?' I asked, as if I was about to pull up.

I gave Fritz a warning nudge with my knee, not that I thought he wouldn't understand.

'I can't handle this load,' said Fritz. 'You know that.'

'You see!' I shouted across to the overseer. 'This bloody thing doesn't drive itself. It's an expert's job. And you leave the expert to do his job.'

We drove on.

They'd got away with eight sacks. When our load was checked in and the fact that we were those eight sacks short, all hell broke loose. Fritz and I stood by, watching and listening.

We hadn't loaded the sugar. We hadn't counted the sacks. We hadn't signed the check out papers as correct. We'd just driven, our normal route, at our normal speed, with no stops between the railway goods yard and the Edeka depot, a German Government overseer sitting with us in the cab all the time.

There was no interview with me about the child. The man had troubles of his own.

We never saw him again. But of course it wasn't an operation that could ever have been repeated.

Anyway, within a few days, the whole of the pilfering business, and my job with Edeka, came to an end.

Fritz and I weren't the only employees on the make, of course. And although the penalties for stealing rationed goods were severe, human nature being what it is, Edeka had to reckon on having some discrepancies. But Fritz and I had pushed the figures up beyond the acceptable limit and a routine stocktaking check showed that the pilfering had gone beyond the point of workers helping themselves to a reasonable 'little extra'.

I was the only foreign worker so, without evidence to support it, suspicion fell on me. Without investigation, the managing director accused me of theft, sent for the police, and I was arrested.

The police, who were short strength and very much overworked, took his word for it, and assumed that the accusation would be backed up by evidence, especially when they were told that if they visited my lodgings they would find all the evidence they needed.

But Frau Bosch had been no fool. There was nothing for them to find, and they had to apologize to me and release me.

It wasn't an acquittal! The Managing Director of Edeka still believed that I was behind the sudden increase in pilfering. And of course he was right.

He could not prove it, but he was not going to withdraw the accusation. I was suspended from driving and given a warehouseman's job to do – under strict, watchful supervision.

It was a challenge, for if I accepted this I acknowledged my guilt. And since the police had washed their hands of the matter, the only other court was that of the labour arbitration court.

He did not have the evidence to take me before this court, but he was challenging me to take him before it and providing me with a reason for doing so. He believed that in such a court the circumstantial evidence would go against me.

So I made my application to the local labour arbitration court, and the whole thing was thrashed out. The incidence of pilfering had increased soon after I had joined the Company. I was the only new employee involved in the handling of supplies. Whatever opportunities there were for pilfering were particularly open to me in my job. I had a criminal record in two other countries.

It was an impressive circumstantial case against me, and I argued my own defence. Could he produce a single piece of evidence that I had ever stolen so much as a box of matches?

To his embarrassment I brought up the incident of the eight sacks of sugar that had vanished from a lorry I had been driving. How fortunate for me that that sugar had been loaded and carried under the watchful eye of a Government overseer and that nobody could blame me, because of my unfortunate youthful past, for its disappearance. But suppose there had been no overseer there, by my side in the cab of the lorry the whole of the time, the court could be certain that I would have been blamed.

Let him give any one case of any theft for which I was supposed to be responsible, and then possibly I might be able to similarly prove my innocence! But how could I defend myself against vague charges that were based upon bias, and motivated by the need to have a scapegoat to blame?

The court decided that I had proved that I was being treated unjustly. I was released from my job with Edeka, with a testimonial to this effect. I was directed by the labour exchange to a job driving for the Markranstadter brewery.

I handled a lot of beer for the Markranstadter brewery, and never drank a stolen glassful. How could I! When I handled it, it was in heavy oak casks which held forty-five gallons.

It was probably the toughest job I ever did, and I did it better than the toughest, strongest men in the brewery. I was the only man in the yard who could take those casks, when empty, and swing them up into the lorry. It gave me a bit of a reputation. The fact was that my gymnastic training had taught me how to co-ordinate the use of my muscles, so it was partly a trick. It had to be a bit more than that. Shifting waggon loads of coal for Max Wendler, and carrying sacks weighing over two hundredweight on my back for Edeka had trained me to use my trained muscles for a new use.

It was through the brewery, through my over confidence in my ability to handle those great casks even when they were full that I had an experience I can never forget and which, as far as I know, may be unique.

Her name was Victoria.

VII

Victoria

Victoria belongs to one night of my life, no more.

Late on the afternoon of that day I had to manoeuvre, single handed, one of the full oak beer casks down a spiral staircase into an innkeeper's cellar.

The barrel should have been secured and steadied by a rope being given new slack for each step.

This correct procedure was tediously slow and I did not bother about the rope, overconfident that I could control the weight of the barrel by balance, taking it down the steps one at a time, guiding it from beneath.

On the third step the weight came fractionally too far forward, and I found myself two steps down below the barrel straining to prevent it coming down on me and crushing me.

I couldn't hold it. It seemed to be pushing my arms back into their sockets, and fraction of an inch by fraction of an inch I was going underneath it. There was a point, and I knew it, when I would be taking the full weight, and then I would be finished. Quite apart from taking the crushing weight on my chest, I would be thrown backwards down the spiral stone steps. My head would be smashed like an egg on to the stone. My back would be broken.

There was only one chance of survival, and I took it while I still had it.

Instead of trying to hold the barrel up, I let it come down. As it came, I pushed it towards the central column of the spiral, and let the force of its fall at the same time push me in the opposite direction.

I was flung against the bannister rail fixed to the outer wall of the staircase, slammed into it with such force that I felt as if my ribs were cracking.

The barrel began to tumble over and over, and I felt it hit my knees.

Then it was gone with a tremendous clattering and banging and I heard it split, the curved oak staves twisting and shattering as they burst away from the iron hoops that had held them together.

The sound of the explosion reverberated through the cellar, and they must have heard it in the bar above like a bomb going off. I was still clinging to the bannister rail, too shaken by my escape to assess my own possible injuries, when the owner of the bar, followed by the handful of people who had been drinking on the premises, came crowding to the top of the staircase.

I pointed down the stairs and gave a breathless explanation of what had happened. I was helped to the bar and one of the customers, who was a doctor, gave me an on the spot examination, said I had had a lucky escape and that all I was suffering from was shock.

There was an immediate remedy at hand for that, and after a couple of brandies I felt sufficiently recovered as well as courageous enough to ring the brewery manager and report what had happened.

I said, of course, that I was sorry about the accident, destroying the barrel, and wasting the beer, which was still swilling about, several inches deep, in the cellar.

'Forget about it. We're lucky you're still alive and not even injured,' he said. 'I'll need a report, of course. The rope slipped; that was it, of course.'

'I'm afraid the rope . . .' I began.

He knew all right.

'The rope *was* on. It slipped. Right?'

'Yes,' I agreed.

I said the report would be in his office first thing in the morning, and he asked what I proposed to do now. I said that I intended to stay on and help clear up the mess. Then I had one more delivery to make. By the time I got back to the brewery with the lorry it wouldn't be worth returning to Leipzig so I would spend the night at the workers' hostel.

He was waiting for me at the brewery.

'You're coming back to my house for a meal,' he said. 'My wife's made up the spare bed, and you can stay the night. . . .'

'I can't impose like this,' I said. 'You're being very kind, and I'd expected to be in trouble over the broken cask and the lost beer. I *didn't* use the rope, you know.'

'I know, but that won't go in the report. To tell the truth, Hoff, I'm damned glad to see you're all right. We're told to use only one man on delivery, at our discretion. But it is a two man job. You'd have been on my conscience if you'd been killed.'

A good meal. A comfortable bed. No trouble over an accident that was my fault! I did not complain.

They had in fact arranged to go out to neighbours to play cards after dinner. I was shown my room, given the freedom of the house, and they went off saying that they would not be back too late and, if I was still up, we would have a drink together.

'You don't know how glad I am to see you alive!' said my host again.

'I'm not unhappy about it myself,' I told him.

It was a pleasant, warm summer evening, and I decided to go for a stroll. Quite near the house I found some open parkland. In the park, I found a girl. All over the world, every night, young men and girls are finding each other in parks. Not all of them, of course, but a pretty high percentage, end up in some secluded place, the girl on her back, and the young man on top of her between her opened and drawn up legs.

Individually these adventures may seem to be unique. Collectively they are so commonplace that, usually, they are not worth mentioning. Certainly the girls don't mention such adventures, later, to the men they marry and to whom they make very good, respectable, conventional and even faithful wives.

Victoria, who had Gretchen plaits, blue eyes and – when I met her – an immaculately white dress, was very, very far from commonplace in the extraordinary experience we had.

Maybe I should have recognized that fortuitously, for reasons I never knew and now could only invent, this casually met girl and I stumbled upon a moment of such compatibility that I should have asked no questions, had no doubts, but thrown everything to the wind and married her.

Instead I never even knew her full name, only her christian name – and *that* she told me afterwards when the white dress was so muddied and crumpled that she had to wait until dark before she could leave the park and go out on the street.

Maybe if I had been older and wiser I wouldn't now have my last memory of her standing, leaning against a tree in that park, saying: 'Tomorrow. Here, by this tree – *our* tree. I'll be waiting.'

I wonder how long, and on how many nights she waited in vain.

I wonder how wrong I was about her then, and how right I am now.

Victoria had a succession of sixteen orgasms during a period of coition that hardly lasted more than a quarter of an hour.

To recall this experience now, in terms of sensuality with a girl known so briefly that if I met her in the street I would not recognize her, would be absurd. It was, anyway, straight 'missionary' sex as some African natives called face-to-face man on top of woman copulation, when introduced to the conventional European method of mating by the early colonists.

I can only be clinical about the experience, and leave it at that.

I know now that there had to be physical reasons and there had to be emotional reasons on the part of both of us for what happened.

On my part I suppose the emotional factor was that I had travelled further away from what there had been for me in that first experience with Hennie. First with Heidi and then with Brunhilde, I had reached two different extremes. All the novelties had been exhausted through exploration, and sex had become simply a matter of physical excitement and sensual relief. I suppose I needed to be wanted, to be important, to me personally essential. I suppose I needed to be given, not simply to take. I suppose I needed a closeness with a woman that was completely natural and uncontrollable.

I have no idea, and never will have, what experiences and what emotional lack of fulfilment there may have been on Victoria's part. She was, and remained, a complete stranger.

But there was one physical fact that may – and I can never be sure of this – have been a contributory cause.

Randy and eager though she seemed to be to make love and to go all the way, she was initially nervous and frightened of our being discovered by other users of the park.

The result was that our precoital love-making was prolonged because of a number of moments of tenseness when she heard someone passing on the other side of the shrubbery where we were. So it ebbed and flowed, ebbed and flowed and when, ultimately, she reached the point where her inhibitions were as abandoned as my own, she had probably reached the 'threshold' point of excitement that is always almost achieved for a man before he can penetrate a woman, but usually has still to be aroused by him in the woman by his act.

By the time I came to enter Victoria she had already reached a point of complete abandon and seemed eager to show herself utterly to me. I never had, and never have since, seen a woman with a clitoris like hers. It stood out from the top of the swollen cleft like a tiny penis.

Tempted by the sight I opened her with my fingers and saw that she did indeed have a phallus that recognizably had the same evolutionary origins as the male penis – the same sort of head as a circumcised penis, the same sort of shaft, about half an inch long.

And when I entered her, I immediately came up against the resistance of the smallest, most tightly muscled vaginal orifice I have ever encountered. The very force it took to penetrate her was such that it robbed me of sensual excitement that had almost reached the point of lost control.

She cried out as she felt me open and go fully through this tight and clasping little opening, and then almost immediately *she* began to fuck *me*.

It took my breath away. Her movements were exactly the same as those of a man who has lost control, except that they were very, very rapid, and very, very short.

I could not possibly have synchronized my movements to hers; it would have been painful and could have been even damaging at the point of maximum withdrawal, so, defensively, all I could do was to bury myself deeply in her and let her use just the root of my penis. And like that, of course, there was no caressive massage of the sensual area beneath the head of my glans and all danger of my own loss of control ebbed away.

It took only a few moments and ended with her changing her movements to a kind of 'stirring', or 'fluttering' after which she became limp and gasping as the orgasm ended.

Immediately I began to move in the ordinary, familiar way but, before my own sensuality had been completely re-aroused, Victoria began again. And it went on like that through orgasm after successive orgasm, the only difference being that with each one she moved faster, more desperately, until finally she had her legs scissored round my body as far up as she could draw them and was rolling from side to side on the ground as she neared the point of those wild explosions of sensuality, to me unbelievable in a woman.

Then suddenly and at last, without any preliminary awareness that it was going to happen, it was as if some volcano within me erupted. And it was all over.

We hardly spoke afterwards.

What was there to say!

I was dazed with near disbelief that a woman could be more aggressive, more savage in her use of a man than a man of a woman, and that she could return to her attack again and again and again.

She was unsteady, soaking wet, muddied, dishevelled and breathing unevenly.

She got to her feet, and when I saw the back of her frock it was not only muddy, but clung wetly to the undercurve of her buttocks.

'You can't go on to the street like that,' I said.

She pulled the dress round, saw it, felt it with her hand.

'No,' she said unsteadily. 'I'll wait here for a bit. It'll be dark in another fifteen minutes, then I'll go.'

'We could walk. Find a seat,' I suggested.

'No. Here. By *our* tree. I'd like . . . I'd like to be alone. You'll come to me again, of course.'

'Of course,' I heard myself saying.

'Then you go, now,' she whispered. And then she added the only other thing I was ever to hear her say. 'Tomorrow. At this time. Here by this tree – *our* tree. I'll be waiting.'

I knew as I walked away that I would not be there.

I couldn't cope with a girl with such a ravenous sensual appetite as that!

Well, of course, although that was only about thirty years ago, it was then undiscovered that maybe there are many women who are themselves capable of giving a man the experience of orgasm after orgasm – that it depends more on the man than themselves, more on the circumstances than the man, or such a permutation of factors that only about fourteen per cent of women ever experience even a second orgasm with a man, and only seven per cent ever experience as many as four. And when people like Kinsey and Inge and Sten Hegeler talk about the phenomena of multi-orgasm in women, twelve is the maximum number ever referred to as being experienced by a woman during coition with a man.

So it may be that my experience with Victoria really was unique.

What I didn't realize at the time was that she could never have had such an experience before, and probably never would have done again, even with myself – although once having discovered such a high level of sexual compatibility Victoria and I, strangers though we were, would probably have had a remarkably good relationship.

As it was, Victoria made this one brief, dramatic appearance in my life and, within the next couple of days, I was up to my neck in woman trouble of a much more commonplace nature as Heidi made her reappearance in my life.

I was still thinking constantly of the experience with Victoria, and wondering if there were other girls like her in whom the abilities of a woman were combined with the desires of a man, half tempted to go back and look for her when, one afternoon later in the week, I was driving my lorry past the Edeka building when I recognized Heidi standing outside the gate.

I had not yet told her of my change of job, and I felt guilty about that. The truth was that my feelings about Heidi were puzzling to myself. It was far too late now for her to hold the threat of a charge of rape over my head. Even though I made the necessary applications to marry her, I didn't really think she could force me to go through with that now. I didn't believe that the child she was having was mine. I wasn't in love with her. I had no desire for her. And yet I felt tied to her.

I could pretend, now, that this was the good side to my character. That I was obeying a feeling of responsibility towards her. That there were depths of compassion in me. I'd be lying.

She was, to me, an unlovely and unattractive sight, standing there alone by the main gate of Edeka's, presumably waiting to encounter me as I left what she supposed to still be my place of work. Her pregnancy had advanced to a point that bloated her body. She was shapeless and badly dressed. Yet, in some strange way, seeing her made her as much mine as a withered arm would have been.

I parked the lorry and went over to her. When she saw me, she began to weep.

'Oh, for God's sake,' I said angrily. 'You look a big enough mess without that.'

'And whose fault is that?' she asked angrily.

'You've a nerve, bringing *that* up!' I said.

'If it weren't yours, you've made up for that enough times.'

'All right! All right. Let's not start off by going into all that again. What are you doing here?'

'Can't you see? I can't go on working. I've lost my job. And I daren't go home to Duisburg like this. My father would kill me. If you were even half a man. . . .'

'Come on,' I said roughly, taking her by the elbow.

I helped her up into the cab of the truck and drove off my

route to my lodgings. Leaving her in the cab, I went in and talked to Frau Bosch.

Poor people live very close to life's realities. I explained that I had a girl friend, whom I intended to marry when the necessary permission was granted, but who meanwhile was pregnant, had lost her job and had come to Leipzig to join me. I had to look after her.

Frau Bosch accepted the situation philosophically. Heidi could share my room. She could perhaps make herself useful around the house.

And so it began again, a second single bed being squeezed into my room, which remained unused that night because, far gone though she was in her pregnancy, Heidi challenged me deliberately. In spite of her conventional morality, modesty had never played any part in our unromantic relationship. 'I know what it's for!' she had said bluntly, more than once, of her genital mouth. And that night it was as if she wanted to confront me with my inability not to respond to the exhibition of invitation to bury myself in that swollen belly. Her eyes were alive with triumph as she watched my tormented penis rear up for its purpose.

'You bastard, Armand!' she said with satisfaction. 'I'll bet *you*'d be like that for it, even if you were watching me having the child. You'd be impatient wanting the child out, so that you could get back in yourself. You really *are* a bastard, aren't you? It's all you ever think of.'

'If I'm a bastard, it's taken a bitch to make me one.'

'So – I'm a good bitch. At least I'm a good something. Come on, and enjoy your bitch, Armand. Bastard! Big, big, *big* bastard, you!'

Heidi during those final weeks was many things.

She was, at times, tormented by insecurity. In other moods and at other times she would promise, over and over again, that she would be a good wife to me.

'You'll see,' she said. 'When this is all over, when we are married and when we get a home of our own, I'll be everything you could want of a wife. Not just in bed, Armand. I'll cook. I'll clean. We'll have a proper bedroom suite, and a proper sitting room suite, and a proper dining room suite. Carpets in every room. A best tea service. A washing machine in the kitchen. Pretty curtains.'

It was all a dream in her mind, absorbed from films and magazines.

She was utterly hopeless, a slut about the house. She did practically nothing to help Frau Bosch. She traded on her pregnancy to be lazy. It was still Frau Bosch who washed my shirts.

The child was born in May, 1943, poor little devil. What sort of experience is birth, we never remember; and yet, because it is the very beginning of independent experience, and because we are creatures of our experience, it must have some formative importance.

It certainly was one hell of a world for Peter Armand Kuster to be born into. A world of bombing, rationing, persecution and a society on the brink of disintegration. Perhaps these distortions had something to do with it, I reasoned afterwards. At least there seems logic in assuming that human nature alters, adapting itself as it were, in times when everything is turned upside down.

It was something of a shock, however, to find that not all women seem to be equipped with a built-in maternal instinct. Touched deeply, at first, by the sight of Heidi with her little bundle clasped in her arms, it hit me all the harder afterwards.

When we returned from the maternity clinic where Peter had been born, it became quite clear that she disliked and resented the child and the demands it made upon her. The best she seemed to get out of it was a continued excuse to dodge helping Frau Bosch with the housework. She did not even keep our one room clean and tidy.

I tried to shut my eyes to the situation. We were committed to one another, and had to make the best of it.

It was agreed that her family must now know about the child and we decided to let them suppose that we were already married. There was a silence of nearly a fortnight before Heidi's mother answered the letter she sent them.

One could read between the lines that they were not at all happy about her news that she had married a Dutchman and had had a child. I don't think that they suspected that we were not married, but they obviously had to believe that their grandson had been conceived out of wedlock. I believe that it was only this realization that prevented her mother from asking when and where the marriage had taken place. As long as they did not know any details about the wedding at least they could go on pretending to themselves that Heidi had remained a virgin, as a decent girl should, until she had had a wedding ring on her finger. I am also quite sure that it was only the fact of a grandson, of whom they accepted, more readily than I did, that I was the father, that made them come to terms with the marriage at all.

I think Heidi's mother had had a lot of trouble persuading her husband to accept the situation, and that this was why the letter was not answered immediately.

Anyway, they suggested visiting Leipzig the next weekend.

Frankly, when I met them, I didn't give a damn whether they liked me or not. And that was just as well. Fritz Kuster was a sour, embittered man in his early fifties, already the victim of silicosis. He should not have still been working at the coal face, but the Nazis were not pretending to run a welfare state. They had a war on their hands and things were no longer going well for them. Lives like that of Kuster were simply statistics of the expendable.

Karen Kuster was a crabby little woman, with a sour mouth and cold, suspicious little eyes. She whined every word she spoke.

But between them, the Kusters had got things all worked out. Peter Armand was their only grandson and the moment they saw the conditions he was living in, they wanted something better for him.

Frau Kuster had no illusions about Heidi. She could see for herself that Heidi was a bad mother for the child. She wanted the child where she could look after it herself – which was in Duisburg. That meant having Heidi in Duisburg. And that meant having me in Duisburg.

Before they left to return home it was all more or less arranged. Fritz Kuster had a cousin in the Duisburg labour exchange. My application for a transfer would be channelled through him and there would be no problems.

'You'll be much more comfortable with us, Armand,' said my 'mother-in-law' in a voice that suggested nothing of the kind, if comfort had any meaning beyond that of creature comforts. 'You'll be able to have two rooms, properly furnished. And you'll get decent food. *We* don't do too badly, Fritz being at the coal face. Some extras. It makes a difference.'

A few weeks later Heidi and I, and young Peter Armand made the train journey to Duisburg.

We made the journey by day, over two hundred miles, travelling eastwards across Germany into the heart of the great industrial areas of the country.

We had had raids, of course, at Leipzig, but the mounting damage that was being inflicted upon Germany by the RAF had been minimized by the press and the radio.

The worst was still to come and I was not to see it. But on that journey the evidence was there to see, from the windows of a train crowded with service men and women, that the country was being savagely hit and this war was a contest that was not going to be decided 'on points', but by a 'knock out'.

It was a sober, frightening experience, that journey, and I wondered what kind of future Heidi and I were taking the child into . . . if any!

One of the effects of bombing a country's cities is, for some reason, never mentioned by the strategists and politicians.

When they plaster a town and kill a few thousand people and lay waste streets of homes they apologize to humanity and explain that they were only trying to hit military objectives – factories, railway marshalling yards, war-supply depots. Why they never point out that town halls, council offices and labour exchanges are legitimate targets and well worth reducing to smouldering rubble, I have never known. For if you can destroy the administrative system of a country you create unholy chaos.

The administrative system of Germany was already in a considerable muddle, and this was much to my advantage. My 'marriage' to Heidi was, of course, without documentary proof since it had never taken place. But because so much documentation had already been destroyed, lost or was not automatically and readily available, nobody questioned our claim to being husband and wife.

I had now a good work record behind me and on the strength of this the labour exchange in Duisburg gave me an entitlement of two weeks' 'holiday' before directing me to a new lorry driving job.

I spent the first days in my new 'in-laws' home. Fritz Kuster had been a prudent man and, before the war, had accumulated enough savings to buy a house larger than those usually occupied by miners, converting part of it into a small self-contained flat which he had let as a source of income. He had no tenants now. Although the street had remained unscathed, Duisburg-Hamborn, as it is called in full, had taken its share of attention from the bombers. The town is a junction – of railways, of canals and of the Rhine and the Ruhr. Apart from serving the Westphalian coalfield it is a heavy-industry town with extensive wharfage – a good concentrated target, about the size of Sheffield. Fritz's tenants had got out and Heidi and I had the flatlet.

Fritz and Karen wanted to know all about my family. I wasn't very forthcoming, but when they eventually learnt that my father was a priest and that I had been brought up in a home with a housekeeper and servants they began to look upon their daughter's marriage in a more favourable light.

Karen said it had been thoughtless and unkind of Heidi not to tell her own mother that she was getting married, and that she was having a child. It was equally unkind to my parents not to tell them that they had a daughter-in-law and a grandson.

It was quite clear that the Kusters wanted to make the most of their new family link with the Hoffs. It was suggested that Heidi and I should spend the second of my two weeks off work with my family in Holland, taking Peter Armand with us.

In Duisburg most nights were disturbed by air raids. It seems odd, writing about it now, to realize that many of my readers haven't the slightest idea what it is like living in a big town or city that was a target for night bombers during World War II.

Yet *this* was what the war was about to the people.

It wasn't a war of armies and navies and air forces, not to the people. To the German people and the British people, the Russians had nothing to do with it, the French had nothing to do with it, the Italians had nothing to do with it.

If you lived in any of the big target cities of either country – and that is where many of the people lived – the war was about being right in the middle of a hit or miss target, on to which, night after night, fire and death and destruction rained down upon you from a sky pulsating with a throbbing drone.

And the noise was enormous and unceasing. The barking roar of the guns – guns everywhere, their locations betrayed by sudden flashes of fire. The scream of bombs coming down – that awful whine that ended in a thundering explosion, if you were not one of the victims. The giant sound of falling masonry, followed by a chorus of crashes as the hurtling debris found a thousand other targets. The hungry consuming sound of fire for everything it could suck into its vortex maw.

This was what the war was about. It was about a thousand personal enemies up there in the night, trying to kill *you*. And if they failed tonight, expect them back tomorrow night. Expect them to keep on coming, however much and with whatever luck you dodged your inevitable fate – and inevitable it was, because they would gradually lay waste the whole city in their search for *you*. And the war would not be over until at last there was the final bomb, the one you heard coming down but never heard explode, to seal you in the tomb of debris in which it buried you in the very instant of your death.

It was the same everywhere. The enemy wasn't another country – that enemy belonged to a different war, not yours. The enemy merely came from another country. And only the place names were different; London or Berlin, Birmingham or Duisburg – you were all the prey of the killer machines in the sky. And it didn't really matter who the men in the machines were, or where the machines came from. They were all the predators; the reality of your war.

The Kusters had a shelter in the back-yard-garden, shared with the adjoining house, but on our first night there Karen Kuster insisted that we went to the communal bunker, built underground in the corner of a nearby children's playground, when the sirens went. She insisted on this for the greater safety of her grandchild.

We spent two uncomfortable hours down there with the garrulous, the elderly, the gossiping, the scared and the crying. Once or twice the earth trembled, and when we came out there seemed to be fires everywhere.

Heidi asked: 'Is it like this every night?'

'Often,' said her mother.

'Well, I'm not going there again.'

'For the sake of the child. . . .'

'*You* take him, if you want to!'

After another night of it, this time spent in the garden shelter, I decided that Duisburg was no place to spend a holiday. I said, the next morning, that Heidi's mother had been right. My parents ought to know about Heidi and the child, and have a chance to meet her and the baby. I suggested that we should pay them a visit at once.

The labour exchange was helpful to me and I had no problem about getting travel permits for the three of us to travel to Bourtange on 'compassionate domestic' grounds.

Heidi made an effort, and she was obviously very impressed by the clean, spacious house my father had taken just outside Bourtange. Rather to my surprise we were made very welcome. My application for family permission to marry had apparently been received and approved by my father some time before, so my production of a 'wife' did not come as a surprise – though of course Peter Armand was unexpected.

My father was delighted with the boy, even though it was

clear that neither he nor my mother thought I had made a wise choice of a wife.

They had still managed to retain a housekeeper and Heidi loved every minute of what was probably the best holiday she had ever had in her life, possibly the only one. Compared to the only kind of background she had known, Bourtange was luxury to her and none of her worst faults, her laziness and sluttishness, showed up.

Indeed, when we finally had to return to Duisburg, I was even beginning to wonder if we might not, in the long run, make some kind of compromise success of the relationship.

It was not a feeling that was to last for long.

As soon as we got back to her parents' home, the sluttishness and the laziness returned, as did the friction between us. And the more I got to know her, the more I had to face it that she was also stupid and unintelligent.

I was given a heavy lorry job with a debris clearing gang, and we worked long, hard hours. To maintain morale it was a policy to clear up the debris of the air raids in the area as quickly as possible. The scars of war can never be concealed, but it is the opened wounds that can have a damaging effect on morale.

I neither liked the job, the place, the raids, Kusters nor my supposed 'wife'. The only person for whom I had any sort of feeling was the child. I was sorry for him. He had been born into a lousy world with not a single thing in his favour. The dice were loaded against him, and it wasn't his fault.

We had been back in Duisburg about a month when, as I left the house one morning, I met the postman. He had a letter for me, redirected from Leipzig. It was from Berlin.

I opened it as I walked down the street; began reading it as I turned the corner. When I realized what it was, I stopped and looked back.

Heidi had come to the door to take in the milk.

She waved to me.

I waved back, knowing it was the last I would ever see of her – with luck.

The letter was from the authorities in Berlin, notifying me that permission to marry Heidi Kuster had been granted.

The time had come to get out.

Now!

VIII

No-Man's-Land

I had made no plans for my abrupt departure. The decision was completely impulsive. I had nothing but the clothes I stood up in and the little money I had in my pockets. The only thing I had of value was a gold ring Heidi had given me.

I sold it to a Duisburg pawnbroker-jeweller and caught a bus leaving the town. I spent the rest of that day travelling, hitching lifts on lorries, and using buses where they were available. It was getting dark by the time I reached Landau, about fifteen miles from the frontier with France. Without ration cards and with little money, food was going to be an obvious problem, but I was prepared to forage – and to postpone doing so until I was safely in France. My most valuable possession was a compass I always carried and a small pocket torch. There was light cloud and a moon and I had the railway line to guide me. I reached the frontier about midnight.

I knew I was near it because the railway was on an embankment about seven feet high and silhouetted on this I could see a German guard, rifle slung over his shoulder, patrolling up and down with a guard dog.

A small stream ran along the line at the bottom of the embankment, and in this lay my hope of getting into France. Then I made my mistake. I didn't want to be squelching about in wet shoes and socks, so I took them off and stuck them into my jacket pockets, rolled up my trousers and slipped my feet into the icy cold, running water.

The stream was running quite fast, and its pebbled bottom was dangerously slippery under my feet. But the water wasn't deep and I made good progress until finally I could see the small guardhouse that marked the actual frontier. Coiled barbed wire was strung down from the guardhouse, across the stream and obviously continued over the open fields beyond. The stream afforded shadow while, in the moonlight, the fields gave no chance of concealment. I felt confident of being able to deal with the barbed wire by putting my folded coat over it and I crept towards it, congratulating myself that the Germans didn't make it too difficult to get into France.

I should have known better. I had nearly reached the wire when the foot I put forward cautiously was suddenly pierced by a barb on a stretch of wire trailing along the stream bed.

I bit the scream of pain back and put my other foot down to try and recover my balance, and it sank into another barb on another trailing length of wire.

The bastards had trailed lengths of barbed wire under water along the stream bed, anticipating that anyone who wanted to cross the frontier at this point would use the stream and would wade in it bare footed.

The agony of the barbs in both feet, and the impossibility of standing, compelled me to cry out as I fell back, my hands going down to my feet to tear the barbs out of them.

Instantly the whole area was a flood of light as the man in the guardhouse switched on the floodlamps strung up on poles all along the frontier line.

There I was thrashing about in the water, in awful pain, with the dog slithering down the embankment towards me. The beast leaped on me, and got me by the ankle with its teeth. I heard a shot, and the sound of a bullet thudding into the bank, unfortunately close to me. Two guards were standing looking down on me, both with their rifles pointed at me.

One of them called off the dog, which obeyed with growling reluctance.

'Get up,' he ordered abruptly. 'Come up here.'

I tried to get to my feet, and howled in pain.

'I can't. Your bloody dog has chewed my ankle off. I've bloody great holes in my feet from your bloody barbed wire.'

'You got yourself bloody down there.' He was a burly man with a belly like a balloon. He had a brutish look, and the tone of his voice said quite clearly that neither my pain nor my life was of any more consequence to him than those of a fly. 'You suit your bloody self. We're not coming down for you. So either you get yourself up here or I bloody shoot you where you are. Suit yourself but those lights go off in twenty seconds, and that's all the time you've got.'

I crawled up that embankment, pulling myself up with my hand, just digging my toes into the avalanching stones and dirt. Then he made me get up on my feet.

'Start walking', he said, pointing back the way I had come.

I didn't move.

The butt of the rifle hit me in the small of the back.

I began walking. He really didn't give a damn what damage he did to me. It was surprising what that knowledge did. I limped, bow legged, putting my weight as far as possible only on the outer sides of the soles of my feet, through the night, from sleeper to sleeper, for two kilometres, about a mile and a half, until we reached a guard-post. Here I was pushed into a small, unfurnished room, and the door locked on me.

There were two other guards on duty at the guard post, and I could hear them talking on the other side of the door. The room was about ten foot square, and must have been intended as some kind of store. There was no window and it was completely dark except for the yellow slivers of light penetrating around the door frame.

I dragged myself round the room, exploring it by touch. The pain in my ankle and in the soles of my feet was agonizing. I banged on the door and called out that I needed medical help. There was no answer.

I spent the night lying on the floor, sleepless from the pain in my feet, and wondering what would happen to me.

When they opened the door it was morning. The guard must have changed because the two men on duty now were younger men. I hobbled out into the guardroom and they had a look at my ankle and the soles of my feet and were human enough to agree with each other that I looked a bit of a mess.

'I need a doctor,' I said.

'You'll get one where you're going.'

'Where am I going?'

'To Schirmeck.'

'What's at Schirmeck?'

'It's a work camp.'

'You think I can work with these feet?'

'That's your problem.'

They gave me a mug of coffee. It was black and bitter. While I was drinking it a van pulled up at the roadside along the track. I managed to get my socks over my feet, but not my shoes. Then I was bundled into the van.

There were two camps at Schirmeck. One was for political prisoners and the other, to which I was taken, was called a 'Work Education Camp'. It was intended for foreign labourers who had been either sent to, or had volunteered to go to Germany, but who had failed to give satisfaction.

The first thing that happened to me was an interrogation.

I knew enough now to understand that all they wanted from a worker who was 'adrift' was to establish some new documentation on him. Nobody was going to check if the story was true. It wasn't important enough to waste any time on such a matter, especially as the original documentation had probably been destroyed in an air raid anyway.

I gave my work record correctly up to the point of leaving Leipzig for Duisburg, but said nothing at all about going to Duisburg.

'You left Leipzig without permission?'

'I suppose so. I didn't think I needed permission. I was a volunteer.'

'Why did you leave?'

'I was fed up with the bombing. After all, it's not my war. I wanted to go back home.'

They were not really very interested. They wanted some details for the new documents on me. I was passed on to the camp doctor.

Such is the nature of war that neither individual people, nor the nations they collectively make up, should ever be judged by their conduct and behaviour during it. All the rules of conduct imposed by religions and by civil law makers are reversed.

One simply cannot take a society in which one outlaws the possession of guns and knives as offensive weapons, and in which one executes the citizen who with hatred kills someone because of understandable enmity, and then overnight issues guns, trains everybody to use them, encourages them to hate without personal reason and not only sends them out to kill but gives them medals for doing so, without upsetting the whole carefully balanced apple-cart of disciplined human conduct.

The only uniformed German I had anything to do with during the war who seemed to be completely unaffected by the circumstances of war was the doctor at Schirmeck.

He examined my injuries. He treated the wounds and bandaged them. He said that I would need to have complete rest for a month or two. He would arrange, he said, that I was given no work until he was satisfied with my condition.

I was taken to one of the fifty wooden barrack buildings. Each block had a prisoner in charge. These selected prisoners were Alsatians who spoke both French and German. Most of my fellow prisoners were French, although there were a few Belgians, Poles and Dutch.

The prisoner in charge of the hut gave me two horse blankets, a tin plate, a spoon and a towel, and allocated a bed to me. Each hut housed about forty prisoners and we slept on straw mattresses on wooden bunks. The bunks were in pairs, one on top of the other. The centre of the hut was taken up with five wooden tables and benches.

In a corner there were hooks for each prisoner to hang his plate, spoon, mug and towel. Every day the prisoners in charge of the huts made an inspection of these belongings. Once a week they were examined by German guards. If any item was dirty the offender was flogged by the prisoner in command of the hut.

I had been in this camp for less than a day when I found my clothes crawling with lice. I had never had to endure body lice before but I decided to accept them as the lesser of two evils. I understood that if a prisoner complained about the lice he was taken outside the hut. He was forced to stand naked in the winter cold while his clothes and mattress were burned. Eventually he was given some old discarded clothes and a fresh mattress filled with new straw, and allowed to re-enter the hut.

Within hours the vermin crawled from the other bunks and bed-clothes of the prisoners and the poor man realized his humiliation had been for nothing. I learned on my first day not to complain but from time to time to undress and hunt the lice for oneself. I remember one day counting no fewer than eighty-seven lice out of my vest alone. After this I gave up searching for them.

We had our meals eight to a table. The prisoner in charge and his assistants were responsible for order. Breakfast was a slice of bread – very thin and dry. They also served red-hot peppermint tea, but that was all we got. At lunchtime a cube of margarine, no bigger than a dice, or a teaspoonful of marmalade was served without bread. So nearly everyone saved his slice from breakfast. It was kept in a linen sack after each man had put his mark on it.

At my table there was one outstanding character – Robert. He was a former swimming champion of France. He was tall and he always wore a sweater, handknitted by his wife when he was forced by the Nazis to work in Germany. He was kind to me. As he was so powerfully-built and strong, the prisoners in charge of the hut treated me with more respect when they saw he had taken me under his wing.

One day when the linen sack was opened at lunchtime my slice had disappeared. It was assumed I had not given it in after breakfast. No one was concerned and the prisoner in charge of my table considered the matter closed. No one except Robert seemed worried as I sat there with a dice of margarine – and no bread to put it on. He did not hesitate. He put his tiny slice on my plate and said in his kindly way: 'You must eat – you are wounded.'

I shoved it back to him but he did not want to take it. We argued. I knew he had to slave all day in the stone-quarry doing really hard labour. Finally he got so mad he swore at me, rose and stormed off from the table. If anyone else, under any other circumstances, had dared to leave the table without permission – he would have been savagely flogged. But as the whole argument had been heard by all, Robert was left alone.

At last I ate the miserable slice but I did so only to show my appreciation of his gesture. The bread was so small I could not even feel it in my stomach. The searing hot tea however did more to kill my hunger.

For dinner we had soup. It was served from a large bowl. To call it 'soup' is to abuse the word. It was, as far as most of us were concerned, hot water with a few boiled potatoes, slices of carrot, cabbage leaves and some tiny pieces of fat from bits of pigskin which had been boiled for hours.

The prisoner in charge dipped his spoon in the bowl which was carried by his assistants. As the plates were passed to him he skimmed the surface off the liquid and filled them. Of course the best part of the watery mixture was left at the bottom and he made sure it stayed there until he and his assistants took their shares. When they had had as much as they wanted, the rest – if any remained – was divided among the prisoners.

Hunger drives men to desperate and shameful acts. On the second week I was there, a young Belgian was caught in the middle of the night stealing some soup that had been set aside for one of his mates who had been too ill to attend dinner. He was beaten with clubs and fists until he fainted. He had to be taken to hospital with severe concussion.

The prisoner in control of the hut, and his assistants, flaunted their power and privileges. They were able to take so much thick soup they could leave it in the bowls for lunch next day. At breakfast they were the only ones eating their bread because they had margarine or jam at this time, and extra bread for lunch.

The sight of them bullying the young Belgian was the last straw for me – along with their indifference over the loss of my

slice of bread – and so I decided to get revenge. As I sat brood-
ing on a wooden bench (lying on the bunks was only permitted
at night time) I had an idea. Each morning after breakfast all
the prisoners, except me, had to go outside for general roll-call
and line-up. As their numbers were called out the Nazi guards
inspected them. I had to remain in sight through the window so
I could be counted too.

Each morning a German guard would come into the hut to
examine our beds. That day I slipped away from the window as
soon as he left the room after finishing his inspection. I knew I
had a few minutes before the roll-call outside began in earnest.
I dashed over to the plates belonging to the boss prisoner and
his mates. Taking them one by one I ate two or three spoonfuls
of the cold soup, making sure to wipe the inside to disguise the
fact that the level had gone down. For the next three months I
was able to complete this operation in the brief time available
before the counting started. At the end of this period my wounds
were healed. I am sure it would have taken even longer to get
rid of the infection if I had not had this extra food. Of course
I got a kick out of stealing from the sods who co-operated so
enthusiastically with the Nazis.

With my wounds healed I was appointed to light duties – I
became the camp toilet cleaner! There were two toilets in a par-
titioned hut with a thatched roof. I had to keep a ditch and a
drain clear by washing them out with bucketfuls of water which
I got from the main kitchen. It was not heavy work – but I never
got used to the stench.

In between trips to and from the kitchen tap to the toilet I had
nothing to do. I started exploring and found provisions were
kept in a cellar under the kitchen building. There were heaps
of carrots and potatoes lying there for the taking – if only one
could get at them. The cellar had windows that could be opened
easily but behind the windows were iron bars which could not be
removed. Eventually we solved this problem. Robert and some
friends smuggled thin rope, pieces of iron, rusty nails and empty
cans into the camp when they returned from the quarry. Patiently,
and after many failures, I succeeded in making a kind of fishing
tackle. By then I knew the time the guards made their rounds
and so with the help of two friends I was able to fish out big
carrots and potatoes nearly every day. I hid them under the
thatched roof of the toilet while I dismantled the fishing equipment. When Robert and his mates returned from a day's hard

labour they were pleased to nibble the vegetables under the blanket. It was something to add to the thin, watery soup but I thought the vegetables tasted awful when raw and they easily gave you the runs.

About two months later the Germans decided I had learned my lesson and I was taken by cattle-waggon back to Leipzig.

It was about the time Leipzig was enduring very heavy bombing. Nearly the whole centre part of the city was demolished. The bodies of thousands of dead rotted away under the debris and every part of the town was infested with the smell of corpses.

When I first arrived I was put up at the reception centre for foreigners. When the bombing started we were huddled together in the cellars and guarded there until the raid was over. One night when we were down there we realized we had forgotten someone in the sick bay – an old Czech who was too ill to move. I argued with a guard that we should fetch him. The guard, a mean-faced, surly fellow did not want me to go upstairs again as he did not trust me and he did not fancy accompanying me. Tired of the delay, I pushed him as hard as I could and sent him sprawling on the floor, and in the dark he lost his grip on the gun.

I know striking a guard was a serious offence but there was no time to think of that. As he scrambled to his feet, I dashed upstairs, took the old Czech on my shoulders, and started to come down as quickly as I could. An incendiary whizzed through the roof and nearly hit me. I lost my balance and came rolling down the stairs – still clutching the sick man.

We landed at the feet of the mean-faced guard. As we landed he staggered and fell again. When both the guard and I had got up we discovered the old man had broken his neck in the fall. This sobered his anger and, as the bombs were still falling, he did no more than shove me back into the cellar.

Later I worked in an aluminium factory where I acted, part of the time, as a translator for French and Belgium labourers. The hours were long – I usually put in ten or twelve a day. It wasn't long before circumstances made it advisable for me to leave the factory and I succeeded in breaking into the director's office from where I stole an official piece of paper which enabled me to make it look as though I had an 'honourable discharge' from my job, and allowed me to return to Holland.

Armed with this forged document I took to my heels and got as far as Erfurth in Thuringen. Along with a Frenchman I was picked up by the police. As my papers appeared to be in order I was released on the condition that I took a job in that area. Once again I became a truck-driver, working for the Edeka firm. My immediate superior was a tall blonde called Christina. She was engaged to be married to a pilot in the Nazi air force. Although he was nearly a head taller than I, she seemed impressed by my strength and skill at handling heavy loads. She had not seen her fiancé for a year or so and we soon started a rather unsatisfactory affair. Neither of us got much joy from our love making but she saved my neck. She sent me word one day that an inquiry about my reason for leaving Leipzig had been answered and the police were on their way to arrest me.

I was on the run again.

It gets easier all the time, that sort of thing. It became easier all the time as conditions inside Germany deteriorated. Although special permission had to be obtained from the local authorities for any travel, there were many uprooted people moving about. Provided one spoke German like a native, knew one's way around and gave the police a wide berth there were no great difficulties.

My real problem was that I badly needed more clothing. I couldn't buy new clothes and I would only have risked stealing what I needed if a safe opportunity had arisen. It never happened.

I had left two good suits, half a dozen shirts and three pairs of shoes at the Kusters' home, and so I decided to take a chance and pay Heidi and her family a visit.

Of course, I didn't expect a friendly reception. On the other hand I was supposed to be the Kusters' son-in-law and the father of their grandchild. Anyway, whether I liked it or not, there was a strange sort of bond between myself and Heidi.

I got a very cold reception indeed from Karen Kuster.

'You can come in,' she said. 'But you'll have to be on your way before Fritz gets back, because the chances are he won't hesitate about turning you over to the police.'

'I can explain everything,' I told her. 'I know it must have looked bad, leaving the way I did that morning. But there was no time to explain. I got a warning that the police were looking for me for leaving my job in Leipzig without getting proper permission. And it was true – that's what I did. Because you wanted it, and Heidi wanted it, and so I took a chance.'

'A likely story. Nobody ever came looking for you.'

'Of course they didn't. But I didn't want Heidi – or you and Fritz, or Peter, mixed up in it. I gave myself up. I spent nearly

six months in the Work Education Camp at Schirmeck. Look.
I can prove it. It's all on my papers. And I didn't dare to write
because I didn't want Heidi to be involved. Then they sent me
back to Leipzig. That's where I've come from now.'

The cold, frozen manner went when I said this.

'What's it really like in Leipzig?' Heidi's mother asked. 'They
say they've had it badly there. We haven't heard from her for
over three weeks, and I can't help worrying.'

'Heidi?' I asked. 'You don't mean that Heidi went back to
Leipzig.'

'Yes. She was given a job there. She went to stay with Frau
Bosch.'

'And I kept meaning to visit the Boschs to see if they were all
right,' I lied, with a note of deep regret. 'Just think. If only
I'd done so....! But there was no chance. I had to live in a
reception centre. She didn't take Peter with her?'

'Of course she did. That's why I worry so much. Is it really
bad....?'

I thought about the streets of uncleared rubble, and the stench
of death of the unburied. I had never liked Karen Kuster, but
I could not tell her why maybe Heidi had ceased to write and
might never write again.

'They've had a few bad raids,' I said. 'But so have you, here
in Duisburg. Mostly it's the city centre, not out where the Boschs
live. But if that's where Heidi is, if she's not here, then I'll go
back. Don't you worry, I'll find her and Peter.'

She wanted that, and could not hide the fact. Nevertheless she
seemed doubtful.

'We know that you and Heidi weren't married,' she said at
last. 'That's what made Fritz so angry.'

'Didn't Heidi explain that we couldn't get married until I had
permission from Berlin?'

'Yes. She explained about that. But that's no excuse for you ...
for you living in sin with her. And under our own roof, too. And
our grandson; not legitimate.'

I knew just how to get round her – I hoped and believed.

'Could you endure all this, what's happened here in Duisburg,
without Fritz? Do you think he could stand up to the kind of
life he has to lead, if he didn't have you? Heidi and I needed
each other. Not just in the way you disapprove of, though God
knows that's natural enough. But to be alone. Can't you at least
begin to understand?'

She did not want to make an admission that was even the beginnings of condoning her daughter promiscuously copulating with a foreign labourer night after night in the room upstairs. Nevertheless she did nod.

'But it's no excuse, Armand! It's a sin in the eyes of the Lord.'

'He looks down on a great deal more of much worse sin these days,' I said piously.

'Yes, that's true.'

'Anyway, Heidi and I can marry now!' I said temptingly. 'I'll pick up the clothes I had to leave here, and I'll go straight back to Leipzig to find her.'

Once again there was that unexplained doubtfulness in her manner.

'When you went away, and you never wrote, she had to think you were never coming back, Armand.'

'I know. I've explained why it had to be like that. But it's all over now.'

'She had no husband, she wasn't a wife, and she had your child. . . .'

'We can put that right. Look, I'll get my things, and be on my way. I'll soon find her, don't you worry.'

'She met someone else. A Czech soldier. I think she's met him before.'

I stared at Karen Kuster, hiding the excitement I was feeling; making it seem like anxiety.

'Go on,' I said.

'They got married, here at the Town Hall. While he was on leave.'

'I see,' I said very slowly.

I still wanted what I had come for; the clothes upstairs.

'He's not with her in Leipzig?' I asked.

'Of course not. He had to rejoin his regiment.'

'Then that doesn't alter the fact that I must go back to Leipzig and find Heidi and – *my* son!' I said sorrowfully, but with a show of determination. 'The truth is . . . and now I must tell you . . . they have had it badly in Leipzig. Whether she married someone else or not because she believed she would never see me again, I must look after Heidi and our child. You understand that, don't you?'

'Perhaps I've misjudged you a bit, Armand,' she said slowly.

'That's understandable,' I said. 'The thing is now to waste no more time. May I have the key? I'll just collect my things.'

'Your clothes?' she said at last. 'Oh, Heidi sold everything – got what she could for them.'

It was only with the greatest difficulty that I controlled myself. I got away from her, after that, as quickly as I could, leaving her with the belief that I was returning to Leipzig.

I never returned to Duisburg. I never heard what happened to Heidi, and whether she and the child survived the holocaust of Leipzig. My responsibility was over.

I was a man alone again, and relieved to be so.

Instead of turning east towards Leipzig I made my way north to Spork, a small town on the German side of the Dutch border. A friend of the family, a member of the Darbinistic Church, lived at Spork and I felt that I could count on his help to get into Holland.

He turned up trumps. He and his children watched out for approaching guards, and then, when it was all clear, he helped me through a barbed wire fence at the bottom of his orchard.

Sneaking through fields, slipping under hedges whenever patrols had to be avoided, at last I reached a village some way on the right side of the frontier. After lying under some bushes until it was dark, I cautiously picked my way through the village, and got home.

My parents were pretty upset when they saw me. But when I explained about Heidi and the boy they agreed reluctantly to let me stay a while with them. Of course, I had to hide in the house and make certain I was never seen by the neighbours, or anyone else. I kept out of sight and a few days later wrote to my brother Louis, who now lived at Rotterdam. I asked him to help me. The letter had to be written with great care because no one could tell when post was being opened by agents working with the Post Office. He replied quickly saying if I could reach Rotterdam he would be able to hide me for a time, and then suggest a further way of escape.

I was grateful for his offer but it was far easier said than done. How on earth could I get to Rotterdam? I did not fancy another spell in a squalid camp like Schirmeck. Some unusual plan was needed to get me to safety. But what?

Sitting at home I had nothing to do but laze around, read and listen to the radio. One day I heard on the wireless the voice of Max Blokzijl, a leading Dutch Nazi. He promised pardon to all persons in hiding, and those who had run away from their jobs in Germany, if they volunteered for the SS. This I decided was my big chance. The Dutch Headquarters of the dreaded SS was in Rotterdam and this coincidence was too lucky not to take advantage of. My parents were dead against the idea. I understood the loathing at this time for the Germans in general and the SS in particular. But I had two good reasons for choosing to make use of Blokzijl's offer.

The Dutch SS must not, of course, be confused with the German SS, although they were organized along the same lines and took their orders from the SS headquarters in Germany.

The German SS were the utterly trusted fanatics in uniform – this is, trusted by the Nazi leaders, disliked by the German army leaders. The hard core German generals had never liked the upstart politician Hitler and his gang, but they were stuck with him. On his part Hitler was far too wise to suppose that he could ever trust the gentlemen-and-officers of the army. Guttersnipes and snobs can never really mix.

The guttersnipe knew it, and the snobs knew it. History is often as simple as that.

In Germany the SS were the Nazis in uniform, which was something quite different from the German army of ordinary human sheep, thinking as they were told to think, doing as they were told, following any leader whose bleating was loud enough. In occupied countries, however, the SS were the self seekers, the rats, the traitors to whatever patriotism is, backing the believed winners.

I wanted to get to Rotterdam and the Blokzijl offer was my ticket there. Nothing more.

There was a snowball's chance in hell of the Dutch SS accepting me into their ranks. I had to be extraordinarily stupid, or unbelievably impudent to offer myself.

Consider! First there was the operated scar that had got me thrown out of the French Foreign Legion. The SS demanded fit, completely healthy men. There would be a strict entry medical, and I would see to it that my operation was known about.

Then there was my criminal record – altogether I had confessed to over a hundred burglaries. I had had forged passports. I had had false documents. I had prison sentences and escapes on my record.

They wouldn't even look at me – but, where they would turn me down would be in Rotterdam.

I made up my mind and went straight to visit the Orts Kommandantur of Bourtange.

'I've just arrived from Leipzig', I said. 'I was working there and at Erfurth. I understand Max Blokzijl has offered a pardon to people like me.' Within a few minutes I was given a free travel warrant to Rotterdam and a letter of introduction to the SS Hauptkwartier there. I wasted no time and was soon saying goodbye to my shocked parents, and on my way.

Next morning I took a bus to the nearest railway station. From the instant I entered the bus and showed my German pass to the driver, the other passengers treated me like an outcast. The contemptuous looks they gave me, and the way they shrank from me as though I was a leper, made it quite clear they thought I was not only a traitor but a degenerate as well. Although the bus was crowded I had the bench to myself. People showed they preferred to stand than share the seat with someone like me. Some of them knew my parents and I overheard two elderly ladies saying what a pity it was for anyone to have a son like me.

The whole journey was a pretty distasteful experience. I longed to tell them I wasn't a Nazi-lover. I hated the thought that they condemned me without knowing the reason why I had to travel in this way. Once on the train I was sent to a compartment reserved for Germans only, and on every station the glares and looks of disgust of the loyal Dutch folk passing by my window reminded me vividly of the dangerous game I was playing. Looking back on it now I can only console myself with the thought that later I did manage to do something for the cause of freedom by fighting with the Maquis – and did then earn their respect.

I went straight to the SS headquarters when I arrived at Rotterdam. I delivered the letter I had been given to the officer in charge and was given a questionnaire to fill in. I was warned that there would be a careful check on my answers.

The questionnaire required details of any convictions. I left nothing out.

When I took the completed papers back to the officer he read through what I had written with an incredulity he was unable to conceal.

'I'm afraid I have a bit of a record,' I said apologetically.

'So I see!' he remarked.

'It won't go against me?'

He stared at me.

'I don't make the decisions. You'll be informed in due course.'

'While I'm waiting to hear, may I go back home?'

'Why not?'

'May I have a rail warrant, then?'

He wrote me one out. I pushed it into my pocket and went to Louis' house.

Louis was delighted to see me and laughed uproariously when he heard how I had got to Rotterdam. We spent an evening drinking while I told him of my adventures. It was a story that kept him very sober indeed.

'Brother, you're a hard case,' he said. 'What are you going to do now? Make a run for it? Where do you think you can run anyway?'

'I'll be best off in France, I think,' I told him.

'That's two frontiers to cross. Suppose the SS accept you?'

'They won't.'

'I think you'd better hang on to be sure of that,' he said. 'If they do accept you, you'd be a deserter. You don't want that hanging over your head on top of everything else. If ever they picked you up, in any country, and that came out, there'd be no arguments – just a firing squad.'

'I can't go back to Bourtange,' I told him. 'I'd probably get a knife in my back. A Dutch knife.'

'You can't stay here with me,' he said. 'Armand, that's not being unfriendly, or refusing to take a reasonable risk. But I'm skating on pretty thin ice myself. It won't take your weight as well. I can fix you up with somewhere else to lie low, though. You're a horny bastard, and it should suit you down to the ground.'

And that was how I ended up in, of all places, a private maternity clinic.

The clinic was run by Lena van Leyden, a big breasted brunette in her early forties, with an assistant called Susie, who was around twenty-three, a slim little blonde. What a pair they were, both real nymphomaniacs.

They were the first nymphos I had come up against – women with not simply an insatiable appetite for the male penis, but an unsatisfiable one. The word is so often misused, the condition so rarely understood. It is both a physical and psychological condition, taking its name from the sensual inner lips of the vulva.

All this I learnt from Lena herself who taught me, during the few weeks I was at the clinic, everything I was to know about the genital anatomy of woman, for one of my jobs was to act as an assistant midwife.

Lena, of course, said Susie was a nymphomaniac. Susie, behind Lena's back, said that Lena was one.

It was no surprise to me to very quickly discover that Louis had regularly, and for a long time, been one of the men trying in vain to give Lena the climax of relief to her sexual excitability that nobody had ever succeeded in giving her. And Louis was doing well out of the relationship. For while society outside was suffering the hardships of wartime conditions, the standard of living maintained by the clinic was well up to pre-war levels. Lena had many 'good friends'. And Louis, as one of her lovers, drew benefit from that.

Food and luxuries were hard to come by. Despite stern penalties for the possession of unrationed goods, there was a booming black market – if you could afford it. Lena did not have to. Her 'good friends' could.

The clinic, apart from the occasional highly paid for abortions, was a completely genuine operation. But it was also, surreptitiously, the background to regularly staged sexual orgies, held for the benefit of Lena's 'good friends'.

It was a weird life. The services of the clinic were used for their patients by several doctors who themselves were among the 'good friends'. There were twenty private bedrooms and I imagine that the fees were very high. The patients were all middle or upper class women.

Lena explained my unusual job to me on that first evening, after Louis had telephoned her, taken me round to the clinic, and introduced me to her. I had absolutely no idea what I had walked into as I sat in her office, which was equipped like a doctor's surgery and used as such by some of the doctors for private interviews with women negotiating arrangements for an abortion.

'First,' she said, 'you've got to understand that if you are to lie low here, you've got to have a job. I've got to protect myself in case the police come looking for you. People with qualifications in midwifery aren't easy to get, so tomorrow we'll give you some papers showing that you've qualified as a male nurse, because that automatically will include a knowledge of midwifery. No problems about getting those forged, but they'll be my excuse for engaging you *if* there's any trouble.'

'But I'd never be any use. I couldn't pretend to know anything about it. Isn't there any other job . . .?'

Lena laughed.

'Oh, you'll be a great asset to the clinic,' she assured me. 'Don't let's be naive. You enjoy showing yourself off to a woman, don't you? Come, now, Armand, you don't have to pretend with me. Every man gets a kick out of showing a woman an erect penis and a good pair of balls. It's human nature. And do you think women aren't exactly the same?'

'It's hard to know about women,' I said.

'We're exactly the same,' said Lena. 'Only while a man has the excuse that he can't help showing it to a woman, a woman's got to find another excuse. The result is that a great number of women find this perfectly natural desire frustrated. They would enjoy being *persuaded* to do so by their husbands, but their husbands, in the circumstances when they could enjoy it, are too impatient. And if they did it deliberately to tease and excite their husbands, their husbands, even if they enjoyed it, would immediately suspect them of being too highly sexed to be trusted to be faithful. Most of these women never get a chance to enjoy exhibiting themselves to men, except for gynaecological examinations, which gives them an excuse. And *I* know what I'm talking about. We don't only have pregnancy cases here, but you'll do the rounds with myself or my assistant Susie, and you'll be present at all the physical examinations, and believe me there'll be no objections to that.'

Then she asked me how much I really knew about the genital anatomy of a woman. I confessed that although I had made love, perhaps in every possible way, to women, I didn't really know much about the unseen anatomy of the female cunt.

'Hardly any men do, Armand,' she said with a regretful sigh. 'If only they did, women would be much happier. Now, when a baby is being born, the girl makes physical efforts to push it out of her body. You do know that much, do you?'

'Yes,' I said uncertainly.

'She is using muscles we teach women to use in the clinic. But they don't only help in child birth. They are essential to really good lovemaking. Especially the constrictor cunni. You know about that?'

I said that I didn't.

'I see I'm really going to have to teach you everything,' she told me with a smile. 'It's a strong, tight muscle that forms the actual hole a man has to open and go through to get into the vagina,' she said. 'It's the most important part of a woman to her when she's giving birth to a child, *and* when she's being

167

made love to, because it can move in and out, up and down. There's only one way to explain. I'll show you.'

She was wearing a white, button down overall-dress. She undid the front. Underneath she was wearing a bra and a small cache-sexe, which she calmly pulled off. She hoisted herself on to the examination couch which was part of the office-surgery equipment, opened her legs widely and drew her knees up, positioning herself so that she was at the end of the couch.

I didn't need the invitation to come and see for myself. She put her hands down, using her fingers to hold herself wide open.

'Down at the bottom, you see the funnel like entrance – that guides the man's penis towards the vagina. You see the tiny opening at the end of it? That's surrounded by the constrictor cunni muscle. Put your finger in, from underneath so that you can see what happens. Don't put it through the hole. Just put pressure around the opening and push it gently inwards and upwards. Now – do you see how doing that stretches these inner lips I'm touching with my finger tips? They're my nymphae. As they're stretched – look, Armand, can you see – they pull the hood of my clitoris down. That massages the clitoris, inside the hood.' Her voice had become uneven. The limp butterfly wings of her nymphae had become engorged, were bigger and were becoming a bright red. 'Are you hot, Armand?' she asked.

As I took my finger from her to strip, she replaced it with her own, unhurriedly giving herself vaginal masturbation. When I was naked, she stared at my penis, the tip of her tongue protruding through teeth gently biting it.

'A practical demonstration, Armand. Remember what I've told you.'

I remembered all right. Picturing every detail of what I was feeling as I thrust eagerly into her, I started coming at once. Immediately she locked her legs tightly round my body, and started using me the way Victoria had done.

But where Victoria's movements had been rapid and small, Lena's were the same pace as my own, and I was aware of her feeling it all from root to head.

'Think of it, Armand,' she gasped. 'Picture it.'

I had begun to soften in her, but she made me stiff again.

'Keep still. Let me do it. Let me show you.'

Then suddenly I was coming again, for a second time.

'Oh, God, no. . . .!' she gasped. 'Not yet. Not yet.'

She went on.

'Imagine it, Armand.'

I did, but this time without effect. I was aware of being limp within her, and suddenly I slipped out. Instantly her hands were on my head, pressing it down.

'Use your tongue. Please . . . please. You can't leave me like this.'

I buried my face into her and did my best, but after a moment or two she pushed me away and put both her hands down to herself, thrusting a finger of one hand up into her vagina and using the first finger and thumb of the hand to make rapid little squeezing movements on each side of the hood of her clitoris.

Almost at once she achieved the results I had been unable to give her, and her whole body began to convulse in a series of violent spasms that gradually died away. When it was over, she looked at me with an almost sad smile.

'I just couldn't make it *with* you. It's not your fault. It's the way I am. Maybe next time.'

She had taught me something that hadn't been part of the lesson. I knew then what nymphomania was – the insatiable search for the unsatisfiable result.

While I was at the clinic I slept in Lena's bed with her about four nights a week, in Susie's bed on two other nights. And Susie was in exactly the same boat except that what she needed and demanded to try and get herself to her threshold was to have the penis in her mouth.

Susie had dentures, and she would very secretly remove these at the last moment. She could, and did, give herself orgasms in this way, but however desperately she tried, and however long one disciplined oneself to make coition last, she could never get the one kind of climax she really wanted.

Between them they took care of six nights in the week. The seventh night, the Friday, was always party night at the clinic. And some of the things that happened at those parties defy description.

The parties were attended by Lena's 'good friends', several of them doctors, and the most outrageous of them a Baron van der Landen who was obviously the most profitable of the 'good friends'. In turn, all the leading black market contacts in Rotterdam took part in these extraordinary orgies.

The parties were held in a vast, low ceilinged room with a piano in one corner, and which had several very large couches arranged around an irregularly-shaped table. On a cabinet next to the door were different cold dishes for a running buffet and many bottles of wine and spirits. Nobody would have supposed that there was a war on.

The parties always began the same way, with a game of strip poker. Nobody ever knew just how they would end, or what would happen during the course of them.

The routine was that every time a member of the party lost, he or she had to discard a garment. Eventually there was a first guest to be completely naked.

When someone who had already become naked had a further loss in the game, having no further garments to shed they had to submit to sexual experience with whoever was, at that point of the game, the winner on points – whether they were of the same or the opposite sex – and the performance took place on the table top with all the other players advantageously positioned to watch. The possibilities were, of course, enormous, being both hetero- and homosexual, and absolutely nothing was ruled out. The card game always became abandoned at this point. Long before the performance was over, everybody was stripped and about ten naked women and ten naked men were tumbling about in twos, threes and even fours in an orgy of exciting each other's genitalia in every conceivable way, watching one another, emulating one another.

How can one possibly describe such scenes, especially when they stimulated the most incredible inventiveness.

When the first orgy had spent itself the exhausted sensualists would drift through in their final couplings, which might well be the second, third or even fourth partnership they had had, to an anteroom to shower or use one of the row of three bidets. It was quite usual, if one was one of the later users of the room, to see three women sitting astride on the bidets with one of them being washed by a man whose penis was being caressed by the free, well soaped hand of the woman on the adjoining bidet in an attempt to give him another erection, while the shower might be occupied by three men and one woman who might have managed to arouse one of her companions sufficiently for a final copulation, all four of them caressing one another's bodies under the water during the standing act.

Eventually everyone was back in the main room, wearing kimonos or bathrobes which were essential to teasing up any beginning for the second round of the evening. Everyone sat around, drank, smoked, ate, talked until someone had the urge to begin again with a solo act.

On one occasion it was Susie, who suddenly flung off her wrap and stood on her hands, demanding to be held by her legs, opened, and to have champagne poured into herself, then crying out: 'This puts drinking out of the lady's slipper out of date. Come on everybody, have a sip of Susie's champagne special.'

On another occasion it was the Baron who got things going again by wandering round the room and dipping his penis in everybody's glass, and then demanding that the whole company drank his health.

The Baron's most extraordinary and ambitious exploit was to transfer himself from one lady to the next, taking each of the twelve who were present on that night in an endeavour to be the only man in the world to have used twelve different women with the same erection to have an orgasm.

The only comparable exploit, he told the company, was the legendary one of Hercules who, as one of his tasks, was supposed to have deflowered the twelve virgin daughters of a mythological king during the course of one night.

'But this,' he told us, as the ladies lined themselves up for him as if for some unbelievable game of leap-frog, 'will be a much more remarkable feat.'

Everyone was more than a little drunk by now. Nobody had any inhibitions whatsoever. At the time there seemed absolutely nothing wrong or improper about those twelve laughing and giggling women presenting the incredible 'chorus line' of petit con.

The Baron no more than impaled the first in line for his attack, patted her on the rump and told her boastfully: 'Stay where you are. I'll be back.' The second got as swift attention. He was slower with the third and when coupled with his fourth partner he remained bent over her, labouring vigorously as if he had completely forgotten his purpose. But no such thing was true. Ignoring the encouraging cries reminding him that he had eight more to go, he was trying frantically to sustain his excitement, and after less than a minute it was all over and he was looking down with regret and humiliation at the limp weapon that had utterly failed in the most exciting situation his mind had been able to devise.

His failure communicated itself to everybody. Back on went the bathrobes and the kimonos and the company returned to drinking and talking and presently the evening petered out.

I decided, that night, that I had to get out of the clinic. It had nothing to do with morality. It had nothing to do with obscenity. It was simply that Lena and her 'good friends', most especially Baron van der Landen, had made me realize that the element of emotion is far, far more important in sex than excitation by novelty. The emotion may be that of tenderness and love as it had been for me with Hennie, or it may be the contrasting emotion of antagonism that had been such a strong force with Heidi.

I rang Louis that evening and told him I wanted to see him. He came round, and I told him that I wanted to get away from the clinic. Of course he was curious about my reasons.

'You could be right at that,' he said. 'I only went to a couple of Lena's parties, and then quit. Not for your reasons. It takes all kinds, Armand. For me, the parties were "sick". They were pathetic. They were stupid. I don't have to be in love with a girl to want her. I don't need this emotional thing you talk about. But I do want to be on my own with her.'

'At least you know how I feel about ducking out.'

'It's Sunday,' he said. 'Give it a day or two. Maybe we'll hear from father that there's been a letter for you from the SS. He's promised to contact me the moment anything comes.'

The letter came on the Wednesday. My father telephoned Louis who got him to open the official communication and tell him its contents. I had been turned down as unsuitable.

Louis had already been making arrangements to get me a permit, under a false name, to travel. It would get me as far as Breda, and after that it would be up to me to cross into Belgium.

I said goodbye to Lena, who was genuinely sorry to see me go, and set off that same day. From Breda I started off on foot due south across the woods and fields towards the Belgian border.

Borders between one occupied country and another exist largely on maps. They do not represent escape from anything.

As I was following the way I knew led towards the frontier, I turned a bend and suddenly came across a platoon of German soldiers sitting there resting, and eating their rations. They were obviously out on an exercise.

For a moment I nearly panicked. Then, because there seemed to be no other way, I decided to brazen the situation out. Their job wasn't, after all, to guard the frontier.

I stepped up my pace and walked briskly through them, calling out 'hallo' and 'good-day' with as much cheerfulness as I could muster. They raised their hands casually, returning my greetings, and let me pass without challenging me.

I turned the next bend in the brook and a few kilometres further on entered Belgium without seeing anybody. Once in Belgium I met up with another Dutchman who worked with a team putting up sharp-pointed poles around the Schelde-tunnel near Antwerp. He told me the times the German guards changed over at both ends of the tunnel. With this vital information I was able to slip through the tunnel unobserved. Before he helped me however he asked me to accompany two girls who wanted to get home to somewhere near Mons. At the last moment, just as we were entering the tunnel, he came running up to join us and became a fugitive as well.

We were very lucky crossing Belgium. The girls knew a lorry driver who used to go regularly to Mons. He hid the four of us under his load. When we arrived in Mons we were invited to spend the night at the girls' home. Their parents were obviously broadminded and did not raise any objections when all four shared one enormous bed. I was so tired I slept like a stone. I remember, however, that the Dutchman and his girl fumbled and explored so much that the girl by my side, a comely brunette called Helga, perhaps disappointed at my lack of enthusiasm, scolded them for keeping us awake.

Next morning when I told her I was determined to get to Paris she asked me to stay for a while. Once I had persuaded her of my urgent need to cross the border however she did everything in her power to help me. The other Dutchman decided to stay. I wish I could remember the names of her family and the others who helped me but all I can say is that I am eternally grateful to everyone.

Helga had a smuggler friend called Gaston who often used to take alcohol and cigarettes across. That evening she brought him to the house after I had kept carefully hidden all day. He was a quiet, elderly man with a sort of inconspicuous appearance but his eye had an alertness about it – the sort of eye that belongs to a skilled hunter. He agreed to take me across and even promised to direct me to the house of a friend in France who would certainly take me to Paris in his van as he did frequent journeys between Lille and Paris. Gaston would not accept any cash for helping me and so I knew I would have some money left to reward his friend who did the run to Paris.

When it was pitch dark we set off. It was so dark Gaston told me to take hold of his coat and to hang on whatever happened. We stumbled along for the best part of an hour until a dog began to bark near us. As there was a strict black-out everywhere he must have estimated the direction to our destination almost to the inch. The barking dog belonged to his friend Bruno and so in the past hour we had clearly crossed the border into France.

Bruno, a sturdy, squat man made us very welcome. He told us he would be leaving that very day before dawn for Paris. Eight other people were already sitting as best they could on the floor of his truck amid some crates and tarpaulins. Bruno decided my Dutch money was enough to pay for a seat. I climbed in and about two hours later we were on our way.

Half dozing we tried to keep steady while the van swayed along. We did not go very fast but we went quickly enough. Every now and then we passed some guard-posts or roadblocks. Bruno managed to allow the guards no more than a peep inside the linen-covered entrance to the rear of the truck by promising them tobacco or by cracking jokes. Sometimes he claimed we were relatives going to a funeral or on others, when they seemed more cheerful, we were said to be going to a wedding and we promised them drinks on the way back!

All these ploys worked fine as long as there were Frenchmen on the roadblocks. But once not far from Paris we ran into a post occupied by Germans. Bruno spotted them just in time and opening the small window in the back of his driving cabin he ordered me to lie down under a tarpaulin. I became a 'bench' for three passengers to sit on. As I was the only one without papers this was the best way to avoid detection. When we halted the Nazis came looking in the back. I was very uncomfortable. I was trodden on and kicked. It was quite suffocating under that tarpaulin and the weight on my body was unbearable.

I could however hear what was said. As their papers were in order the Germans asked about the contents of the crates but this was shown on the papers. Then one guard asked them to stand up so he could see what they were sitting on. Luckily one of the passengers was an extremely pretty young blonde. She managed to adjust her skirt in a most provocative way showing a flash of thigh, and this distracted the guard so he forgot about getting his question answered. He never asked again for the tarpaulin to be lifted – underneath I was sweating blood and tears. After some jokes, a little flirtation and a kiss, we were allowed to continue.

The rest of our journey was uneventful and we finally reached Paris after some twenty hours on the roads. Once again I was in a foreign country some way from home. Once again I had escaped from the Nazis – but I was still on the run.

IX

Mireille, Jeanine, Madeleine, Yvonne, Manon, Yvette – and the Maquis

Paris in February 1944, when one arrived as an alien, a fugitive, penniless, hungry and literally wearing nothing but shoes, socks, a pair of underpants and overalls, was not the place written about in guide books and tourist brochures.

I suppose it could only have happened in Paris, though, but I landed up like that, almost immediately, in a girl's bedroom.

I dropped off Bruno's truck as near as I could to Saint Denis. It was better to be in a district I knew than one I didn't. I had vague plans of making for the street where I had lived with Polja. I didn't expect to find her still there, but there were shopkeepers and barkeepers I had known and I had to have some kind of help from someone.

I was a suspicious looking character, and I knew it. I wanted to go to ground as soon as possible. So when I spotted a German patrol coming towards me down the Boulevard de Bonne Nouvelle, I darted into a side street, the Rue de Poissoniere.

The way I hurried down the street, and the way I kept glancing over my shoulder, would have made it clear to anybody who observed me that I was on the run from the authorities.

The only person in sight was a girl standing outside a cheap hotel. She was as much type-cast as I was. She was obviously a prostitute on the look out for business.

She looked at me as I approached, gave me no more than a glance, then went on looking beyond me. It was quite obvious to her that I was not a potential client.

Just as I was passing her, her hand shot out and she caught me by the shoulder and pulled me into the hotel doorway.

'The patrol has turned into the street. Are they after you?'

'No. But I can't afford to be questioned,' I said.

'Come on then,' she said.

She took me up two flights of stairs to her room, and I breathed with relief. I told her something about myself, and of a few of my adventures since leaving the Nazi camp at Schirmeck. She left me in the room for a while and then returned with food, wine and cigarettes. I ate greedily. Then she told me to strip off my overalls and have a wash while she fetched me some decent clothes. When I had scrubbed the grime of my journey from every pore, I delayed her search for new clothes by showing my gratitude in the way she understood best. I made love hungrily, as the wash had aroused me, and it had been a long time since I had had the chance to enjoy a supple young body like Mireille's.

Mireille explained that her pimp was in prison, and she was being looked after by a friend of his. This friend was rather busy most of the time, and so she felt deprived of love with affection. She missed love which was exciting and pleasurable, and nothing to do with business. I must have pleased her. I kissed her slowly all over with passion, and carefully led her to her peak, using all the techniques and tricks I had learned in the years since Polja had first taught me not to rush my lovemaking. I was gentle and fierce in turns, and she grew more and more aroused as I drove myself on, reaching a perfect rhythm, and then finally lifting her to the summit of joy.

As I lay back exhausted but delighted, she rushed out of the room saying she was going to fetch her friends. It turned out she wanted to tell them about my 'performance'. Within a few minutes I was sitting, stark naked, on the bed surrounded by five girls. Apart from Mireille, there was Jeanine, Madeleine, Yvonne and Manon. Jeanine was the only girl who worked on her own. She had a room at the hotel and found her customers in expensive night-clubs. She used to bring them from the clubs to the hotel by taxi. Madeleine, a statuesque blonde, was rather stupid but very attractive to Germans. She used to pour out her child-like whimperings to them whenever her pimp had beaten her. She also used to confess her hopes and dreams to me while I sat listening patiently for hours. She was not interested in sex and seemed to lack desire, as prostitutes often do. Yvonne, on the other hand, was vivacious and lusty and constantly sought satisfaction and always wanted to be aroused and caressed. Manon was more interested in drink than sex. She was gay in the evenings but moody in the mornings, when she often suffered from a hang-over. She chattered a great deal, but hardly ever made sexual demands on me.

Sex for these women was their job and their living. Their clients ranged from middle-aged husbands, grown bored and tired with the perfunctory lovemaking of their wives to the occasional priest who had been excited by something he had heard in the confessional. There were schoolmasters from the local high school, and even policemen who dropped in for a quick one while on duty. The policemen did not even have time to undress, and the teachers came during their hour's lunch-break at noon.

Apart from the fact they gave pleasure to these men, some-times in unusual ways, these women behaved and responded normally like any other mature females. It always struck me how grateful they were for simple acts of friendliness and companion-ship. They would sit and chat for hours once they realized I was sympathetic and trustworthy. Their gratitude for even small gifts or demonstrations of affection was often quite touching. As they were used to being treated roughly, and without consideration, they had, of course, learned to endure such treatment. But when a man approached them politely and gently, they reacted, once they had overcome their first suspicions, with the spontaneity and sincerity of children.

There were seven girls living at the hotel at that time. The Hotel de l'ABC was run by a Polish couple. I was given an attic room. It was very narrow and so tucked away at the top of the building it lacked even one window. Soon afterwards the girls introduced me to the two pimps, Andre and Pierre. They soon saw how useful I could be to them all, and so they decided to pay for my room. They agreed I should act as a 'go-between' for them in their dealings with the Germans. They were always buying and selling food, clothes, silks, wines, jewellery, ciga-rettes, pornography and so on. Andre and Pierre also asked me to make sure the girls did not take any friends up to their rooms for love. All the visiting men had to be clients.

Everyone going up had to be noted in a book. The pimps took it in turns to collect the money, or goods, owing them. I managed to impress them with my reliability, even though I sometimes had to close my eyes when one of the girls made love for love's sake. I had to permit this because, if I stuck to the rules, the girls would insist I satisfied them, and I soon grew tired of being called to 'do my duty' at any hour of the day or night, whether I felt in the mood or not.

When the pimps were convinced I was reliable, they started asking me to help them plan raids in the countryside. These raids were essential to their activities in the black market. They were the leaders of a gang which made raids wherever they could to get hold of whatever goods were most in demand.

On one occasion there was a heavy demand for pork, and the prices on the black market went rocketing up. They knew of a farmer who had plenty of pigs, but he also knew what they were worth. His farm was surrounded by a very wide canal, and it could be entered only through the main gate, which was heavily bolted at night. It was also guarded by a ferocious watch-dog. The farmer used to dabble on the black market quite a bit, and liked to buy gold.

Andre and Pierre thought the problem of getting the pigs was insoluble so they came to me. This farm seemed to be the only place with enough pigs to make a raid worthwhile and it was not too far from Paris. I told them to get a plan of the farm, so I could study the layout to see if a raid was possible. When they managed this I discovered the pig-stys were at the back of the farmhouse, apart from the main building, and separated from the open countryside only by the canal. When they also told me the vicious watchdog was male, I got an idea.

For several days I got their gang to pass by the back of the farm. On these journeys they hid empty bottles, tightly corked, and empty tins, which had been soldered so they too were water-tight in a ditch.

The gang also collected wooden crates, ropes cut to length, and they kept their eyes peeled for a bitch dog who was on heat. When all these preparations were completed, the raid got the go-ahead.

As soon as it was dark about six of the gang crept along the canal-bank at the back of the farm. The wooden crates were then fastened together with rope. These crates were then turned into a raft by being put into the canal with their open sides facing downwards. Underneath the crates were placed the cork bottles, and soldered tins. These pushed the raft upward until it floated well enough to carry two men. A long rope was then attached to the raft at each end. One man swam the canal to haul the others over, while another remained behind to pull them back again. I was not allowed to see how the plan worked in practice. There were two good reasons why I could not take part in this raid. Firstly I did not have the right papers and documents, and so I could not get past any roadblocks, which might be set up any-where. Secondly Andre and Pierre thought the rest of my ser-vices to them were too valuable to be jeopardized.

When the raft was ready, two other members of the gang ap-proached the main gate. One had a little bitch under his coat.

The other had a battery-operated, portable radio and some gold. They rang the bell and the farmer came out. When he saw the gold he let one man enter. The other stayed outside. When the farmer went inside to negotiate, the man with the dog tied the bitch with a leash to the gate. Soon the giant watchdog was completely fascinated by his new girlfriend, and ignored the sounds of the rest of the gang stealing the pigs from the styes. As the farmer sat haggling with the man with the gold, the portable radio blasted out dance music which drowned most of the other noises made by the raiders.

At a given signal six pigs were killed almost noiselessly. Normally pig killing is a noisy and barbarous business, but these animals were hit on the head with a sawn off shafted sledge hammer to which a pointed steel head had been welded. The pigs were then quickly hacked into pieces and hauled, one by one, to the other side of the canal. By the time the negotiations in the farmhouse had concluded in a deal, the last raider had been hauled to safety, the little bitch was safely hidden once more inside the coat and the operation was over.

It all went smoothly, and it was profitable. My share of the proceeds were sufficient for me to be able to buy a made-to-measure suit from a tailor still able to satisfy such demands, and who was introduced to me by Andre.

It was a long time since I had been decently dressed, and being smartly dressed gave me greater self confidence than I had had for a long time.

And so there I was, the day I took delivery of and for the first time wore my new suit, standing outside the Hotel de l'ABC into which I had slunk as a disreputable looking fugitive only weeks before, sunning myself in the afternoon sun and ready to look anyone in the eye.

While I was there a very beautiful and very smartly but ostentatiously dressed girl with raven-black hair passed the hotel. I would have paid her a compliment, but a young Nazi officer, walking in the opposite direction, got in first.

She ignored his sexually-loaded remark.

The opportunity was now mine. I translated it into French for her.

Beyond giving me a glance, she ignored me, too.

The next time I saw her was when I awakened in the middle of the night, and there she was, sitting on the edge of my bed, chin in hand, studying me.

'I did not understand what he said,' she told me with a smile, 'but thank you, just the same, for the translation. In French it is a little more delicate, don't you think? And your translation was quite subtle. Well – here I am!'

She told me that she knew the hotel proprietor. The subtle difference there is between courtesan and prostitute was the difference I recognized there to be between her and the girls who lived in the hotel. She said that she had been given a room for the night when she had decided that it was becoming too late to get to her apartment conveniently. They had given her a spare room in the loft. She admitted she had been curious about me, and had been asking the girls who I was. She said she was also made more interested when she heard how fond of me the girls were.

She then offered me a gold-tipped German cigarette from a gold cigarette case, gave me a light, and fell silent. I had, by this time, propped up my pillow, and was leaning against it. As we smoked, we both watched each other for some time. I was most impressed by the lustre of her hair, the perfect smoothness of her skin, and the poise of her figure.

I sensed she was getting a little nervous. She seemed to be a bit unsure of herself, and this was unusual for someone so sophisticated. She was not accustomed to not being totally in control of the situation. The men she met were in her power, and they behaved totally predictably.

She gave a small nervous laugh, and stubbed the remains of her cigarette in the ashtray. As she bent down to do this, as it was on the floor, she made sure I got a glimpse inside her white blouse, which was carefully opened at the front. Instead of a bra, she wore two black straps, one over and one under each breast. Her firm, white breasts and full, red nipples were most attractive. I began to warm towards my mysterious night-time visitor.

Then she rose, and asked abruptly whether I already had a sweetheart. When I told her I had no particular girlfriend, she frankly admitted she had already been told as much by the proprietors. Then she added she had heard I had a reputation of pleasing nearly every woman in the hotel. I pretended to be rather embarrassed by this notoriety, and when I looked so bashful she seemed less nervous. She slowly leant forward and slid her slim, soft hand underneath the blankets until it rested between my thighs. She stopped for a tantalizing second or two, then she suddenly moved it upwards until she had me in her grasp. It was easy for her to find my most sensitive part as I always slept stark naked. When I stirred swiftly into life at her touch, she looked relaxed and pleased.

Then, as unexpectedly as she had started this stimulating opening gambit, she withdrew her hand and said bluntly: 'Will you share my bed in my room?' Then she added coyly: 'I get cold very easily on my own. I would like it very much if you warmed my bed for me.' What could I do, I thought with amusement, but be gallant and polite?

I agreed to join her. She told me her room number and left me. I quickly put on a shirt and trousers and went out. She had left the door ajar. I entered her room quietly as she stood slowly drying her arms after a wash. She was naked. She held her right arm in the air as she dried it, and her legs were taut as she stretched. I could see her plump, white buttocks in the half-light given by a tiny bedside lamp. Her stomach was as smooth and firm as a flat pebble in a stream. Her legs were perfectly formed, and she had the most feminine feet I had ever seen. Women usually look less attractive in bare feet, but Yvette had small, delicate ankles and short, shapely feet. Her nipples were rampant. They thrust out with desire after her cold wash, and after she had thought of our moments of lust to come. Her breasts were just as firm and full as they had appeared when I had glanced inside her blouse, in my room. I thought again of her ripe, inviting mouth which was soon to kiss my thighs, and I was glad I had taken that opportunity to act as her interpreter at the hotel steps.

Although she had taken the initiative, I was full of enthusiasm by now. I crossed the room and almost brutally walked towards her so she stepped back and sank on to the large bed. I ripped my shirt off, and she tore at my belt, forcing her hands down over my buttocks. I kissed her, and we tore at each other like starved tigers. There was no need for me to remember my lessons from Polja and Nadia in how to take my time, we both knew how to pace our lovemaking so that both of us would be triumphantly satisfied at the same second.

By now I too was naked and we explored each other ravenously. Unlike some women, she was silent as she sought to please me. She seemed to save her breath for the great effort which would soon be needed. She clawed at my back and gripped me with her gloriously soft legs. I kissed her hard, red nipples and stroked her moist thighs.

Then, sensing I was free to be selfish because she was as near to relief as I was, I savagely forced her on to me, and impaled her. As I had had so much lovemaking in the past few days, with the other girls, I had no difficulty in controlling myself. I thrust at her and she seemed content for me to take the initiative in this way. But suddenly, and ferociously, she sprang to the attack. As she felt her release near she dug her long nails into my bottom with such venom that the blood ran. This held up my peak but, as soon as the pain wore off, I rammed again at her until I had drained every bit of energy I had, and then I collapsed, almost unconscious, across her.

Mournfully she eased herself from underneath me, and began kissing and licking my wounded thighs and back. Then we fell asleep. Next morning she asked me to come and live with her at her apartment. She told me she was the mistress of one of the highest Nazi commandants in Paris. She was careful not to mention his name, and she always referred to him as the 'Commandant'. Judging by the luxury of her apartment, and the level of her spending, it was obvious that only some very high-ranking officer could afford to keep a mistress so comfortably. He looked after her so well she was able to give me a handsome allowance out of the money he gave her. She said she wanted me to provide what 'that fat, German pig' could not in the way of lovemaking.

I agreed with her proposition and moved in with her. A few days after I settled down, a girl friend, Adrienne, turned up. She was even more beautiful than Yvette. She was the leading dancer at a fashionable nightclub 'Le Perroquet au Nid', on the Champs Elysees. While we were chatting the telephone rang. It was the porter warning Yvette that the Commandant was on his way up. She urged Adrienne and I to slip out of the back door. We managed to get out without the 'fat German pig' spotting us, and Adrienne took me to her home where she lived with her father.

Her apartment was small. As we approached it I noticed a bicycle, obviously hers, because her father was very old, leaning against the wall in the corridor. It gave me an idea. I was not satisfied with the arrangement I had formed with Yvette. I was on the run, and without resources, or documents. This recent incident had confirmed how dangerous it was to be living with a top Nazi's mistress. I could not go on relying on the vigilance of her porter to save me from detection and the harshest punishment.

I made love to Adrienne that night. We were both quite tired and our loving was brief and unmemorable, even though she had the sort of gorgeous limbs and breasts you would expect to find on a dancer. I was preoccupied with my plan and I did not arouse or satisfy her as I had Yvette. After a few hours' sleep, as Adrienne dozed soundly, I crept out of the flat, took the bike and headed out of Paris going south.

It was now early April 1944. I managed to reach the village of Salbris in Sologne without mishap. There I found a farmer who was willing to take me on as a farmhand. At the farm another couple of boys, one from Paris and one from Romorantin, were also hiding from the Germans. We made friends and I taught them to swim in a nearby brook. Of course I had to tell them most of my adventures and soon my history was relayed to the Maquis who occupied the woods for a hundred miles or more around the farm.

One day when we were having lunch a couple of cars suddenly surged into the farmyard. Out of one jumped some shabby-looking young men wearing black berets, and holding pistols and Sten-guns. They ordered everyone to line up against the wall, and then they took me with them. Soon we were driving through what appeared to me to be inaccessible woods to their camp. They were the Maquis of that region. I began to wish I was back lying in the comparative safety of Yvette's bed in Paris.

But I need not have worried. The captain of the Maquis had heard about me, and thought I might be able to help them in their struggle against the Nazis. Before we reached their camp we first had to cross a large meadow, and there before us loomed the giant figure of a German captain, standing erect in full uniform. He was a doomed man. His hands were tied behind his back, and he was staring fixedly into the distance. Just as our cars halted, a shot cracked out, and the Nazi officer toppled over into the grass. His limbs still thrashed about convulsively.

I was forced to get out of the car, which had stopped near the body, and to look at him. As I was pushed nearer to the quivering officer, a tall, thin, dark-haired youth with piercing black eyes stepped forward, pistol in hand, went over to the German, and shot him twice through the heart. One bullet passed through the centre of the Nazi's hand as it clutched at his tunic covering his heart. It left a blue-edged, irregular hole in the bloody hand.

I was nearly paralysed by the sudden drama of this scene and was still stunned as I was lugged before their captain. He was surprisingly young, about thirty-five, and very distinguished-looking. But he was obviously a hard-boiled, tough character. Bluntly and briefly he said I could help them operate the wood-gas engines of the German trucks they had captured. I could also teach his men how to maintain and work these engines, and act as interpreter whenever necessary. There was no need for him to spell out or even mention what would happen to me if I refused to co-operate. I had just seen the fate of the giant German officer, and so I could have no doubts about how they would react if I showed the slightest reluctance to assist them in their fight. I had no intention of refusing, however. Helping the Maquis was a far more satisfying life than comforting whores in Paris, or running errands for pimps.

They had recently captured three trucks which needed servicing. They did not take long to fix. Then I started instructing several of the group how to understand the working of the engines. The young earnest patriot, with the prominent eyes, who had put the Nazi officer out of his agony, was called Dede Rousseau. His sixteen year old, younger brother Riri, was also one of my pupils. At the beginning they kept a strict watch on me and were vigilant to find out if I was totally trustworthy. Even when they trusted me enough to invite me to their home, I was still not above suspicion.

They lived in the village of Salbris. Their mother reminded me of Pilar in Hemingway's 'For Whom The Bell Tolls'. When everybody was cheering and feasting at a real family re-union on one of my visits, I suddenly felt very lonely and went into their large garden, for a stroll. I found some bushes bearing tasty, ripe berries and I sat down to eat some. Suddenly I heard someone stealthily creep up on me. And there she was – Madame Rousseau, flushed and embarrassed. She had one hand under her apron. Years later she confessed she had spotted me leave the party, and had come after me with a loaded pistol, ready to shoot me if necessary.

The captain of the Maquis in that district, I never knew his name, everyone always referred to him as 'The Captain', commanded an adventurous, hardy group of men. The day after this incident in the bushes a magnificent Horch-car with twin rear tyres drove into our camp. In the front seat were two Nazi chief-staff-officers, and in the back was a small boy, looking very fierce and huddled in the corner, holding an enormous Luger in both hands.

The German officers had passed through a nearby village and had stopped to ask the boy the way. He had offered to show them and they had let him climb into the back seat. There he had found the Luger. His father and brother had been killed while working for the Maquis. Now his only request to our Captain was that he should be allowed to shoot one of the Nazis himself. This wish was quickly granted by the Captain.

First they were interrogated, with me acting, as usual, as the interpreter. Then they were sentenced to death, and I translated this grim verdict. As I finished telling them their fate, one fell on his knees and begged for mercy. He was promptly shot by our Lieutenant. The other behaved with more dignity. He was led to the meadow I had seen on the day I had joined the Maquis. There he was blindfolded and the little boy stepped forward. He was forced to his knees so the boy could reach his head. Holding the Luger with both hands, he got it into position, and pulled the trigger. The Nazi slumped over – killed instantly. The boy threw the pistol away, and rushed off into the woods. I never saw him again.

We slept in tents made from the parachutes used when planes dropped our provisions and ammunition. It was very boring to be out at night waiting for these parachutes to land. We had to lie in the bushes for hours on end, wet, cold and hungry. When the planes had passed over, and dropped the supplies, we had to search frantically, stumbling about in the dark, for the canisters. We would fall into pools of slime, or muddy water, or cut ourselves in thorny bushes. It was a tedious, frustrating, often painful business, but we depended on these 'drops', and so we took it in turns to watch, and gather up, the parachutes.

One night there was suddenly a sound of a gun going off, and then a cry from someone saying he was shot, and going to die. We quickly ordered the bleeding man to shut up. He was bleeding quite badly. Two of us carried him back to camp where they made arrangements to take him to hospital.

Later we heard he had put his cocked pistol into the back pocket of his trousers so he could warm his hands in his trouser pockets. He had stumbled, and, in falling, the pistol went off, and shot him in the bottom. After the Liberation we met him in Romorantin, where he was telling everyone how heroically he had fallen in a life-or-death struggle with the Germans. The bullet hung on a gold chain round his neck.

It was not much fun sleeping in parachute silk instead of

blankets on cold nights. We did not, however, have much chance to sleep. We had plenty of food, drink and tobacco, but sleep was a luxury. Every two weeks we had to move our camp. This was a sound security precaution because we could never be certain whether or not someone had betrayed us to the Nazis. Not only were the Germans very keen to kill us, but they also offered high rewards to any traitor who helped them catch a member of the Maquis.

For this reason only the best and most trusted members of the group went on secret missions. The Captain was, at first, very enthusiastic about my going on raids, because I spoke German so well. We always needed information about the enemy, and the Captain recognized I might get a chance to eavesdrop and pick up useful facts. But, from the very first night I spent in the Maquis camp, it was obvious I would never be sent on such a mission. I had started talking in my sleep! Perhaps because of the horrors I had endured before reaching France, the air-raids, and the squalor of Schirmeck, and perhaps because of the scene in the meadow when the tall Nazi was shot by Dede, I became a security risk, by babbling while I slept. As I spoke in French the others in my tent were able to repeat everything I had said while I slept.

Once the Captain heard about this, he realized it was impossible for me to go on secret raids. He knew that whenever one of our group was captured during a mission, the Nazis carried out reprisals and executions soon afterwards. They tortured those they captured and it is only in romantic books that torture is heroically endured. But in my case they would only have to give me a sleeping pill to discover whatever they wanted!

But, even though some missions were considered too secret for me, I saw plenty of action while I was with the Maquis. As soon as I had fixed the captured German trucks, and given the lessons in how to maintain, and drive, them, the Captain put me in Dede's platoon. Dede was a sergeant, and the most daring member of the group. It was soon clear his orders were to test my courage and fighting abilities.

A few days before I joined them, they had raided a Nazi train, and freed about thirty Sudanese prisoners-of-war. They had been hiding in the woods but now they were sent for as our group had been depleted through losses, injuries and sickness to only twenty men. They were all giants. The biggest was their leader, Abdoul. When they were relaxing, he would grab me by my belt, telling me to keep stiff, and would lift me up into the air above his head. Soon I became their 'weight' in a sort of weight-lifting exercise. Although I was the smallest member of the platoon, weighing only 50 kilos (7 st 11 lb) it was still quite a test for even a brawny African giant to heave me up using only one hand.

They used to spend their time off swimming, exercising, and sharpening their pocket-knives which they used even for shaving. I learned to know them well. I got to like them very much. We taught each other many tricks with ropes, knives, cards, and so on.

They taught me how to hunt, read footprints, follow trails, to fish, and many other skills of gymnastics and swimming. My varied life so far, even though I was still only twenty-three, had enabled me to pick up enough knowledge to teach them things they did not know, but they certainly taught me more than I taught them. We became very close friends. We had some happy times together, and since I had first run away to Paris in 1937, I had not enjoyed such friendship.

One day Dede's platoon was ordered to attack an army convoy of trucks crossing our part of the forest. The day before we had attempted to do this when led by our lieutenant – but we had failed, either because our information had been inaccurate, or because we were not properly prepared. On this occasion, however, as we drove through the woods in four trucks loaded with armed men, stopping now and then to drop off some to take up positions overlooking the road, we suddenly burst through the bushes and found a road facing us.

Dede shouted frantically for me to stop and turn the truck round. This was impossible. I was caught between two German tanks and so I did the only thing I could. I pressed the accelerator and shot between the tanks across the road. I gave the truck so much gas we jumped over a ditch on the other side and went into the bushes. We pressed on, made a detour, and headed back to camp. There we found the others waiting for us, anxious about our fate. They had been driving behind us and so had been able to stop, and turn around before they got to the road. As they had not expected such a strong convoy, they were doubtful about our chances of survival. Once we had crossed the road, they had returned to camp. For the first time I was warmly congratulated by the Captain, and he promoted me to the rank of corporal.

Several days later we got the order to attack whatever trucks were still coming on this route following yesterday's convoy.

Word had come from a nearby village there were still some trucks crossing one road in particular. Dede's platoon went there in a truck. We took five Sudanese and there were ten of us in all. I was armed with a Sten-gun. The others had rifles, but Dede took his enormous Luger. When we arrived at the road, we hid the car, and scattered among the bushes which overlooked the curve of the road.

Soon we heard a truck coming along. It was a steel-plated Dodge. It was open at the back, where about a dozen German soldiers were sitting. As the truck drove past us we fired at random. I aimed my Sten low at the driver's door, hoping my bullet would pass through the steel-plate and hit him. The others shot at the soldiers sitting in the rear. But the truck went on as though nothing had happened.

It disappeared around the bend. We were called together. Dede suggested we should get into our truck and try to attack another vehicle further up the road, in the direction the Dodge had come from. I still could not believe we had completely failed to do any damage to the Dodge. I stood there watching the telegraph poles beside the road and only just listening to Dede's suggestions. Suddenly I saw the telegraph wires tremble, as though they had been caught in a storm. I pointed and shouted triumphantly: 'We got them – look!' They must have hit a pole. 'Let's go after them,' I yelled.

Of course, as soon as Dede saw this, he changed his plan, and left the truck where it was. We then went up the road on foot. He divided us into two sections; one on each side of the road, which was well-screened by bushes. After we had rounded two bends, and covered about two kilometres we saw the crashed Dodge. It had smashed a telegraph pole, and had two wheels in the ditch. As there was no sign of any Germans, we swiftly ducked out of sight. Dede thought for a while and then signalled to the five Sudanese to attack from the back.

The rest of us were to try to keep their attention to the front. We reckoned they were, like us, hidden in the bushes, and waiting for the enemy who had attacked them earlier. Stealthily we crept from tree to tree, from bush to bush. None of us knew how near we were to death. The Nazis had had time to take up good positions and they could have a pretty clear idea how strong our party was, and where we were.

About a hundred metres from the Dodge, Dede ordered his men to fire their rifles, without damaging the vehicle further, as it would be useful to us. They fired – but no fire was returned. Then he looked at me, and motioned his men to remain where they were, covering us if necessary. We inched forward together. My heart seemed to be beating in my throat. I kept my head as low as I could, but I still felt I was a huge, naked target for the worst marksmen in the German army. I crept up with Dede until we were about thirty metres from the Dodge. We had a good look at it. We were nearly level with the silent, stranded truck, on the other side of the road. Nothing moved. We looked at each other. I guessed what Dede had in mind. I shouted in German: 'Surrender – we will not fire any more!'

When I had repeated this three times, a weak answer came from inside the truck. I translated two words: 'Wounded' and 'surrender'. We waited no longer but dashed across the road, and leapt into the rear of the truck. A German soldier, badly wounded, stiff with fear and looking like a maimed deer hounded by savage dogs, lay there. He told us most of his comrades had fled, leaving him where he was. Dede then called the rest of our men to join us. I opened the driver's door. I had already noticed the bullet holes in it, now I saw the driver. He was dead behind the wheel. The bullets from my Sten-gun had torn the arteries in his leg, and he had bled to death. The floor of his cabin was covered with blood.

The stench made me feel sick. I lugged his corpse out on to the road. The others examined the crates in the rear of the vehicle. The Dodge must have contained a group of retreating soldiers because it was packed with loot: perfume, silk, money, tinned foods, as well as handgrenades and wine, were there. Dede kept a stern watch to ensure there was no pilfering. It was too much for us to carry in our truck, and so he suggested we burn as much as we could.

But I had managed to have a close look at the Dodge, and had seen that apart from a few bullet-holes, no vital parts were damaged. I volunteered to drive it back to our camp. I managed to get the engine started but we could not risk following the road in either direction. As the ditch alongside the road, at this spot, widened like a small canal, so that it was ten metres broad, and about six metres deep, we were at a loss to decide how to get the captured truck back to camp.

The Sudanese, however, came up with a bold idea. They had spotted a crude bridge, about a hundred metres back down the road, made of logs. I turned the Dodge round while the others returned to the cover of the bushes. At a point where the bridge was half-hidden by bushes, Dede motioned me to get out of the cabin. 'You'll never make it,' he said. 'The bridge is much too narrow, and definitely too weak to bear that truck. Come and see for yourself.'

I went over. At first glance he appeared to be right. But when I had a closer look, I saw that, if I was well-guided, I had a slight chance of getting the Dodge across. The rough-and-ready bridge was just wide enough. Whether it was strong enough was a risk I would have to take. Dede agreed to guide me across. When all the others had crossed the bridge on foot, I edged the truck slowly towards it. Luckily I managed to steer the front wheels into the right place at my first attempt.

They only just covered the logs on the outside of the bridge. I kept the door open – just in case I had to leap clear. Then off we went. Dede was magnificently calm. He did not even sweat. He walked backwards in front of me, guiding me so accurately, as if he was deaf to the sound of cracking, crumbling, breaking boards beneath his feet. We were almost at the other side, I had just got the front wheels on to the firm ground when the bridge finally sank slowly beneath me.

Fortunately the Dodge had a four-wheel drive, and so I was able to put a last bit of pressure on the accelerator which enabled the front wheel to get a good grip, and pull me to safety. My legs wobbled under me when I got out, and staggered over to my comrades who rushed to congratulate me. Back in the camp the Captain promoted me to full sergeant. From that moment Dede accepted me as his equal. I was now in charge of the Sudanese, as well as of the maintenance of transport.

It seemed strange to me how easily they were all impressed by the day's events. It had been quite a feat to bring the Dodge across the rickety bridge. But I could see little heroism or merit in our sneak attack on the truck. The exploits of the day had been exciting and spectacular, but I was the same man I had been twenty-four hours earlier, and yet they saw me in a new light. I thought of the great change my life had taken since that moment outside the hotel when I had first seen Yvette. But for her, I might have still been in Paris living in comparative safety, waiting for the Liberation. I could still be working for a black market gang, instead of risking my neck daily.

X

Love With Mother and Daughter

From the time the lovely Adrienne's bike collapsed beneath me on the road south from Paris, I was caught up in the dirty business of war. When France was liberated by the Allies, there was a lot of talk about bravery and heroism, in this period. But my overwhelming memory of my time with the Maquis is of the sickening waste, and awful cruelty, of war.

When the Captain promoted me to full sergeant I began protesting openly about the ruthless execution of prisoners by the Resistance group. On the very evening of my promotion, the Captain told me to translate to a wounded German his sentence of death. I refused to do so, arguing that such murders were contrary to the Geneva Convention. He looked at me sternly, and asked me to assure him the Nazi would not continue to fight against France, when he came out of hospital, which was where I suggested we took him. Then he asked me how we could travel about, moving each fortnight to a new camp, with all the captured Germans with us. I could neither give him the assurance he wanted, nor answer his question, and so the wounded man was shot a few hours later.

Many more captured Germans were shot in the days that followed. Once a whole group of six prisoners was led into our camp. I had the job of collecting their belongings, and papers, and then I had to tell them they were doomed. I even had to lead them to the scene of their death in the woods. Once there, a volunteer from our group, or some local patriot, claiming a grudge, was allowed to shoot them through the head with a pistol.

One very young, tall, blond lieutenant was sentenced to be shot. I asked him whether or not he would consider joining us, in order to save his life. He proudly shook his head – and was dead within seconds. Others fell on their knees, and begged us to think of their families back home. Most, however, were dumb, and slaughtered like cattle. Sometimes I still see the faces of the prisoners butchered during this time. Not one tried to escape, or flee for his life. Sometimes I was amazed how easily they were resigned to their fate.

Only one, an Alsatian, who spoke fluent French, offered his skill as an armourer in exchange for our sparing his life. The Captain agreed, and he was put in the charge of Robert, our master of arms. He was given the job of cleaning rifles, and other guns. Robert also allowed him to load guns just before they were distributed to the men for a raid. The man was clearly warned not to try any tricks, and to be very careful with the working of the different weapons. For example, we had Sten-guns and Tommy-guns. Both took nine mm cartridges, but not the same kind. If a Sten was loaded with the ammo intended for a Tommy-gun, it would jam immediately, and the man whose life depended on it would be helpless. One day, Robert saw the Alsatian deliberately loading a Sten with the ammo intended for a Tommy-gun. He immediately took a pistol and shot him through the head. We examined the gun's magazine, which was still clutched in his hands, and found Robert had done the right thing. He was also proved to have acted wisely when we looked at the other magazines just filled by this man. With one snap pistol shot, Robert had saved several of his comrades' lives. After this incident, the Captain did not accept any more offers of this kind from condemned prisoners.

As I was not only the interpreter for doomed prisoners, but also in charge of supplies, I was very busy after my promotion. I used the best truck, and selected a team of four, keen Sudanese. When Dede told me the rules of the game, about getting supplies from reluctant farmers, and shopkeepers, I realized how simple it all was. Those who co-operated were given an IOU cheque, which would be honoured by the French Government, after the war. Those who refused to accept this arrangement, and those who were reported to us as black-marketeers, were forced to give into our demands. Every operation went quite smoothly. We would line up the farm-workers, or shop assistants, talk with the farmer, or shop-keeper, and then, after handing over our promissory note, we would load up the truck with cattle, or goods, and disappear into the dense woods.

When I became a full sergeant, I was allowed to sleep in a tent with Dede, Robert the Breton armourer, and the Captain's secretary, Claude. Whenever we were lucky enough to be able to turn in early at the same time, we used to discuss every conceivable topic before going to sleep. Since the Sudanese joined the group, we no longer had to take turns keeping watch at night. They were on guard night and day. It was very rare for any of us to spot where they were hidden in the bushes or trees, before we were noticed by them, and the alarm promptly sounded.

The Captain had a special personal tent for storing officers' gear and documents. It also contained some rare titbits; such as many different kinds of wine, tins full of delicacies, cigars, cigarettes and sweets. Our menu was plain to the point of tedium. We had meat, beans, eggs, bread, an occasional tin of sardines, accompanied by whatever wine was available.

Claude told us about these private provisions hidden in the Captain's extra tent. No one was allowed to enter it alone. The Captain insisted he accompanied anyone who went in. He slept in another tent which he shared with the Lieutenant.

We decided to do something about this private store of luxuries. We rolled dice to decide who was to creep into this tent at night for some special items of food and drink, to liven up our evenings. Taking it in turns, we carried out several raids, until the Captain noticed things were missing, or disappearing faster than he was consuming them. He decided to post a Sudanese to guard his tent.

Abdoul, the leader of the Sudanese, must have guessed we were the guilty ones, because when the Captain gave the order for the new sentry, he came to me and told me the news. He boasted that no one would be able to pilfer anything from the tent while one of *his* men were guarding it. I agreed with him, and told my tent-mates of this depressing development. To my astonishment they also agreed with Abdoul. I had only told Abdoul that I thought further thefts were now impossible in order to give him a false sense of security. I argued this was probably our last chance of getting some of the luxuries, and so we should make one extra raid, to obtain more than we needed, so we should have a little in store.

Dede was the only one to agree. The other two, however, not daring to back out, for fear of losing face, were assigned the task of attracting the new sentry's attention if necessary. Dede and I crept up to the tent. It was my job to crawl inside, and pass out bottle after bottle of wine to him. The giant Sudanese sentry was humming a tune quietly, and all seemed safe, when suddenly Dede beckoned for me to get out of the tent. Abdoul was on his way to inspect the guard. As we now had six bottles, we took three each.

Then we disappeared into the bushes. Next morning, when I returned from a trip to get supplies, a general order had been given for the group to muster together. The Captain made a furious speech – about there being thieves in the camp who had dared to steal his private property. He spoke of the special sentry, and the missing bottles. He thundered that, if anything else was stolen, the thief would be flogged in public. If the thief was not exposed, he said, the sentry would be flogged instead. It is possible he suspected one of the Sudanese of stealing. Everyone stood rigidly at attention while he made this threat.

After the group had fallen out, Abdoul came up to me. He was obviously angry, as well as being uneasy. I told him bluntly it was his own fault. 'You shouldn't have boasted,' I said. 'I merely wanted to teach you and your men a lesson.' Then I added: 'I don't know who did the stealing before your man took on the job of guarding the tent – so I reckon you should keep a pretty sharp look out in future in case you let the Captain down again.'

I will never know whether he believed me or not. As he was a Moslem I could not offer him a bottle of wine, so I slipped some packets of cigarettes into his hand. 'There's one for the sentry,' I said, adding an extra packet. With this we were friends again. I believe he was relieved to think I was the only member of the group who had not been awed by the almost legendary ferocity of the Sudanese. I did not enlighten him further.

This incident was not the only lighter moment during the months I spent with the Maquis. It was not all killing, danger, and futile inhumanity. On one or two occasions we were invited by a trustworthy farmer to organize a dance in an empty barn. The Captain used to point out the men who could attend. When they arrived, it was amazing to find precisely half the number of the selected men had young women and girls, waiting to partner them.

Only half the number were needed because half the total were required to guard the barn, while the rest enjoyed the dancing. And dance we did – without any music! As we twirled about, the only accompaniment was the crackling of dry hay, or the noise of some material being torn or split, and the sighing of everyone in the half-dark barn, letting off as much steam as possible during the brief time available. After a while the male dancers changed places with those on guard, and there was never a quarrel. The women were just as friendly to their new partners as they had been to those who were lucky enough to dance first. We never knew who they were, we never met them again, as we shifted our camp so frequently, but these were truly wonderful interludes in the long, sad tragedy of war, and we felt it was a real honour to be chosen to enjoy them.

By the middle of July, however, there was no time for such amusements. The Germans were on the retreat, and as they travelled on the main highways, some of which passed through our woods, we attacked them suddenly from the bushes, only to withdraw to set up other attacks further down the road. When we took prisoners, they were duly registered, before being shot, and buried. Then we would move our camp, and our operations would start all over again.

One morning at the end of July news came that about ten Germans had occupied Salbris, the village where Dede's family lived. By this time the previous occupying force had already left the village. Our Captain gave his orders. He took his own car, and Dede and I, along with five other men, took a truck. Off we went to Salbris.

When we arrived it turned out that the inhabitants had already been trying to force the Nazis out of their village. They had been quite successful. The Germans had been pushed out to the outskirts of Salbris, and were holed up in a garage, standing apart from other buildings, at the crossroads. About a hundred metres closer to the village was an old farmhouse. The field all round it was open, and gave hardly any shelter to anyone near the garage. We had only a Bren-gun, no mortars, and we were in the same position as the villagers, unable to do much to shift the Germans in the garage.

Then an old farmer came to our rescue. He went up to the Captain, who immediately motioned me over to him. He told me he lived in the farmhouse, which had an old pipe which led directly to the garage. 'A very small man,' he said, 'might squeeze through and get underneath the garage so he could place ex-plosives, or detonators, to do such a job.' This suggestion was a non-starter.

Then the Captain turned to me and said: 'A small, German-speaking volunteer might get through, and persuade them to surrender.'

Well, there I was – and everyone was waiting for my reply. I managed a grin, and then remarked that *if* the pipe was not blocked, for it was a long one, *if* one could make oneself heard, once in the cellar beneath the garage without being shot by the Germans, while trying to think of the best form of words to use to make them surrender, then it *might* be worth trying.

The old man hurriedly started to give me the details of the layout of the garage, but I stopped him and said: 'But Captain, I haven't agreed to do it yet!'

'Well?' he asked.

'They won't agree to surrender – unless I can promise them their lives will be spared,' I argued.

'Of course, of course,' he replied impatiently.

'No,' I answered. 'I am not going on the strength of you just saying "Of course". I must have your word as an officer, or I won't go.'

This was my last chance of avoiding this crazy mission. I thought this argument would get me off the hook. He had been dead against sparing the lives of prisoners, since Robert had exposed the treachery, and ingratitude, of the Alsatian, and I thought he would refuse to give his promise to save these prisoners. But I did not know the front lines of the Americans, chasing the retreating Nazis, were near at hand, and the Captain realized he could hand over any prisoners to them.

'OK,' he said. 'You have my word as an officer of the FFI (Force Française Interieur). But only because you are a foreigner, and not a regular soldier, do I give in tō this request.' He was piqued, I could see, and I noticed the Lieutenant glare at me.

Well that was that. I was stuck now. I had to go ahead with this mad plan. I let the farmer continue with his directions. Then, leaving my gun behind, in case anything went wrong, taking off my basque beret, and my FFI armband, I set off. First I had to jump into the ditch where the drainpipe started.

The pipe was full of excrement, filth, and minor obstructions. It smelt foul. I edged along, trying to keep my mouth clear of the muck and slime. Once again I began to regret I had ever taken that impulsive decision to borrow Adrienne's bike, and set off into the unknown. 'After all,' I told myself, as I slithered through the shit, and rotten leaves, 'you could always have left Yvette and returned to the Hotel de l'ABC to look after Mireille and her friends. Why did you have to be a bloody fool, and end up risking your neck in some exploit like this – when the war's almost over in France?'

Muttering, and cursing my stupidity, I finally emerged, filthy, but unharmed, in the cellar underneath the garage, and I could hear the Germans talking to each other. Immediately above my head, in a wooden ceiling, was a large trapdoor, under which, the farmer had said, was a staircase, leading upwards. Luckily a helpful villager had given me an electric torch. I crept up the stairs.

There was no way of locking the trapdoor from beneath. My hands were soaked with sweat at the thought that they only had to open the trapdoor to hurl in a grenade, and that was the end of me. But I decided I had got this far, and the best move was to return to the exit of the drain, in case I had to dive for safety, if a grenade was hurled at me. Of course the drain would not give much protection if guns were fired into it, but in such a situation, I thought, one cannot have everything!

I started to yell. The voices stopped. They were at least listening. I argued and pleaded in my very best German. I told them we could easily have put explosives under them but I had been sent to give them a chance to save their lives. At first they would have none of this. They said it was nonsense, because the FFI always shot their prisoners. Then, to my horror, I heard one suggest they threw a grenade downstairs. I immediately shouted that, at the first shot or explosion, our troops would open up with mortars, and kill us all. Then, to add more weight to my huge bluff, I told them I was an Alsatian and had been forced to crawl into the garage. I said this party of the Maquis were in touch with the Allied army, and had been ordered to avoid unnecessary killing.

At last I convinced them I was giving them a chance to save their lives. I heard them throw down their weapons, open the main door and step out of the garage. My comrades arrived minutes later, running as fast as they could, and lined up their prisoners. There were seven in all. The two other Germans in this group had been hiding in the Church tower, and they swiftly gave in when they saw their fellow-soldiers surrender. Dede was the first to open the trapdoor and congratulate me. The Captain kept his promise, and the prisoners were transported into the hands of the Americans. But we had a great deal of trouble getting them away from the villagers. Some women claimed they had been raped by them – although, looking at a few of these women, it was hard to believe any man would actually imagine he would get any pleasure from violating them. Others tried to kill any of the Germans they could get their hands on. We were only a small force, and so it was tremendously difficult to impose our will on a group of villagers, who outnumbered us. But we managed to force them aside. Not one of them thanked us for helping them.

My reward for my crawl through the filthy pipe was a gun belonging to one of the captured Germans, along with a leather holster. It was a Walther 7.65 mm. Later I changed the barrel to a 9 mm with the help of Robert the armourer. This made the weapon even more effective, and deadly. I was certainly glad to have such a good gun during the days that followed.

This period was one of the most dangerous in my life. I came nearer to death more often, in these few weeks, than at any time either before, or since. We were engaged in constant attacks, and counter attacks, in and around the town of Romorantin. We liberated it, lost control, re-conquered it, and then saw it reoccupied by the Germans in a series of confused, and nightmarish guerrilla raids. The Germans were on the retreat throughout France, and we kept being called on to chase them out of the town. When we had done this, we had to leave to take part in other raids and missions. Then new Germans would appear in the town, and we would get orders to drive them out again.

We hardly slept for days. I was half drunk or drunk most of the time as we had only wine to quench our parched throats. My comrades sometimes managed to grab a short nap but, because I had to drive the trucks, while they had a snooze in the back, I had to keep going. We seemed to be always on the move, and apart from the driving and the fighting, I had to repair, and maintain, the vehicles as well. I had to change trucks time and time again as one broke down – and another was shot to pieces. When a driver was shot, I had to remove the corpse and hop in, not knowing whether I was to be the next victim. One body which had to be lugged out of a cabin, before I could get the truck on the move again, had no head.

Like most guerrilla actions the battles were confused and disorganized. Much of the struggle for Romorantin was the fiercest type of hand-to-hand street fighting. It was man-to-man stuff, with each soldier using everything he could grab, in the split second, as a weapon. On one occasion I found Abdoul, shot in the leg, lying in the front garden of the Town Hall. A German was advancing on him; just as I came running round the corner. He stood with his back to me and, as I spotted Abdoul, I saw the German start to take aim. I leapt on his back and light as I was, he toppled over, and as he started to fall I rammed my knife in his throat.

Abdoul's kneecap was splintered, but he did not utter even a slight gasp, or groan, as I hastily examined his leg. I shall never know how I managed to drag him to the nearest truck. He was as heavy as an elephant. I drove him to the infirmary. I never saw him again. I hope he got back safely to his village in the Sudan, where his father was the chief.

On another occasion we were moving through some houses hoping to get a pot shot at some enemy who were well-placed at a cross-roads, where they had a machine-gun post. There were only three of them, but they were defying all our efforts to dislodge them. Once Germans got dug in, in a strategic position, they often took a hell of a lot of shifting.

The only way to get at them was indoors – through the houses on either side of the streets. I had two men with me, Dede and his brother, Riri. We had just entered a room, overlooking the machine-gun post, and Dede was carefully trying to open the window when they spotted us. They reacted with incredible speed. A grenade crashed through the window, we ducked, and off it went. We had amazing luck. The grenade fell on the table, and the main force of the explosion went upwards. We were unhurt, but remained deaf for hours afterwards. When we crawled to peep out of the shattered window, the Germans below had vanished.

During such unnerving escapes, and horrors, one loses all sense of time, or place. I cannot recall the details of the events of this hectic period in Romorantin. But I shall never forget the moaning of corpses when they were thrown on top of each other. The weight of the last one thrown on the pile presses the air from the lungs of the body beneath, making a sound as if it was still alive. I shall also remember, for ever, the first time I was under fire, with bullets whining past, and the grenades bursting just a few metres away. At such times one is aware of a sickening, terrifying feeling of total loneliness, and the kind of stark fear of death an animal must experience when confronted by some larger beast, in a place of no escape. Facts, names, times, numbers are lost in the swirl of the insanity of war, but smells, especially the stench of gunpowder, blood, and corpses starting to rot, remain with those soldiers lucky enough to survive to the end of their days.

And one day, when it seems centuries since the whole foul madness began, you suddenly discover you are no longer frightened. You realize you have subconsciously become a fatalist who recognizes the uselessness of fear. You seem to take the illogical position that: 'As long as I can hear bullets whistling, as long as I can see others blown apart by grenades, I am safe.'

One tells oneself: 'I won't hear the bullet that gets me, and I won't feel the impact of the explosion which rips my body apart, and so worrying about the destiny of each bullet or bomb is a waste of time.' When fear diminishes in this way, a man's chances of survival seem to increase. I did not consider the possibility of being crippled, or wounded, once I had adopted this stoical attitude to the bullet that kills. Such an outlook certainly helped me. As long as one is afraid, one is apt to hide away, to take cover, to lag behind or to move too slowly. Such tactics increase the danger, I told myself. One of my comrades, Dede, agreed with me on this point as we talked it over while we drove together. We decided that facing up to danger, and trying to conquer the enemy before you, lessened the risk of being killed, or wounded. It may sound muddled and emotional, but this philosophy helped me to survive.

And then, miraculously, the bleeding, the stench of death, and the daily hell were finished. Suddenly the war was over for the Maquis. The Americans met up with the Resistance forces, and there was a huge demonstration in the market-place at Romorantin. For the first time we slept, not in parachute silk, but in a proper Army barracks, and were paid regular wages.

When I had explained and accounted for the vehicles and equipment in my charge, I was asked officially if I would like to join the regular French Army, retaining my rank, and having the chance to become a French citizen. I had heard, however, of the possibility of being sent to England, and so I declined their offers as I fancied applying for a pilot's training with the RAF. And so I was officially discharged from the FFI with a paper signed by Claude, the Captain's secretary. It was also signed by the Captain. And for the first time since I was brought before him that day, after having witnessed the tall German's execution in the meadow, I learned his name – Gauthier.

While my discharge was being arranged, there was the lighter side of the aftermath of war. There were many parties to go to, girls anxious to be ours for the asking, and all the delights of peace for those who had been fortunate enough to end on the winning side. For some of the discharged Maquis, this new freedom and absence of war was all too much. They went wild, and started looting and stealing from nearby castles. The authorities had a devil of a time rounding them up, because they were still armed. But, one by one they were captured, imprisoned or killed.

Dede and Riri were among those who were unhinged by the sudden peace, and they had a chance to calm down during a spell in prison.

I made friends with a Parisian, Renee. His family still lived in Paris, so we decided to go there. I still had my Walther, with its 9 mm barrel, which had served me so well during the fighting in Romorantin. It hung from a leather pouch attached to my belt. We hitchhiked, and even hoboed on the trains, and arrived in Paris in September 1944 – five months after I had taken Adrienne's bike while she slept in her flat.

For the first few days I lodged with Renee's parents. His family were very kind to me. Of course I had to pay a visit to the Hotel de l'ABC but nearly everything was changed. All the girls, except Jeanine, and the Polish proprietors, had left.

Soon the money paid to me when I was discharged ran out and I decided that it was time to visit the Dutch Embassy in the Rue de Grenelle. There I was registered, and told I was, as an applicant for the RAF, under full military command. I was ordered to move to quarters at the porte de Clignancourt, where the Dutch shared an enormous building with a detachment of Americans. I met there other Dutchmen waiting to be sent to England by plane. Of course, although Paris was liberated, the war was far from over. Weeks went by, and from time to time a few of us were told we could fly over. This meant each man's identity had been checked through the secret radio links with Holland.

These were difficult weeks for me. I had some trouble adjusting to the change from the exciting months I had spent with the Maquis, to the long days with nothing to do but wait for my turn to come for the flight to England, and listen to the gossip, or boasting, of those I was forced to live with. Money was scarce, and so I decided to do something about this problem. I found where the storeroom was in the American building on the top floor, and it was accessible through a window that was always open. This window could be reached via a drainpipe, which was climbable from the floor below. This drainpipe was at the back of the building, and overlooked by another block, which was deserted. Soon I was able to get hold of various goods in ce n d, such as military greatcoats, which I sold to cab drivers, who were happy to get hold of warm clothing now that the nights were long and cold.

Soon I had a steady income, and was able to go dancing and

drinking. On one of these outings I met Mathilde Foret at a cafe I had gone into. She was thirty-three years old, small, slightly plump and blonde. She had been married for five years to a butcher whose first wife had been killed in a traffic accident. He worked hard on nightshifts at the slaughterhouse, and, after a heavy stint there, he had little energy left for Mathilde, who was bored to tears by his constant tiredness, and by being left on her own, night after night. I soon gathered, during the dances we had, that this was the picture and so, when the cafe closed at midnight, we went to her flat.

As she unlocked the door, she begged me to keep quiet, as her daughter was asleep. I remembered she had said she had a step-child, but no children from her marriage. We went straight to her bedroom, where she swiftly undressed, and we started to make uninhibited love. I was delighted because she was a comely, if buxom woman, and I had had very little lovemaking in the past five months.

Her bed was on the far side of the door. As I lay on Mathilde, who seemed near to achieving the summit of her pleasure, I decided to delay my peak by examining the surroundings of her room. Suddenly I spotted a face peering through the glass panel above the door. I could see it was a girl's face. I caught a glimpse of dark, unruly hair falling across a forehead, and then the face disappeared.

Mathilde was still panting, and groaning with joy, and did not appear to notice the slight interruption in my attentions to her. After she had been satisfied several times, I heard her give a deep sigh of contentment, and she finally relaxed her grip on me. I decided it was time to get dressed and return to my quarters.

As we went through the corridor leading to the front door, the door of the second bedroom opened and a light went on.

There stood the girl whose face I had seen at the transom window of Mathilde's bedroom door. And only now did the enormity of what had happened hit me.

This was the step-daughter Mathilde had told me about. There was no knowing how long she had been up at the window, watching her step-mother being fucked. I sweated, remembering Mathilde on that bed with her legs wide open and her knees drawn up, her hand reaching out to feel my balls and the stiffness of my cock for her as I stood at the bedside before mounting her. I remember how, after my long period of celibacy, there had been no restraint but a vigorous, almost savage assault. Dear God, what *had* the girl seen!

I feared to look at her, yet could not resist it. Screwing with other people watching had been quite, quite different at Lena's parties. All there had been there had been excitement. This was utterly different because of all the unknown currents of human emotion that had suddenly and terribly become involved.

The girl had dark-brown curly hair. She wore a short, transparent nightdress. One hand screwed up the hem of it, pulling it back and taut against her body so that it stretched across the prominence of the pubic mound. You could see her breasts through the thin stuff, with the nipples standing out. Her eyes were wide and curious as she stared at me. Her mouth was slightly open, and she was running the tip of her tongue round the moist lips.

Mathilde, who didn't know about that window-watching, began abusing her.

'What are you doing out here, Louise? Get back into your room at once. A fine thing if I can't invite my cousin back for a chat about old times without you snooping. I've a mind to tell your father . . .'

The girl gave her step-mother a scornful glance, then looked at me again with that strange, speculative stare. Then without another word she turned, and her bedroom door closed on her.

'I'm sorry about that,' said Mathilde anxiously. 'Don't mind about it. There's nothing to worry about. You'll meet me again tomorrow. At the cafe, about three o'clock.'

I promised, and made my escape.

I was, in fact, a bit uncertain about keeping the appointment. In the end I did so, less out of any desire to be further involved with the mother, but irresistibly curious about the daughter. I wondered if maybe, later, she might have had things out with her step-mother. I would always want to know exactly how much she had witnessed. Her uninvited involvement in the sexual experience was, in a strange way, far more important than Mathilde. It was the thing I would always remember long after I had forgotten exactly what the experience of Mathilde had been like.

Finally I went to the cafe. At that time the cafes in Paris provided music from noon until midnight. The place was crowded with youngsters, many of them dancing. I ordered a glass of wine and sat at a table watching them.

Suddenly I was aware that I was no longer alone and that

someone had joined me at the table, and I looked round expecting to see Mathilde. It was the girl, Louise.

'She couldn't come,' she said, with a grave smile. 'So I . . . I came instead. Do you mind?'

My first impressions of her had not been wrong. She was a pretty, attractive girl, and I guessed her to be about seventeen or maybe a little older, although she had seemed more of a child the previous evening.

I offered her a drink, but she refused. I didn't quite know what to say, but I knew that what there was between us, and why she was here, was what she had witnessed the previous night. I said, lamely:

'I'm sorry about . . . about last night. You probably imagined . . .'

'Oh, I didn't *imagine* anything,' she said gravely. 'I saw it all, right from the very beginning, until you noticed me. I'd never watched it before. You're terribly big, aren't you? It must feel enormous.'

'Look!' I said awkwardly. 'It must have been a shock to you. Your own mother . . .'

'She's *not* my mother!' said Louise quickly.

'All right. But she's your father's wife, and I . . .'

'I want you to do it to me,' Louise broke in.

I stared at her. I hadn't known what to expect, but I could never have expected this.

'Oh, no,' I said quickly. I beckoned the waiter, and put some money on the table to pay for my wine, and got up. 'Oh, no. No! You can't mean it, anyway.'

She got up, and walked closely by my side out of the cafe.

'I've never been more serious in my life. Wouldn't you like to? Don't I attract you that way?'

I was walking hurriedly, in no particular direction. She was almost having to run to keep up with me, holding on to my arm and looking up into my face with those wide, wide eyes.

'It's not that,' I said. 'Mathilde's your . . .'

'She's *not* my mother. And I'm not fat like her. Ugh, I don't know how you could have wanted her, with all that hair. I'm not like that. Or *couldn't* you do it to me? Not again? Not yet?'

'Of course I could,' I said, nettled.

'Well, then! I thought a man like you wouldn't have needed to be asked twice. I'd have thought you wouldn't have needed to be asked at all. Does it worry you because I've watched you doing it to someone else? I'd have thought it would have excited you doing it to a girl who'd already seen you doing it. Seen how strong you are with that thing of yours.'

She was giving me an erection with her talk. And there, in the street, very briefly, she dropped her hand from my arm and felt the evidence of it.

'See!' she said triumphantly. 'We're still in the street and you want to do it to me.'

'Just because a man . . .' I began.

'This hotel,' she said abruptly. 'Men bring girls here. You can just take a room . . .'

She guided me round, turning in front of me towards the hotel entrance so that I had to turn with her or collide into her. Then, dropping my arm, she propelled me towards the desk where the proprietor was waiting.

Suddenly my mind did a kind of somersault, and I was seeing the whole situation from the point of view of a man with an erection which isn't just a physical state, but a mental one in which the mind can justify whatever ideas and desires and purposes that are obsessing it.

I booked the room and followed her up the stairs keeping three steps below her so that my eyes were on the pretty little bottom under the tight dress, letting my thoughts dwell underneath it.

I remembered the previous night again, but now with excitement. And now it wasn't an excitement for Mathilde but for the girl watching at the transom window of the bedroom door. Yes, from where she'd been at the window I'd given her a good profile view of it lifted right up in full stand. No wonder she had wanted it herself. And I'd shown her a splendid, strong performance – maybe something much better than anything she'd ever had with her boyfriends; obviously much better. And when she was getting it, she'd be picturing it happening to her in a way she'd never done before and it would be easy to make her go crazy with sensual ecstasy. And suddenly I couldn't wait, and when we reached the bedroom door I fumbled so much with the key that she took it from me and opened the door herself.

There was nothing to wait for. We'd done all our preliminary love-play with words, out there in the street, walking from the cafe to the hotel. I began getting my clothes off as I shut and locked the door.

Louise had come out prepared for it. As she kicked off her

shoes and pulled her dress over her head, all she had on was a narrow little suspender belt and long stockings that made a teasing display of the last three inches of those splendidly graceful legs before they flowed into the sweet vortex decorated by no more than a blonde, soft down. I couldn't wait as she fixed those calm, steady eyes on me and sat on the edge of the bed to lift and open first one leg then the other to peel off her stockings. I knelt on the floor in front of her, my penis standing stiffly, openly and unashamedly enjoying the tempting view of the pouting little mouth.

She didn't laugh. She wasn't coy. There was something incredibly calm about her. The calm, I thought, before the storm in body and mind. She swung herself up on the bed and drew her legs up, thrusting her knees apart.

'Do I lie like this? Is this right?' she asked.

I must have been very stupid, my common sense dulled by excitement, for I still didn't understand, and believed she was simply asking for an exact repetition of the act she had seen performed with her step-mother.

'That's fine,' I said breathlessly. 'You'll feel it all with the very first thrust.'

I positioned myself above her.

'*I* put it in?' she asked, reaching out with a strange uncertainty.

Our talk was too provocatively exciting and stimulating for me to be analytical about it at the time.

'You know where it goes. Where you want it. And look at it. Look how eager it is for you. It's got to be pulled down, and I can't do that *and* hold myself in position. Surely that's the exciting thing, putting it in yourself.'

'*She* felt it first, didn't she?'

'*You* feel it.'

'Oh, God,' she said softly, doing so. 'It's too big. Let's get it over but . . . but be gentle. This is my first time. . . .'

I was into her by the time she said that, thrusting and discovering for myself the taut barrier of an unpenetrated hymen.

'You're a virgin!' I gasped, incredulously.

'Yes.'

'I can't stop now,' I said breathlessly.

'You mustn't. It's got to happen to me, hasn't it? And I made up my mind last night that it was going to be you. Oh, God, that will fix her. Oh, God, what a hold I'll have over her now . . . straight from her to me.'

I shut my ears to it. I didn't really hear her actually saying this, my mind rejecting it. I only remembered afterwards that this was the unbelievable thing she was saying as I tried to subdue the demands of sensuality and to be gentle.

'You press down,' I whispered. 'It'll probably hurt. I don't want to hurt you. You must give yourself the hurt.'

Then suddenly, because I was stimulating the very seat of my sensuality between the butterfly-caress of her lips, I lost control and began to erupt. She felt it and seemed to understand that if she was to lose her virginity to me it couldn't be delayed.

I felt her take a deep shuddering breath. I was aware of the determination and purpose that was what was obsessing her, and she thrust herself up violently on the implement, and then cried out sharply with pain. I went all the way into her, now unable to stop myself, now heedless of her moaning pain, and savaged her briefly until it was over for me.

Her face was white and drawn as I looked down on her, withdrawing from her. We were both red with blood, and the sheet beneath her had a spreading red stain, too.

'I'm . . . I'm sorry,' I mumbled, meaning it now.

'Don't be. I asked for it, didn't I?'

'But you *did* like it? Just a little.'

'It's filthy! It's disgusting! It's horrible! And, oh God, I didn't know it would hurt so much.'

'You're making me feel ashamed.'

'How do you think I feel? To know I was being like *she* was with you? Ugh. But you can't help yourself, can you? I don't blame you. I can't blame you. I asked you to do it. I almost forced you to do it. I made you get stiff. I put you in. I made myself no longer a virgin, not you. You're just the animal I watched you being last night with *her*, but that's not any more your fault than being a bull is the bull's fault. I want you to go away now. I'm not . . . I'm not ungrateful, but I just want you to go away and leave me.'

'The bed . . .' I said.

'I'll deal with everything. Just go away before I start hating you for doing what I wanted you to do. Just go. Go . . . go . . . *go!*'

I sensed hysteria building up. I was right out of my depth. I needed time to understand. I felt awful about the whole thing. She had cut me down to size, and I was limp and bloody and without my pride in maleness. And I wanted to escape from that, even more than from whatever scene remaining with her might have led to.

I scrambled into my clothes.

'You're sure . . .?' I said, half way to the door.

She was off the bed, naked, bending over it, tearing off the undersheet, presenting me with the view I could never forget of the blood streaking the inner thighs from the soft mouth I had despoiled and ravaged.

'*Get out !*' she shouted at me.

I got out, and found a bar and began drinking brandy.

I felt sick. It wasn't shame. It was the humiliation of knowing that I had disgusted a woman by being what a man cannot help being, but must feel pride in being. I could have wept, almost literally. In that moment I felt that I would probably never be able to have another woman in my life. This damned girl had killed it for me, destroyed it for me.

Another brandy.

'Garçon, autre. Brandé!'

I remembered, and remembered. I felt her feelings of disgust as she had watched me fucking her step-mother. Like having to see a dog and a bitch in the street. Like watching any two farm-yard animals. But a man as an animal with a woman as an animal. For the first time in my life, sex was dirty, obscene, disgusting. And this girl, God damn her, had made me feel like this.

'Garçon, une autre!'

I sank, slowly, descending deeply into the pit of self-contempt. Hemingway once told the story of a young priest who ampu-tated his own penis in an obsessional disgust that I had found it impossible to believe in at the time. Now, briefly, I understood. Give me a knife, and I could do it, just as she had thrust herself down on the obscenity with which she had been impaled.

'Garçon . . .'

Just a wave of my hand.

I don't remember how many double brandies I drank. More than enough! I have no recollection of ever paying for them, of ever leaving the bar, of getting home and to my bed, and falling into the stupor of recovery.

I only know that I had a hell of a head when I wakened the next morning, and that there were traces of dried blood still caking among my pubic hair.

I took a bath, and felt better – both in body and, more im-portant, in mind.

I remembered, and looked at my penis and it began to enlarge and erect at the memory of Louise with it in her hand pulling it down to the very last cunt it had enjoyed. I was all right!

I lit a cigarette, and inhaled with real feelings of relief. What an incredible, unforgettable experience to have had. But she'd remember me. All her life she'd remember me. When she was older, and experienced and mature, she'd remember me better than any other woman remembers the first man and the first time.

What a situation. What a role to have played in a woman's life.

That afternoon, back to my normal self, without even considering the possibilities, I went again into the cafe where I had first met Mathilde and then her step-daughter. I was on my second drink when Mathilde came in.

She marched straight up to me, and stood glaring at me.

'You! Come outside. I want to talk to you.'

I swallowed hard, and realized that I had been a fool ever to come near this place again.

'No. I'm sorry. I'm quite comfortable here, thank you.'

'You won't be, if I say what I've got to say here.' She meant it. 'Do you want a scene in public? Here? In the street? Or are we going to be sensible and have it out in private?'

I paid my bill, and followed her. She said nothing – not a word. We walked. The route we had taken together two nights earlier when my desire had been something and she had been exciting. Back to the house. Into it. Into a living room I had not been in before – a very ordinary, dingy, typical living room where Louise was sitting, listening to a radio she now switched off, waiting for what was obviously a promised confrontation.

'Is it true, what she tells me?' Mathilde demanded, speaking at last.

'What have you told her?' I asked Louise – although I knew that answer perfectly well.

'That you did *exactly* the same thing to me yesterday afternoon that I watched you doing to her the night before – only she was a whore being unfaithful to my father, on his own bed, while I was a virgin being raped a few hours later by the same prick.'

'You vile little bitch!' said Mathilde.

'Whore!' said Louise, spitting the word out. 'Whore ... whore ... *whore*!'

I had never seen such hatred in anybody's face.

'You wait till I tell your father.'

'What'll you tell him? How you lay there on his bed, with your legs open, putting another man's prick into yourself. How many other men have you had – *mummy*! God, I've got you where I want you now. You did *that*! *You* made me a tart. You did that to *his* daughter. He'd kill you.'

'*I'll* kill you.'

'*You'll* leave me alone from now on. No more, don't do this, Louise. Don't do that, Louise. No more running errands for you. No more clearing up after you. No more, Yes, mother. No, mother. We've had the same man. After you, me! Exactly the same thing. Exactly the same way. You just remember that, *whore*!'

'You little slut!'

'*Big* slut!'

I got out. They never heard me go. I didn't matter to them anyway.

I found a cafe.

'Garçon. Cognac!'

I never saw either of them again.

XI

How Lucky Can You Be

I arrived in England in November 1944, nine months after reaching Paris, two months after being discharged from the Maquis, twenty-four hours after making my escape from Mathilde and Louise.

I had two ambitions – to be a pilot in the RAF as part of the regular Dutch army and to discover if English girls were really as frigid as they were supposed to be.

After eleven days of the screening process I was one of a group sent to a big house in Wimbledon taken over by the Dutch. Here we were treated 'like millionaires'; waited on, given civilian clothes, pocket money – and freedom. What an odd, unappreciated word that word 'freedom' is. I could hardly remember a time or a place when and where I had been guilt-free and able to look any man wearing any uniform of authority between the eyes without some sense of anxiety.

We were often invited to dances in the neighbourhood. I had moved out, after a week or so, to private lodgings – a 'billet'. After one of these dances I got back very late and the landlady was furious. I had taken out a land girl and taken her home after the dance. It had turned out that she lived nearly two hours' walk from the dance hall. When we reached her home she told me she dare not invite me in because her parents were very strict. The more important invitation, however, was not denied me.

Her name was Ellen, and she was my first experience of an English girl, and she was very far from being frigid. But making love in a back alley in freezing cold, with all the problems of her thick khaki underwear, made the experience less than satisfying to both of us. When I got back at dawn to the house in Prince's Park I got a lecture from the landlady. She said such adventures made me run the risk of disease, shotgun marriages, and breach of promise actions. I laughed and promised not to embarrass her any more in this way.

Although I was healthy enough the medical inspection revealed I was too thin (weighing a mere 47 kilos) for active service. They made me a clerk in the paymaster's office in Earls Court,

West London. For the next five months I had lodgings nearby in Gloucester Road. They reckoned that after this period I would have a medical again and this would show whether a diet of vitamins and halibut oil capsules had increased my weight.

There were three of us working in one room for £1·50 a week. We had every weekend off from midday Saturday until Monday morning when we started at 8.30 am. It was quite a pleasant life. The work, typing out numbers on salary lists, was boring but our evenings out and the weekends made up for the tedium. The normal dances, arranged for soldiers by hospitals, fire brigades and so on, bored me stiff. I had to spend so much time interpreting for my comrades I did not get much chance to enjoy myself.

When I was not helping out my mates who could not speak English well enough to chat up the girls, I had to answer questions from the hostess about life in Holland and Europe. I decided to copy the example of others who had been in the country some time already and to make a social life of my own. This, I reasoned, would also help me to improve my fluency in the language.

It was, however, at one of these hospital dances that I met Maureen. Our relationship was brief, beautiful and it ended tragically. She was the second girl I made friends with after flying from France. She was Irish, short, dark and vivacious. During a 'ladies excuse me' she approached me, and we hit it off right away. She was about twenty and worked as a nurse about nineteen miles from London. As it was her night off we went to her sister's place in town. Her sister was married, and did not mind a bit. After several nightcaps we went to bed. As there was no blackout curtain we undressed in the dark. Shivering we crept into the bed but it was not long before we forgot all thoughts of the cold. She was as lively and passionate as any man could wish, and just before we fell asleep exhausted, I thought I had found a marvellous girl to brighten my stay in England.

But soon afterwards I lost her address while moving to my new lodgings in Gloucester Road. Several times I went by bus to the area where she had taken me, but I could not find her sister's house. About two months later I bumped into her sister while changing tubes, and she began by being very angry with me. She accused me of breaking Maureen's heart, and of letting her down. 'You took advantage of a young girl,' she said, and was obviously very upset. I calmed her down as we stood on the platform and I explained about losing the address and my repeated attempts to find her.

Eventually she believed my protests and then broke the sad news. Maureen was now a patient in her own hospital, suffering from cancer and about to die. An operation a fortnight ago had failed to save her, and she had not long to go. She gave me the address of the hospital and at the weekend I took a train there. As it was the spring I took a bunch of tulips and asked at reception for her. The nurse immediately recognized me from Maureen's description. She was a close friend of hers. It was soon clear that she felt the only thing she could do for Maureen was to fix it so we would be able to have long, undisturbed visits.

It was the saddest afternoon of my life. I can hardly describe how painful it was. Words seem now so inadequate, and I shall never forget how helpless and agonized I felt. The young, lively creature I had danced with and loved so warmly lay there with her huge dark eyes sometimes shining with happiness and then brimming with tears. She wanted and deserved so much to live but what could I give her but company and sympathy? At last, long after visiting time was over, I had to leave. She begged me not to come back.

'Thank you for that lovely night,' she said, making her first reference to the night we had spent together at her sister's house.

'There will be more, when you are better,' I said. I had to say something, and what else was there to say?

Her eyes shone, yet no tears came. 'I'm not fooling myself now – about *anything*!' she said. 'Not about what's going to happen to me so very soon. Not even about us, on that first night. I was just another girl to you. And you *could* have been just another man to me. Maybe you would have been if I hadn't had a good idea even then what was happening to me. I'd never felt love before. I wanted to feel it, just once. Silly isn't it? I'm telling you I love you and saying goodbye to you in the same breath. Oh, God, its so damn silly.'

She gripped my hand. She hurt me with the strength that came from somewhere beyond her physical weakness.

'I'll come back. Tomorrow. Every day, somehow.'

'No. *No*. You must never, never come back. That's the kindness and the cruelty. I've seen what's happening to me happening to others. I don't want you to see.'

'I don't mind.'

'But *I* do.'

I don't honestly remember how that scene ended. She did weep, finally. She did cling to me, as if there was a whole lifetime left in just those moments.

When I got outside the hospital finally, I was weeping myself, like a child. And it took me some days to get over it, to realize that for me it was not the life and death matter it was for her, but just another experience.

By May 1945 I passed the medical board examination, but they had two reservations. I was still under weight but I signed a paper absolving the army of any responsibility if my health suffered from active service. Also, some small defect in my sense of balance ruled out the possibility of my becoming a pilot. As I no longer had the patience for office work and was still eager to help chase the Japs out of the Dutch East Indies, I chose to be a soldier instead and began initial training at Warley under the command of a Lt. Col. T. C. Hearn.

They put all the Dutchmen in one platoon and they made me interpreter for my comrades who did not even understand the words used in simple commands for drill. The first few days were killing, as I had had no exercise for the past six months, apart from my efforts in the bedroom, my muscles shrieked out for relief but there was no let up. Our NCO drove us remorselessly. One night a barracks dance had been arranged but most of us were so exhausted we decided to give it a miss and got ready for bed. I was already in my bunk when the sergeant came in and told us the Colonel expected us to turn up and be presented to the officers' wives and ladyfriends. Of course, as one of us had to be able to talk to them I was dragged from my bunk, and hauled to my feet.

Once I had got there, and the official introductions were over, I started to look around to see if it were possible to escape to my room. As I glanced about I saw a blonde girl of about sixteen. She looked so beautiful and radiant I quite forgot about my aching muscles. I set about getting a dance with her and discovered that her name was June and that her parents owned a cafe in Brentwood.

Unfortunately, she was actually only about fourteen, but I became very good friends with her and her family and during the rest of my stay in England they provided a home for me, and treated me like their two sons, Ronny and Bernard.

The whole family were absolutely marvellous to me. I have kept up the friendship to this day and it was Ronny who pressed and persuaded me to set down my adventures in this book.

When my training at Warley was over I was sent to Catterick in Yorkshire for a six month course in Reconnaissance. Every leave I went down to Brentwood to see June and the rest of the Wright family. They always gave me a fantastic welcome and when there were long leaves such as at Christmas, we had many trips together.

It was on the famous 'Flying Scotsman', at the start of my Christmas leave, that I had a further insight into the British character. I had always heard of their calmness and ability to carry off awkward situations but this incident really confirmed things for me.

The train was so full I had to walk the whole length of the train before striking lucky. In the last compartment there was an empty seat beside a stern looking, tall, thin, Wren officer. It was a small compartment with only four seats on each side. Opposite the Wren and I, were a soldier, a sailor cuddling his girl and an elderly gentleman who started to snore as soon as I sat down. On the other side of the Wren was a captain and on my side in the corner was another sailor. The train shook along. The lights were only at half strength and sometimes they went out all together. The curtains were drawn because of the blackout, and it would have been cosy if the heating had been working properly.

It grew colder and colder. I had tried to start a conversation with the Wren but her response was stony. Eventually, however, as she drew her greatcoat over her knees, she relaxed a bit and let me have part of it over me. I whispered a 'Thank you.' Nearly everyone else had by this time dozed off, or at least had their eyes closed. She cuddled up a little and then suddenly let her head rest on my shoulder. As her breathing became regular, a mischievous thought struck me. I thought being so thin and spinsterish – there was no ring on her finger – she might welcome a friendly gesture. I slipped my hand under her greatcoat, and began stroking her thighs softly.

As she was so tall, and her head on my shoulder, her long legs were stretched well out, in front of mine. I slowly moved my hand upwards and gently began stroking inside her panties. She kept breathing regularly but then as I increased the excitement for her she suddenly woke up with a start. As she gasped at the joy I had brought her the great coat slipped to the floor! Her gasp made the elderly gentleman and the sailors opposite wake up. There was I in full view of them with my hand in her pants! They stared at me, and for a second or two, it seemed as though the lights grew brighter than they had been for the rest of the journey. The Wren shuddered, replaced the greatcoat, curled towards me, and closed her eyes as if to lock out the world.

Never before have I seen such clear evidence of how tactfully the English can behave. Not only did those opposite resume their positions, without a word, the sailors even managed to avoid smiling. In my mind I saluted them and wondered how other nationalities would have reacted. When everyone had settled down I decided it was safe to withdraw my hand. The Wren had made no gesture of wanting me to take it away, but I assumed it was certain that, after an embarrassment like that, she wished me to stop. But to my astonishment she gripped my hand firmly, and scolded me in my ear for being a 'naughty boy'. Then she asked where I was spending my leave. Of course I had to disappoint her as I had a date with the Wrights, but I hope she remembers that incident on the train with as much pleasure as I do.

There was not much fun in between leaves at Catterick. But we did manage to make our own excitement out of the most routine things. In the course of our training many of my Dutch comrades were looking forward to becoming officers. When at last the few chosen were made known, to my great astonishment I found my name had also been put on the list. In all truth, however, nothing had been further from my mind. Not that I too did not feel ambitious or frightened by that kind of responsibility, but simply because of the disastrous consequences if I were repatriated. Imagine me returning to Holland bearing the rank of lieutenant! The former jailbird and burglar an officer in the Royal Army! Already I pictured myself being court-martialled because of forgery and so on. The false information I had given at the Dutch Embassy in Paris, when specifically asked whether I ever had been in trouble with the police, would be enough already.

Naturally they would never have sent me to England in the first place had they but known who I really was. The information taken about me by the Dutch officials in Paris seemed to have covered my political background only. My fighting with the Maquis, along with time spent in the labour camp Schirmeck, perhaps had induced them not to take things too seriously in my case. Who can tell exactly how in such times scraps of information are obtained and pieced together?

As long as I remained abroad, this did not matter much and being only a small part of this vast army I could be fairly sure of being left in peace. Once an officer, however, the game would be up. Before long I would meet someone who knew me, and that would be it. Even here, in England, the military authorities would not look kindly on an officer without a clean record who had wilfully led them astray. My refusal, however, would have contrasted so much with the enthusiasm of the others chosen that I judged it best to let the matter rest for the moment. Instead of protesting or talking it over with my CO, I pretended I was honoured, but I secretly decided to play the game my own way once the time was right.

I went on one of the last leadership tests, a twenty-four hour march, with two Englishmen, Jim and Jeff, and a Dutchman called Ben. We had to travel as a group across the wild Yorkshire moors after having been dropped miles from anywhere from a car. Each of us had to take turns to act as leader. We started very early in the morning armed only with maps, compasses, iron rations, and carrying a full pack and equipment. We had to find our way to the next map reference, where a dining truck would provide meals. Points were given for sticking to the timetable and for arriving with iron rations intact. If you reached a map reference too late you missed your meal, and this left you with the choice of either marching on an empty stomach or else losing valuable points.

Jim and Jeff ganged up against Ben and I. It was clearly a matter of national pride and rivalry with them that they should be the first two to act as leader. 'It's our country and so it's our right to go first,' they said. 'And anyway if you leave it to the British you'll get your hot meal all right.'

As there was only a short distance to cover in the first twelve hours Ben and I let them have their way. This was a mistake. Jim used the compass clumsily and set the wrong course to start with, when we had been dropped from the car. When it came to Jeff's turn six hours later it was obvious we were lost. We had been supposed to find our instructions at this time so we could work out the next route which led to our dinner. It was clear that if we returned to where we had started we had no chance of getting to the dinner truck in time.

Jeff tried to work things out again but in the end he gave up and tossed the compass into my lap. I managed to find the way back to our starting point. When we reached our instructions for the second stage it was certain we would be an hour late.

We were all so anxious not to miss that meal that we agreed to press on even faster to make up for lost time. We did our best and almost made it, but the dinner truck had left ten minutes before we arrived. Two other groups jeered at us as we turned up, and they were just scraping the last of the hot food from their plates. The officer marked all four of us as losing three points. Ben and I had agreed to take our share of the blame to avoid the Englishmen losing six points each.

They were grateful for this and I urged them not to linger like the groups who had enjoyed their food. I knew we could complete the twelve hour journey in ten hours if we did not lose track again. After a while our empty stomachs started to protest, but I kept pressing them on. I had spotted on the map a farm-house ahead of us – dead on course. I hoped to find something to eat there so that we did not lose points by eating our iron rations. As we had already lost three each, eating the rations would definitely mean failing the course. I was determined not to let that happen.

Jim and Jeff were conscripts and so they were not as anxious as I. Soon they were demanding that we stop and eat our rations. When I told them my plan, they laughed and said we would only be able to find food if we paid for it – and that was strictly forbidden. Ben was also doubtful, but in a quick burst of Dutch I persuaded him. At last the Englishmen gave in and struggled on until we got to a hill overlooking three farmhouses.

After reconnoitring on my belly in the heather I spotted a vegetable garden and some chickens. Ben went to get the veget-ables while Jeff and I searched for the poultry. Keeping out of sight from the farmhouse he managed to 'shoo' a chicken in my direction. I leaped on it and managed to grab a leg. It cackled loudly. With one quick movement I wrung its neck. When we had made certain we had not been heard we rejoined Ben. He had plenty of potatoes and onions. Jim had found some empty tins and soon we had a fire going. Luckily they had filled our water bottles at the last stop. After skinning the chicken and removing its guts, we buried the bits we did not want along with the vegetable peel. After an hour's cooking we were soon enjoy-ing a delicious meal.

As Jim said: 'Only the salt's missing!'

The unexpected meal stimulated us to even greater efforts,

and we covered the rest of the course in fast time. They gave us bonus points for being so quick and we passed after all.

However, I still had to appear before the War Office Selection Board before a final decision could be made. The tests lasted three days and were rather simple. I soon found the proper way to sabotage them without arousing the curiosity of the examiners. If I were to fail it should be because of lack of officer qualities and not because I was dumb.

I took great care to give answers that were unusual and in the end they rejected me as officer material saying I was too 'individualistic'. It suited me fine and there were really no ill feelings when I congratulated the other Dutch comrades who all passed with flying colours. I even remember their marvelling about how well I seemed to take my own failure.

I was given the rank of sergeant instead and made a messenger at the Dutch HQ in London while awaiting transfer to Holland.

Soon afterwards I met up with my two brothers who had been on a special course in Wolverhampton. This incident was the first to confirm how right I had been not to accept the chance to become an officer. We met only briefly but I managed to introduce them to my good friends the Wright family.

Early in 1946 I was shipped to Holland as an instructor to help train a regiment at Amersfoort.

I left England with many regrets. Whenever I think of the good time in that country I feel a warm glow of satisfaction. It was perhaps the very first time I had been taken at face value and been found worth the friendship of normal honest people, as well as the recommendation of my superiors to higher office than I would ever had dreamed of.

Although my first ambition had not been achieved, the second left no doubts. It is definitely not true what they had said about English girls!

XII

On the Run in Africa

When I learned my regiment was to be sent to the East Indies to crush the Indonesian freedom fighters I decided to desert. I did not mind fighting and risking death in the struggle against Hitler but I had no intention of dying for such a cause. If I simply refused to go to the Far East I would get three months in jail. If I deserted and was caught the military courts would punish me very severely. The only thing was to desert and not get captured – but that would take money.

I got in touch with a black marketeer who was keen to buy military uniforms, and other clothing. One night when I was on guard duty I worked out a scheme that would enable me to go missing for some time without being noticed. In that time I loaded up a truck with clothes and shoes from the store to which I had a duplicate key. It was of course out of the question to drive the truck out of the main gate, so I arranged with the fence that I would deliver the goods to him at the rear of the camp outside the barracks. This meant driving the truck straight through a high barbed wire fence which surrounded the camp. Then I had to go about two kilometres along a country road for my rendezvous with him.

Everything went to plan and he was waiting for me when I got to the spot but he did not have all the cash on him. He claimed he would have to sell some of the goods before giving me the rest of the money. I was in no position to argue so I just had to accept the cash he offered. Leaving the truck for him to take care of I got back to the barracks just in time to reply to a check by the officer in charge of the watch, and no one had noticed my absence. But I had to explain the state I was in. Breathless and sweating I told the officer I had seen some suspicious-looking shadows moving about at the back of the camp. As it was a bit foggy, I said, I thought it best to investigate before sounding the alarm. He had no way of knowing how long this had taken me so he asked me to make out a report. After being relieved as guard I went to my bunk.

But before going to sleep I hid my money. Next morning I was awakened by the military police. They had discovered the theft, the missing truck and the smashed fence. They had also read my entry in the watch-log. So they questioned me about what I had seen. Answering all these questions while I got dressed I pretended to be very angry when they began to turn over my cupboard. When I protested I was carted off to their HQ at Utrecht. There a much tougher interrogation started, but all they had to go on was suspicion and conjecture. By now they had however learned of my criminal record from the civilian police and this made them put me in custody while they carried out further investigations. They locked me in a cell and took my paybook from me. As a military prisoner you have no right to escape in the way an ordinary crook can. You have to obey military orders even when you are arrested. My guard therefore raised no objection when I asked to go to the toilet. There I climbed through the window and walked out of the barracks receiving a salute from the guard at the gate; who acknowledged my rank of sergeant.

Having some cash in my pocket I took a taxi back to Amersfoort. There I went into the camp and hurried to my hiding place. I had there not only the money from the black marketeer, but also a paybook under a false name which I had organized while working in the paymaster's office in London, just in case such an emergency should arise. Within a few minutes of entering the camp I was out again and on a train to Bordeaux. There I found a Dutch steamer which carried half cargo and half passengers. It was about to leave for Africa. Here was my chance and I took it.

During the night I hid among some cargo on the quay near the prow of the ship, studying the watch on the deck. It was February and freezing cold but long after midnight I had an opportunity to find some warmth on board. Taking off my shoes I slipped up a narrow gangway. Crossing the fore deck I hid among the shadows on the port side. When the watchman had passed again I crept over to an iron door which, luckily, was open. Having had the foresight to buy a torch in town that day I was able to see my way down three flights of stairs. Another iron door was open and soon I was in a hold. It was loaded with Renault trucks and the labels showed that they were destined for Dakar, West Africa.

Closing the door behind me I found the truck with the largest cabin and made myself comfortable. I was woken by the sound of someone locking the door with a key.

It now seemed safe to take a better look at my surroundings. Over by the wall were several crates full of bottles of champagne. I had brought a few packets of dates with me and now I was able to have a drink as well. I had to spend six days in that hold before I judged it safe to attract attention. We had sailed on the third day but I was pretty dozy most of the time because I drank greedily from the champagne. Using an empty petrol tank and some steel drawers as a toilet I was able to survive without too much unpleasantness.

On the sixth day someone was climbing the metal staircase to the hold when I made enough noise to attract his attention. He was quite astonished to find me locked up like that. I must have looked pretty scruffy. He took me at once to the captain. Captain Bosman his name was; a burly man with kind blue eyes and a short blond beard. He was well thought of by all the crew, and he treated me very sympathetically. Being a fellow-Dutch-man and a lover of freedom he warmed to my tale about deserting rather than going to the East to fight the poor Indonesians who had long been suppressed by our nation. He refused to mention me in the log and assured me that if I kept myself inconspicuous, and was discreet when talking to passengers, he would let me slip off the ship at Dakar. I agreed and was told to help a lad in the mess with his duties. They gave me an empty sailor's bunk in the forecastle. The ship was called the *Amstelkerk* and the voyage to Dakar lasted a week.

When we arrived I was told to keep out of sight until the cus-toms officers had left the ship. Next morning they tipped me off that the coast was clear and, carrying my few possessions, I step-ped ashore just like a member of the crew off to enjoy a few hours' leave. One of my childhood heroes had been Tarzan and I re-member feeling in high spirits as I walked for the first time along the coast of his homeland. Strolling about, I studied the quayside characters. The sometimes grotesque and exotic Arabs and natives who lingered in the shadows fascinated me. Noticing how strong the sun was I set off for the town. I had changed my last coins on the ship so I stopped at a cafe for a cool drink.

There I met an old Dutchman called Panache who had eked out a living in Dakar for the past twenty years by occasional car repairs. He introduced me to his friend Mr Vincent, another old fellow and former Foreign Legionaire who designed and painted posters for the town's cinemas. He owned the house where they both lived. Being bachelors and fond of booze, the place was usually in a mess. That night Vincent invited me to a party, held by former members of the Foreign Legion, at the Hotel de France. During dinner I told him of my attempt to join the Legion and why I had been rejected. They all agreed I should be 'elected' to their 'club' because of my ambition and bad luck. Then when they heard why I had deserted from the Army they said Vincent should give me free board and lodgings until I got on my feet. The local police chief was also at this dinner and he was told to ignore my presence in Senegal, and he promised to do so for as long as he could.

For several days I helped Vincent with the painting and putting up of posters. He was drunk most of the time and not very agreeable company. Panache, whom I used to see in the evening, was also usually very drunk. One night when we were enjoying an aperitif at the Hotel de France we heard the manager had had an accident in the market and broken both his legs. He was in hospital and his wife was very worried because she had no one to replace him. She was a monstrously fat woman – so large, indeed, she could not reach her feet and put on her shoes. Well over sixty, and a former Austrian dancing girl, she had married the manager while on a tour of Africa. She was delighted to meet me especially as I could speak to her in her native language. She quickly agreed I could act as manager while her husband was in hospital. As he was an old man it took three months before he was able to get back to work.

Bernard, a young, homosexual civil servant, was a useful friend at this time. He was a knowledgeable guide and I got around quite a bit. On one of our walks through the Armenian quarter I met Elise. Her parents lived at Santos in Brazil. Her father owned a cigarette factory and she was in Dakar seeing relatives. Her uncle knew my friend and he invited us to his house for a drink. I was very interested in Elise. Nineteen, small, slim, with a ripe young figure, and bright, dark eyes, she was quite enchanting. She had been educated in Brazil and spoke only a little French. But we were able to get along fairly well in Spanish. From the day we met she used to come regularly to the hotel. She took her lunch out of sight behind the bar so she could not be seen by the customers.

It seemed she was head-over-heels in love with me and she had a scheme to take me back to Santos where her father had contacts in the immigration office. Her idea was that he could fix me up with all the required papers, we should marry, and I should work in a factory. I liked her a lot and because my prospects were so poor I began to warm to her plan. She even imagined she could smuggle me on board her ship in one of her trunks. Her relatives, she said, would be glad to carry the luggage to the docks when she was due to leave.

But the crazy idea came to nothing. The police chief tipped me off that people were beginning to talk about me and he would soon have to notice my presence officially. The boat to Brazil did not leave for a week. At first I thought I could hang on but the next day the chief said I could not stay even that long. I would have to give up my idea of the lovely young Elise and life in South America.

Some time before one of the guests, a Swiss, had offered me an office job in his trading post not far from Kaolak. Bernard got me a railway ticket as I would have needed identification papers to buy one myself. I set off without having the guts to say goodbye to Elise. I had walked out of too many women's lives already not to have learnt that the best way is just to go.

The Swiss and his wife met me at the station and it was soon clear he had no idea I had entered the country illegally and had no papers. He said it was out of the question that I should work for him. The district officer was arriving next week and he would be bound to ask about me. They suggested I acted as though I was a tourist, and pretend to be a cousin of the book-keeper's wife, who had just arrived from Dakar.

She was a young blonde of about thirty with two children. Her rooms were next to mine and we shared the same maid, a comely negress of about seventeen. I soon took a fancy to the maid but that bit of fun ended rather abruptly. As she spoke only her native language we had to communicate in gestures. This made courtship difficult. She let me pat her magnificent breasts but refused to let me lift her skirt.

I tried to impress her with the size of my penis but that only set her off in a fit of giggles! One day I tried to relax her by showing her a bottle of eau de cologne. She smiled delightedly. Carefully I put it on her breasts. She was as meek as a lamb. Then by signs I told her she could have the whole bottle if she undressed and took a shower. When she came out of the shower a beautiful brown statuesque princess dripping with water I began massaging the eau de cologne into her breasts and thighs. I was just kissing her breasts when the door opened and one of the shop-keeper's children ran in – followed by her mother. The

Swiss gave me a strict telling off. The girl was working for him while she awaited her wedding. She had been promised to a local young man. The Swiss was responsible for her welfare and this did not include what I had had in mind!

But he did me a further favour by introducing me to a business friend of his who was known as the King of the Salmoun because of his power and influence among the natives living around the Salmoun river. He owned a trading post and I was taken there by boat.

When this trader heard my story he offered me a partnership in his plant down river where the fish were caught and smoked. It was on a small island near where the river flowed into the Atlantic. About fifty natives with their families lived in huts on the island. The buildings which were needed for the smoking process were in ruins and needed repair, but I soon got things working properly. I taught these natives how to use bows and arrows. The beach was swarming with crabs of all sizes. They scurried fast back into holes if anyone came near them. I found some boxes of rusty nails and hammers. After making a fire I was able to forge the nails into arrow heads. It was easy to make bows and arrows from the tough wood from the mangrove trees. Within a week all the boys and some young men were shooting crabs, and the meat was really delicious. We were also able to catch shrimps and find oysters.

After a month on this island paradise my partner sent an urgent message down river to say the police were on their way looking for me. They were coming in a government boat and he advised me to flee to Bathurst in British Gambia. Everyone on the island seemed as sad to see me leave as I was to go. It turned out that the police had decided to come after me after one of my letters had fallen into their hands. I had kept a promise I had made to my friends in Dakar to let them know how I got on but one of these friendly letters was my undoing. I heard later that the hotel owner at Dakar was heavily fined for having employed me without a permit. This was very sad because he had barely recovered from his accident and had acted from the best of motives.

It took me only a few hours to reach Bathurst in a canoe. As soon as I landed I went straight to see the police chief, an Englishman in his early fifties. He promised to see the Governor on my behalf and gave me a room at the fire station. His wife was in England at the time and he expressed his regrets at not being able to entertain me properly. I got to know his mistress however, a young black girl. She was obviously quite fond of me because one day, a few weeks later, she came and warned me the Governor had decided to send me back on a steamer which was arriving the next day. It was impossible for me to get a job because the English and the Dutch had an extradition treaty which included military deserters. She also described the lay-out of the inside of the police station for me. That day I burgled the house of a wealthy Syrian merchant and found some cash. I used this to persuade an Arab, whom I had been giving French lessons, to hire a canoe and some oarsmen who would row me to Portuguese Guinea.

On the journey, however, I became very ill. I passed out and awoke in a hospital in Bissao. I was told I was suffering from dysentery, a vicious form of malaria called paludism, jaundice, scabies and tapeworm. It took me two months to get well again.

I was a first-class patient and the hospital authorities accepted the letter I had written in the police chief's office about losing my papers on a hunting trip. When I was fit enough to get up and about I was able to roam all over the hospital grounds. The staff were friendly and often let me watch them perform operations. The knowledge I gained in the hospital stood me in good stead later when I had to care for sick friends or cure myself. It was partly my experience in this hospital which enabled me to claim the role of nurse when my future wife, Jo, lay grievously ill for weeks.

When I was ready to be discharged they were shocked to learn that I had no money. That afternoon I was granted an audience with the Governor of the colony. Speaking in French he reacted with some good humour to my story and he agreed to let me stay until I had earned enough to pay the massive bill I had run up at the hospital, and my fare to wherever I wanted to go. This seemed very generous of him but I soon found how impossible it was to carry out this plan. All the trade was in Portuguese hands. The head offices were in Portugal and the regulations concerning health insurance stopped them employing anyone who had not been passed by the board of health in Lisbon! I was however given a room at the Government's expense at the Hotel Miramar.

One of the guests there, who worked for the big firm, Casa Goveia, wrote on my behalf to a large insurance company to see if I could have a medical examination in Bissao. But they said it was impossible. His name was Maurice and he taught me Portuguese and in return I taught him French. We got along very well and whenever he was free he spent time showing me around and explaining things.

The Governor had told me I was to report every day to the officials at the Town Hall, and I also had to inform them if I left town for the night.

One night a local mechanic called Lemon visited the hotel to have a drink. I was out with Maurice taking a stroll but the owner told Lemon about me. Lemon lived opposite the only other hotel in town. He often took me with him when he had to leave town visiting addresses where car repairs were needed. He had a car of his own and was glad to have someone to talk to on the long trips. It was rough country, marshy and barren, with rivers and swamps full of crocodiles. We often had to pass shallow water in the car where the beasts watched us – too close for comfort.

Once a month a steamer came into port directly from Portugal and on one visit it brought a Syrian family who were finishing a European tour. With them was their eighteen year old daughter Pauline. She had glorious long black hair and a good figure although, like most Middle Eastern girls, she was a shade on the plump side. Her lively personality, beauty and ability to speak English as well as Spanish made her a great attraction for all the young men in town. The great wealth of her father of course made her even more of a prize.

That evening I was visiting Lemon's house for a game of chess. The hotel opposite was ablaze with lights. A band played and people were dancing on the terrace. Lemon had seen the girl and he challenged me to go over and get a dance with her. This was not fair of him. I was shabbily dressed and still pale from my recent illnesses. But when he offered to lend me a tie and to pay for the drinks I took up his challenge and we went over to the hotel.

Eventually we were introduced to the girl's father who seemed upset by all the young Portuguese men strutting around his lovely daughter. Lemon played chess with the father while I tried to amuse the son, aged about fourteen, with a few card tricks. After being introduced to Pauline I carefully ignored her. I ignored her as much as the young men were trying to attract her attention. At last this provoked her into walking straight up to me and asking, impatiently tapping her foot, whether I danced.

I kept very cool and merely had a brief conversation with her.

As we left a little later, after having agreed to pay them a visit next day, Lemon congratulated me on my approach. Her father had already told him she would soon get bored with the young men who spoke little Spanish or English. Lemon had learned that they intended to stay for a week before getting a boat to Freetown. Next evening we went to the hotel and Pauline was sitting reading to her smaller brother while a few of the more persistent Portuguese hovered around. We chatted in English and Spanish and she grew so interested that none of the young men were able to get her from my side for the rest of the evening. Lemon played chess again with her father and from that night on the drinks were on him. This was to be the routine until they left for Freetown.

Two nights before they left she was very sad. By now we were very fond of each other and she proposed some mad schemes, such as stealing her mother's jewels and eloping with me. I pointed out the folly of this but she said our friendship could not end in such a flat way. I said that if she felt that way, there was no need for it to end without some pleasure and excitement. She asked me what I meant and we soon had a plan made for the night. She would go to bed early and she reckoned her parents would follow quite soon. When everyone had left and all the lights were out, I would sneak back. She let me know where her room was and promised to leave a window open for me. When Lemon heard of our plan he offered the use of his front room to watch the hotel unobserved to see when the lights went out. When we judged it was safe, I crossed over to the hotel and slipped into the garden. Suddenly a spear-point was thrust flat against my chest. We had forgotten about the native guards who protected most buildings at night. After some swift talking I persuaded this one that I was welcome and expected. He could see this for himself because Pauline had already appeared at her open window. I gave him some money to buy himself and his mate a drink, and that settled it.

I quickly climbed into Pauline's room and she closed the blinds behind me. As her parents slept next door we had to keep our voices down but we could keep the light on. She was not shy at all and undressed as easily as I did. Her breasts were even larger and just as firm as those of the young negress maid in Dakar. We started to caress each other and I soon learned she had never touched a man between the thighs. She examined me there with a child-like fascination and I had to warn her not to excite me too much because I had not been with a woman for quite a while. Then she lowered her head and took me in her mouth, her eyes shining with joy, and she swiftly brought me the greatest pleasure. She told me she had learnt how to make love orally when attending a convent school in Spain. The nuns had stroked her and the girls had grown fond of satisfying each other orally. Now, for the first time, she had a man to love in this way.

She had to be a virgin when she was married or her family and friends would treat her as an outcast. She told me she did not care about this, but I told her not to be silly. I kissed and excited her but when she begged me to take her I refused. At first she was amazed at my restraint but, after I had reminded her of the consequences, she hugged me and asked me to start intercourse and go only so far. I agreed and entered her very carefully. I managed to give her some pleasure but withdrew before damaging her marriage prospects. At dawn I left her and she gave me a ring as a token of friendship.

When I made my daily visit to the Town Hall the clerk looked at me strangely and told me I must see the chief of police that morning. I saw Lemon down by the harbour and he laughed when I told him the clerk's message. 'They just want to put you in jail for your own protection,' he said. 'That Syrian has found out and really means business.'

I had other ideas. There was a steamer in the harbour sailing that very afternoon for the Cape Verde isles and then on to Portugal. This might give me a chance to switch ships and reach South America, and maybe the lovely Elise, after all.

Lemon took me out in a rowing boat and soon had us both aboard the steamer. Mingling with the passengers I found an empty cabin, and slipped into one of the bunks. Lemon locked the door with a key we had found in a steward's jacket hanging in one of the cabins we had explored earlier. That was the last I ever saw of him.

During the voyage I had another bout of malaria and became so noisy that I was detected long before we reached the Cape Verde islands. The captain had me locked up until we reached Lisbon, where he handed me over to the immigration officials.

Soon everyone had left the ship except for myself and one of the Immigration Officials who had been left behind to keep an eye on me until a car came to pick us both up.

However, he didn't keep quite alert enough and at the first

opportunity I slipped away, returning to the docks later to try and find another ship.

I learnt from some local sailors that there was a ship now in from Spain which was heading for Brazil. I decided that this was all right for me and easily managed to slip on board with the other passengers. Once at sea, however, to my horror, I discovered that this ship was in fact bound for *Spain* and had come from Brazil, not the other way round. My Portuguese, which was not that good, had let me down badly.

In Spain, stowaways get sent to prison and it was not long before I found myself in La Coruna jail.

XIII

'So You Won't Talk'

The best scheme for avoiding being deported to Holland was suggested by a fellow prisoner at La Coruna jail who was a lawyer from Madrid. He said I should become a Roman Catholic.

It seems the law allowed anyone to enter and remain in Spain if two Spanish residents, recognized as good citizens, were willing to vouch for you. The young lawyer told me that if I said I wanted to become a Catholic but had never been baptized I had a good chance of staying in the country. They would have to find me a godfather and godmother who would be guarantors to the authorities for my good behaviour.

So I took lessons in religion from the prison chaplain who was delighted at this unexpected chance to win a new soul to the only true Church. I studied hard and soon knew by heart the prayers and some long sections from the Latin Mass.

The lawyer, like most of the other political prisoners, had treated me with suspicion until I responded to his advice. It was quite understandable that they distrusted each new arrival. Some prisoners were not prisoners at all but spies planted to gain information about plots and rebels. The Church backed these informers and gave them absolution if they managed to unearth some threat to the State. But the lawyer and some of his friends started to show they trusted me.

Many of the prisoners had been put away without trial and without even knowing the evidence or charges against them. My friend the lawyer had been in prison for about two years and still did not know what crime he was alleged to have committed. Occasionally a prisoner was tried but he was never given any warning or a chance to prepare his defence. If there was the suspicion that a man was a major threat to the security of the State he was handed over to the Inquisition. Franco was of course powerfully protected by the Vatican.

The tortures ranged from electric shock treatment to mediaeval thumbscrews. No means were neglected, no matter how uncivilized, if there was a chance of making a man talk.

One form of torture was a type of garotte. The wretched man

was strapped into a chair and an iron ring was closed round his neck. At the back of the ring there was a screw which could be driven slowly into the top of his spine. Two priests stood on each side of the victim and an executioner took his orders from them. As the screw edged into his vertebrae, the priests tried to persuade the man to confess. I was told the theory was that their best chance of getting him to talk occurred just after he had ejaculated. If he kept silent the screw was driven on – until the poor soul was out of his misery. My natural curiosity led me to try to verify these tales of torture and horror but although I sometimes played chess with the chief guard it was impossible to obtain real proof – without being tortured myself. Although I attempted to peep into the death cells which were strictly out of bounds, I was unable to get near them.

When I finished my religious lessons the Chaplain told me I was to be confirmed and baptized the next Sunday. The Bishop of Santiago de Compostela was to conduct the ceremony.

It never came off. The next day I was transferred to the Caravanserail in Madrid – the largest prison in Spain.

There were two possible ways my embarrassing position could be resolved. They could get me to sign a passport with a picture and I could be sent from the Dutch Embassy back to Holland or I could be kept in prison. While I had been in prison at La Coruna, the lawyer had helped me to write a request to the Government asking to be allowed to live in Spain. So far I had received no answer to this. When they took me to the Dutch Embassy to sign a passport I refused, as I knew it would mean a one-way trip from Madrid to Amsterdam.

I was in a dormitory with about twenty military prisoners, mostly Germans, who had deserted from France and Africa. As these prisoners regarded me as being of the same race, and as I was able to speak their language, they soon accepted me. The food was not bad and we played games and cards to kill time. One game was a bit childish but very popular. A prisoner would stand with his back to the others with his hands against the wall. The rest stood in a half circle behind him. They would take it in turns to slap his behind. After each smack he would have to turn and point out who had slapped him. If he guessed right then he was replaced by the man he had caught. But if he failed the game went on until he guessed correctly. They were all very fit and strong with large hands. Their blows hurt like hell. Their idea of fun was to try to swipe the same spot each time. After each smack your bottom grew more painful and if you failed too often to locate the culprit the game was more like a torture.

One of the soldiers, Hans, a young, fair-haired fellow, never took part in this game. Although he was popular they never pressed him to play. One day I discovered why this was.

A boy of about seventeen, a Spaniard, was put in our dormitory. As I was the only one who could speak Spanish I soon learned his story. He had come from the sick bay and was walking with difficulty. He had been in a cell with two older prisoners who had raped him so badly he had had to have stitches.

When I translated this to the Germans, Hans suddenly flung himself on his bunk and sobbed like a child. The senior officer then took me aside and explained the young man's misery. When serving Rommel in the desert, Hans had been part of a platoon captured by some African soldiers. After being disarmed they had been lined up and searched. When it came to Hans' turn they were delighted by his blond looks and white-skinned body. They ordered him at pistol point to bend over and, one by one, they had violated him. All this had occurred in front of his comrades who still felt deeply ashamed at the humiliation he had endured. When each of them had tried to intervene to stop his suffering they were knocked to the ground and told they would be shot if they caused any more trouble. Hans was still acutely affected by this shameful episode and his comrades treated him with great gentleness and sensitivity.

At last the Spanish decided to put me over the border into France. I was sent on a train with two guards to Bilbao where two plain clothes policemen took over. From there we went by car to San Sebastian where we had dinner. They gave me a food parcel and when it was dark they escorted me to the French frontier. They did not use the road. We travelled on foot through the woods, climbing rocks, and scrambling through bushes. Suddenly one stopped and pointed north. I was to go in that direction until I reached France.

My first task was to find some cash and, if possible, some clothes. I approached a farmhouse but soon realized a break-in here was out of the question. A noisy, barking dog alerted a farmhand who came to see who was about. I ducked away into the bushes and made for the next building. After investigating a summer bungalow which also seemed unpromising, because it looked as though it was too early in the season for occupants, I tried another bungalow.

After ringing the bell to make sure no one was in, I circled the building until I found an open window at the back. On the kitchen table the remains of breakfast were still evident and so it appeared I was in luck. In the bedroom I found a few thousand francs and some clothes that fitted me. I stole a bag to carry these in, and I also took some food from the kitchen.

The whole raid took less than fifteen minutes and I reached some bushes near by without being spotted. There I changed my clothes, threw the bag away and tucked the food inside my shirt. Then I skirted round the edge of the village and found the road to St Jean de Luz where I struck lucky again. I got a lift from a car all the way to Biarritz. There at the station I found I had enough money to buy a single ticket to Paris. In the train I ate the food and slept for a few hours. It was nearly midnight when we drew into Paris.

With my last franc I bought a Metro ticket to Bonne Nouvelle, the part of Paris I knew best, and where I hoped to find a room for the night. Coming out of the station I had the astonishing luck to recognize Bertrand who had worked with me on the farm at Salbris before I was forced to join the Maquis. Sipping red wine together in a cafe he listened to my adventures over the past two years. He offered me a bed for the night and said he might be able to get me a job. Knowing he had done some wild things in his time I naturally asked him for more details. He studied me thoughtfully for a while and then said: 'Are you in good working condition?' Without waiting for my answer he laughed and explained that for the job in question it was important I was not suffering from any sexual diseases. I told him that I was clean and he said that next morning I would find out what sort of job he had in mind.

After spending the night on a couch in his room, we had breakfast in the cafe downstairs and he took me to a small private massage parlour in a four-storeyed house next to a shabby hotel. It turned out the hotel was a brothel and the cashier in the parlour was one of those fat ladies who always seem to be in charge of red-light places. I quickly learned that Bertrand already had a job at the parlour as a masseur. There was a vacancy for another masseur as one of the richer clients had lured one away so he could devote his time totally to her needs. Hence Bertrand's idea was that I should apply.

Women clients used to have a bath at the parlour and then many liked to be massaged afterwards by a lusty young man. The fat lady needed three masseurs to keep up with the demands and she was delighted with Bertrand for using his initiative. As soon as she understood I was applying for the post she called her assistant, Nanette, who with her husband, Josef, looked after the cleaning and tidying. Asking Nanette to take her place at the entrance she ushered me into her office. There she explained my duties, outlined how much I could earn if I gave satisfaction, and described the lay-out of the place. I quickly agreed to everything. I was in such desperate financial straits I could not object to anything. Here was a chance to stop running and get off the streets for a while. I could earn enough money to buy time so I could decide my next move.

Then she told me to undress so she could examine me. When I had taken all my clothes off she reached between my legs and took me in her hand. She studied me for some time until she was satisfied I was healthy. Then she began to stroke me and because I had not been with a woman for so long I swiftly came to a climax. She was angry and slapping me away she ordered me to get dressed. This puzzled me, but I soon found out why I had failed her little test. The massage side of the business was just a front and the customers came for a great variety of sexual satisfactions. Any man working as a masseur needed to know a few tricks to stop himself getting too excited and spoiling a client's pleasure.

In a firm voice she told me earnestly: 'You have a lot to learn, but I like the look of you.' If I wanted to earn the kind of money she had just mentioned, she said, I had to be as good as the other, more experienced, masseurs. I soon discovered what a strange life it was inside that tatty parlour. On the ground floor there were two bathrooms and two massage rooms, as well as the cashier at the entrance. On the first floor there was the women's section with four bathrooms and their adjoining massage rooms. Josef and Nanette lived on the next floor, where there was also a spare bedroom for me. The fat Madame lived at the brothel next door. Bertrand and Andre, the third masseur, had digs elsewhere.

Bertrand was a handsome blond man, while Andre was more of the dark Latin type. Of course, I was the smallest of the three – Bertrand was the tallest. To the rear of the cashier's box we had our own room where we awaited the clients. Madame decided which of us should look after each customer after recognizing whether they were regulars or not. It was easy for her to make these decisions when she knew the ladies and their individual desires, but of course some clients were new. They had usually come on some woman's recommendation but sometimes they drifted in by chance. With these strangers it was up to us to find out what kind of 'treatment' was required. Fat Madame quickly discovered at the entrance whether a masseur was needed. Most of the men clients asked for a masseuse and when this happened Madame pressed a button connected to the brothel next door and one of the tarts slipped into our building, donned a white coat, after having taken off all but her bra and panties, and dealt with the man's demands.

The baths were raised and stood on quite high legs in order to save the assistant from getting backache as he or she bent over and bathed the customer. Few women asked for us to bathe them, but the men quite often requested this service. Over the massage tables there was a mirror and there were several other mirrors round the room. The table was adjustable and we could swing it so that the client's head or legs could be lower than the rest of the body. A special hinge in the table made it possible for the masseur to open the lady's legs and give more intensive treatment and extra pleasure if requested.

Of course massaging is a recognized profession and special training is required, but we knew nothing about that. Most of the time we merely stroked their bodies, concentrating on those parts which gave them the most excitement. Starting at the shoulders and upper arms we worked up and down to their breasts very slowly. When their nipples showed their desire increasing we used to pass our hands softly over their bellies until they settled on their thighs. If they seemed to be enjoying themselves we lowered the hinge and parted their legs. At this stage some would ask to be turned on their stomachs and the masseur would enter them while matching his rhythm to the motions of his hands as he stroked their thighs and buttocks. When the woman reached her peak we had to watch without gaining such satisfaction ourselves. I soon learned how to avoid coming to a climax on such occasions.

As I was an addition to the team I thought I might be a new attraction but I was mistaken. The customers were conservative and usually asked for their usual masseur. My turn came only when Madame judged Bertrand or Andre could not cope.

My first customer was an elderly, plump lady. When she rang

the masseur's bell I was told to go in. She seemed a little shy as she asked me to massage her breasts. Soon after I began she started fumbling at my thighs. When I sprang into life she gained the courage to ask me to take off my coat. Then she half knelt and placed one of her legs around one of mine pressing her chest against my thighs. She clearly wanted us both to reach a climax. As we did she waved me away. I can still remember her crouched on the floor with a look of almost mystical joy on her face as she gazed at her breasts. As I slipped out of the room quietly I remember feeling sorry for her. There was something tragic as well as grotesque about a woman having to have pleasures in such a way.

One day we were playing cards in the waiting room when a beautiful young woman entered. I expected either Andre or Bertrand to be called to attend to her but to my astonishment they both asked Madame to let me look after her. It was only my second day and I had no suspicion that they might not be doing me a favour. When I got into the massage room she looked very friendly and inviting. She asked my name and kissed me. Then she hugged me as if I were the one to be massaged and satisfied. My spirits rose – perhaps this job was not quite as degrading and squalid as I feared! Then she dropped her towel from her and displayed the full glory of her naked body. This was too much for me. I stiffened at the sight and she stared at my rigid manhood between my thighs. Then I opened my coat and smiled invitingly. At this she screamed: 'Get out! Get out at once you dirty bastard! Leave me alone!' As she was trembling with rage, I beat a quick retreat, confused and puzzled by this amazing reaction. Downstairs they were roaring with laughter because it was well known this was how she liked to get her kicks!

It was soon clear that this place served for women the same purpose as a brothel provides for men. It gave them a chance to release bottled-up lust and to act out fantasies. And it was obviously better that emotions and desires were catered for in such a way instead of remaining stifled and causing neuroses and sickness.

Every day, I suspect, innocent people, usually wives or small children, suffer because men and women do not find release for their needs. But after a few days I grew fed up with the job. I had never been really keen on it but a couple of incidents involving a really ugly old woman who bit me savagely, and an attempt to involve me in a small orgy centring round an aged homosexual, were too much for me. Disgusted and angry, I stormed out of the parlour telling the fat madame to go to hell.

This was an impetuous thing to do but I could not stomach the work any longer. I found myself on the streets practically broke and with poor prospects. After taking the Metro to Neuilly I broke into the first reasonable-looking country house I came across. There was nobody at home and I soon picked up some cash and jewellery. After leaving the grounds I was walking along a canal when I spotted a car and motor-bike pursuing me. Without being seen by them I chucked the jewels into the water just before they reached me. It turned out the owner of the house had noticed me coming out of his garden while he sat having a drink with a neighbour. They took me to the nearest police station where they found the stolen money in my wallet. But it was impossible to prove it was not mine. As I had no identity papers I was remanded in custody and a few days later found myself locked up in the Sante Prison. I was to remain there for the next ten months.

At this time there were about eight thousand prisoners in the Sante. In some cells there were eight men who had to sleep on straw mattresses on the stone floor. In one corner there was an open toilet with a single tap above it. The window was high up near the ceiling and had bars. There was no protection against the elements in either summer or winter. Many times we awoke to find what appeared to be a layer of snow over our blankets – they were bugs – millions of them. When it was light they hid in cracks and holes but at night they attacked us. Occasionally they would be gassed in one cell but they would move to the next cell and quickly return to the one they had left. When we tried to avoid them by putting our mattresses together and sprinkling water around us, they dropped from the ceiling.

I can still smell the stench that was caused by a sleeping prisoner turning on his mattress in the night and crushing dozens of bugs. Fortunately they were not too keen on my blood but the others were not so lucky and got bitten all over. The bugs were some use, however, as they gave me a chance to get some free smokes. If anyone could produce the corpses of ten bugs on a piece of paper, they got a cigarette from those who were well supplied with tobacco. In this way I managed to get ten to fifteen cigarettes a day during the ten months.

As the food was poor and as I did not receive any parcels I had to try to get some extra by winning at chess or doing the odd favour for richer prisoners. When I first went there I had another bout of malaria. The senior prisoner in our cell reported me sick and I was lined up with about twenty others before a doctor. He merely gave me a glance and ordered his assistant to give me an aspirin and the 'treatment'. I quickly found out what this meant. I was locked in a cell with five others, along with a jug of water and one toilet bucket. They left us there for forty-eight hours. We had to sleep on the bare floor. No food was provided for the whole two days. When we were let out, only three of the original twenty 'sick' men lined up before the doctor again; the rest reckoned the cure was worse than the disease! I stood there, weak and trembling with fever. This time my condition was properly investigated, the doctor prescribed quinine, and I was sent back to my original cell.

Because of the scarcity of food I decided to devise a plan for improving our rations. The primitive toilet in the corner of my cell was central to the scheme I came up with. By now I was the senior in our cell because of the rapid turn-over of prisoners. None of us was getting food parcels. It was not difficult to persuade the others to take part. The plot was quite simple. At six each evening two corridor cleaners brought soup in a large container and while a guard opened and closed the cell doors, the soup was served up with a spoon. As each prisoner had his own plate there was no need for the guard to count the servings. As long as an empty plate appeared at the door it was filled. The soup was served as quickly as possible because there were so many prisoners and everyone was eager to eat it hot.

We had a washbowl in our cell which fitted neatly into the top of the toilet, about twenty centimetres below the rim so it could not be seen easily in time of danger. Two or three of us would stand in the doorway passing the plates to the guards and when they were filled they were passed back to two of us by the washbowl. There we would empty the hot soup into the bowl and swiftly rinse off the plates under the tap. When the bowl was full it was placed in position in the toilet and one of us would get in position to cover it if the guard's suspicions were aroused. If any guard did count the plates he would come in and find the toilet occupied and the number of plates would make him think he had made an error. Afterwards we divided up the extra soup equally among those without food parcels. The plan worked smoothly for about three months. There were some close shaves but we grew to spot the guards who counted and those who were careless. Eventually however we were caught.

A new guard took over but we carried on with the routine because we were so hungry. The strange guard looked young and innocent – but, he could count.

I was on duty at the tap doing the rinsing. Everything was going to plan until he suddenly appeared inside the cell, just at the moment I was placing the bowl inside the toilet basin. I just had a few seconds to sit over the basin. The guard looked around for more plates and then came over to me. He said: 'Are you ill sitting in such a place at dinner time?' I was just about to answer when he spotted I was sitting there with my trousers firmly belted around my waist!

As I was the senior and the author of the trick I took the blame and next morning I was taken to the Governor's office for punishment. No one could have tried the ruse before because he made me describe it in detail. While he heard the evidence and listened to my case I thought I detected the beginnings of laughter. So I started pleading that for six months I had been without proper food.

The verdict was no punishment at all. He banned all my food parcels for a month!

When I got back to my cell everyone cheered. Next day I was taken to the sick bay and the doctor prescribed extra rations and bread and potato mash for the rest of my stay in custody.

During those ten months about sixty different prisoners spent some of the time in a cell with me, and some had strange stories to tell. There was a man, a Negro from Martinique, who, driven mad by a guard, waited for three days and then managed to stick a steel pen in his eye as he peered through the peep-hole. Then there was a youngster who spent thirty days there for some minor offence and after he left we learned 'he' was a 'she'. A sister had taken the place of her brother because they were fatherless and the boy was the only breadwinner, and he risked losing his job if he did time.

Twice during my ten months the guillotine was used.

There is, in all of us, a taste for the macabre, and France is the home of the Grand Guignol. Paris is the city of the guillotine. Hangings, beheadings, lynchings, burnings at the stake, crucifixion have always drawn their morbid audiences. There isn't a civilized country in the world which, if it reverted to public executions, wouldn't have its vast audiences. The quality of being human, and of culture, is the thinnest of thin skins developed by a species which is really still one short step, that has taken a few million years to take, away from a primeval beast.

It is the usual thing for writers to describe the sweating fear within a prison at the time of an execution. To describe how, because there is a strange bond between them, there is a pandemonium among the prisoners that is their frantic farewell to a comrade.

Forgive me, but – balls!

There's a sweating all right, but it's the excitement of kids watching a western movie. It's the prickle in the scalp and the wetness under the armpits of the audience watching a gory, spine-chilling horror movie.

There's pandemonium – just like there is at the ringside when someone is smashing the face of a world heavyweight champion into his come-uppance defeat; just like there is in the football stadium when the winning goal is scored in a cup final. There isn't much outlet for letting off the steam, that stews and stews inside the primeval beast in a prison. And when it is there, it explodes.

Those writers, they've never been there. Those prisoners who have told those writers what they think it is like are being prompted by what they think the writers want to hear. If you'd pushed Freud into a prison cell, let him live there, let him be there on a day when someone was being topped, you'd have got the truth.

As it is, you have to take my word for it. And I'm only an amateur, doing my unqualified best to portray things as they really are.

In the Sante the man is led – unless they've changed things since I was there – to meet his last visitors on the day before he dies. He is chained hand and foot. I wonder – do they think he's going to run away?

But that's the way it is. That's the way they do it. And everybody knows: 'Tomorrow a man is going to die, and it isn't going to be *me*. A blade is going to slice through a neck, and it isn't going to be *my* neck. Tomorrow's going to be different. Tomorrow's going to be exciting. The tick on the wall that marks off the days is going to have an individual meaning tomorrow.'

The guillotine blade falls at six in the morning. That mystical alarm clock that is somewhere in every human skull ensures that nobody oversleeps that morning.

A man is going to die. A man? What man? Who really cares? He is a killer. He is a violator. He is a stranger. The value of his life belongs to him alone. But his death is drama to all those whose day is made tense with excitement by it.

Excitement? You wouldn't call it that? Then what else is it?

Not sympathy! Not pity! Not nice, comfortable, Christian feeling. Men locked away in vermin-infested cells do not have such emotions.

During that hour before the blade falls you may learn if you wish that there is a measurement of time that has nothing to do with clocks, with the sun rising and setting, with the seasons. Time is in the mind, where a moment may be a lifetime, and a lifetime may be an instant. You may learn the whole new philosophy that all your life, from birth to death, has all its time compressed into the moment of experience through which you are living.

For that hour moves through your consciousness like the head of a bird, in periods of motionlessness and in sudden jerks.

And in the moments before six o'clock in the morning even breathing stops. But somewhere down there below, the lifers in the cells nearest to the drama actually hear the sound of the blade falling between its guide channels, and its thud when it has cut cleanly through a human neck so that in one brief instant it is like a stick of seaside rock, patterned with red arteries instead of the characters that spell the name of a resort.

And then, they announce it. They have no bells to ring. They have no cannon to fire. They have chipped enamel plates to bang against iron bars. And – note this well – they are not deprived of the use of these.

And the sound is taken up, like a chorus, spreading as the silence did when the dead man went the previous day to say his farewells.

Premeditated, judicial execution is shockingly and unforgettably exciting. It is an experience one can also do very well without even remote involvement in.

The evidence upon which I had been imprisoned was flimsy. While I was in the Sante, a Dutch Embassy official came to see me, and I refused to apply for extradition.

This put the ball in their court and France, unlike Spain, had an extradition treaty with Holland. The law said that the Dutch Government had to prove not only desertion from the Army, but that a crime had been committed as well.

It took those ten months for my case to reach the French courts. I was finally charged with the trivial offence of stealing twenty revolver bullets found in my possession when I deserted.

I could not answer this charge. The French court found it to be proved, and ordered that I be returned to Holland. Handcuffed they took me to the Belgian border where the Dutch police formally arrested me.

I was tried by a Dutch court, found guilty and sentenced to a year and nine months, the ten months spent in the Sante to be deducted from this.

I came to a decision as yet another cell door clanged behind me. I did a little arithmetic. I looked at the situation realistically. For stealing twenty bullets – twenty-one months in prison. That worked out at twenty seven and a half days for every bullet. And that was just myself.

I talked to other prisoners, and accumulated similar statistics on the basis of their sentences and the value of their thefts.

I knew it was nonsense, and a game I was playing, but I amused myself by building up a case that said that thieving was grossly underpaid for those who were caught.

Resolution: If they got me back in jail ever again – and, face it, they would – I'd have my money's worth.

Second resolution: Think big.

It did not happen overnight, but I believe that this is when the Panther was really born.

XIV

Career of Crime

My decision to desert from the Army and try my luck in Africa and Spain almost certainly saved my life. I discovered that only twenty-three of my regiment who had been sent to the East Indies returned alive. The year and nine months' sentence was a small price to pay for avoiding such a fate.

While I had been in custody in the Sante my family had written to say my father had died. I must confess I felt no regret – only relief.

When I served my short sentence John, who was now married and a manager of a firm dealing in glassware and laboratory equipment, invited me to stay at his house in the Hague. The time with my eldest brother and his wife was a most miserable period. They had the crazy idea they could convert me to a life of piety and virtue.

I had to go along with the idea. A friend of the family, and a member of the Darbinistic Church, owned a firm producing wall-plugs and I was persuaded to take a job there. They said the firm would soon be needing a sales representative and I would have a good chance of getting the post if I worked my way up from the bottom. So I soon found myself sitting among about half-a-dozen boys twisting wire around plugs. We were paid by the hundred and my basic pay was five guilders a week. They said I could boost this to twenty-five guilders if I worked hard.

I took a small room in town for ten guilders a week and John allowed me to eat free at his home until my finances improved. I discovered quickly the chances of that sales rep's job were remote. The boss had four sons and the eldest was very keen on the business. It was clear I had been put in this ill-paid dead-end job because they felt they had me over a barrel.

My suspicions were confirmed when I challenged them about my low pay. As I was over twenty-three I was entitled by law to be paid at least thirty-five guilders a week. The boss wanted me to sign a paper confirming I got this minimum wage to avoid him having trouble with the authorities. Both my brother and his wife urged me to sign. I reminded them of the teachings of their church about the telling of lies, and pointed out the trouble we would all be in if the fraud was discovered. The matter was dropped and I never signed. This was further evidence for me of the gap between the practice and preaching of John and his plain, evil-smelling wife.

She was a dreadful woman. She never seemed to wash well enough to get rid of body odours, and she was always at me with her bible texts and sermons. As she was childless she seemed to have the idea she was carrying out her Christian duty by reforming me. But her notion of Christian duty did not prevent her from putting margarine on my bread while they always had butter. I was used to margarine as it was served in prisons – but it was an indication of their meanness. My days with them showed how they spent their time talking about the evil in the world. This obsessed them so much that they had no time to appreciate the good things in life. Their minds were as barren as their marriage.

On Sundays I used to drive them to church in their car. On one of these trips I met Mary. Her parents were old friends of my family and my sister-in-law and Mary's mother thought up the idea of inviting me to Mary's home. Her father did not approve of me. He was a high-ranking civil servant whose marriage was a failure. His wife told me later that they had nearly always slept apart and he had to practically rape her in order to produce their three children. She hated his guts for this and I suspect she was keen for me to see Mary, just to spite him. Their eldest child, a son, was in an institution for the feeble-minded, and the daughters lived at home. Mary was eighteen and anxious to learn more about the facts of life. She was small, slim, dark-haired and had marvellously firm breasts. Ours was not a deep relationship. We were attracted to each other in a purely physical way.

Her stifling home background, with its constant bible readings and sermons, had held up her sexual development. As I had been brought up practically with a bible in my cradle I was able to counter the biblical texts she used against pre-marital love with a few of my own in favour of the pleasures of life. But although I could hold and defeat her in these discussions, it was a much harder task to loosen up her body.

She had been stiffened and inhibited by her mother's constant talk about sex being dirty and degrading. It was obvious she was a virgin and I thought the best way to give her her first lesson in love was to find a suitable time and place.

When John and his wife went away for a weekend they left the side-door key with me so that I could pop in to stoke up the coal for the central heating. On the Sunday afternoon I told Mary's parents I had to slip back to check the level of the coal. Mary asked, and got, permission to accompany me.

As I had already examined the coal-stocks before going to church we went straight up to the flat. She was a little scared at first as we lay on the couch in my brother's living room. I started to caress her and in between kisses I reminded her of the texts urging us to enjoy life and love! She relaxed and gradually loosened up. Slowly I slipped off her pants and began kissing her between her thighs. Again she went very tense but then she forgot about her mother's warnings and texts and really let herself go as she writhed and enjoyed the journey to her peak.

After this we had little opportunity to be on our own. The weather was too bad to take walks and we had to rely on a rather dangerous charade in her home. In the evenings her father used to stretch out for a snooze while his wife knitted at his side. This front room was divided from the back room by a wooden partition which had glass from the ceiling to about waist-level. It was therefore possible for her parents to peer into the back room where we sat. We however devised a routine which reduced the risks and heightened the excitement. I would get up and walk out as though going to the toilet. Then, on all fours, I would creep back in, and satisfy Mary by kissing her. Then I would creep out again, flush the toilet and return to the room upright.

After a reasonable interval she would go through the same subterfuge in order to look after my needs. I still shudder in horror at the thought of what would have happened if either of her parents had stood up to search for a newspaper or a knitting pattern just as Mary had her head between my thighs!

My friendship with Mary gradually slackened off, when I got a job as a truck driver salesman with a large lemonade firm. I had to take digs away from where she lived and what with working long hours, sometimes even on Sundays, it was difficult to see her as often.

I was beginning to think it was time to get some real money by returning to the profession I was best at – thieving.

I began work choosing an area of prosperous villas. I noticed a well dressed, elderly couple coming out of a front door, presumably going out for the evening.

All the windows of the couple's house were in darkness. The

small window over the kitchen door had been left open, and so within five minutes of their leaving the house, I had already entered their kitchen.

As I slipped across the hall, however, the lights went on outside the front door. A key was inserted in the lock and I heard voices. Desperately I looked around for somewhere to hide. I spotted a coat-stand on the right-hand side of the hall, and I crouched behind it. Pulling an overcoat round me I got down behind the umbrellas at the bottom. The front door opened beside me just as I ducked down. The lady of the house hurriedly entered the drawing room and picked up a purse she had obviously forgotten. She crossed the hall, without even looking at the coat-stand and went out, locking the front door behind her. The porch light went out and I stayed in hiding until the car drove off. As I stepped out from behind the umbrellas and coats I noticed for the first time that I was soaked in sweat. It had certainly been a close shave.

Then I cheered up. My luck had changed. Downstairs there was some money in a purse which the lady of the house obviously used for her housekeeping. I began a thorough search of upstairs. I found an iron box, screwed down to the bottom shelf of one of the bedroom cupboards and camouflaged by an old shoe-box put loosely over it. The bottom of the shoe-box had been cut out and the lid glued down so it looked just like the other shoe-boxes in the row. I managed to open the iron box with a large screw-driver. There was about three thousand guilders in cash and several jewellery boxes full of trinkets. Then I left the house by the front door, as the road was empty, and went back to where I had left my bike.

As I cycled off in the cool night air I felt elated at having earned more than a year's salary in just a few minutes. Then thought: 'If luck is really on my side why not try another house?' I decided to make at least one more raid before people would start returning home after a night out, and the police patrols would be about.

My next target was a villa in total darkness. I hid my bike and went into the front garden, and around the house. I entered the house noiselessly by scraping away the lead around the panes set in a window. Once I had found there was no money lying about I concentrated on the dressing table in the main bedroom. With experience a thief gets an intuitive feeling which tells him whether the occupants are really rich or just struggling to keep up appearances. He can also tell whether they are secretive people who lock away everything, as in the case of the first house I broke into that night, or people who leave things lying around. In this house it was clear there was a fairly young couple who made little effort to hide their valuables.

I found some jewels which looked to be worth quite a bit. I was just pocketing them when I heard someone coming up the stairs. Through the crack in the open bedroom door I could see the swaying light of a torch. 'Christ!' I thought, 'another burglar! Who said this was my lucky night!' I dived under the double bed and waited, expecting to see a partner in crime creep into the room. Then I heard the low murmur of a woman's voice in the adjoining room. I had earlier glanced in there and judged it to be a children's bedroom. Now I guessed the person on the stairs was a neighbour who had promised to look after a child while the parents were out. In order not to wake the child by switching on a light she was using a torch. Eventually I heard her go downstairs and leave the house by the back door. As she was locking it behind her I crawled out from under the bed, crossed the room, and went into the next one. There indeed was a child, aged about two, sleeping soundly. Through a slight crack in the curtains I could see the baby-sitter, torch in hand, passing through the garden into the house next door. Then I saw, by the way lights went off and on in that villa, that she was climbing the stairs to her bedroom.

Then I had a daring thought. If she was the housekeeper and all alone for the night, why not try her house too? With my torch I found she had left the key in the lock on the inside of the back door. There seemed to be no better way in and by breaking a small pane I was able to reach in and turn the key. I took the risk that the sound of the falling glass could not be heard upstairs. I also took the risk that she might make another visit to see if the child was sleeping soundly. Locking the door behind me, I crept through the kitchen into the corridor. There was a light under her door and the sound of music so I was probably safe for a while. I discovered several pieces of jewellery in the main bedroom. Compared to the takings from the other two houses this loot turned out to be the most valuable of the night. The papers next day said my haul was four thousand guilders in cash and over sixty thousand guilders' worth of jewels.

The couple I rented a room from had contacts in the under-world and they gave the address of a well-known fence. He was willing to buy the lot for five thousand guilders, paying me two thousand in advance.

With money in my pocket I chatted up a girl cashier in a small warehouse in town. I had bought some clothes there and was making eyes at her while she counted my change. She grew flustered and this probably accounted for her mistake. I made a date with her for that night. When I got outside I found she had given me two hundred guilders too much in my change. As I was seeing her that evening I did not bother to go inside and return the money. Back in my room I was sprucing myself up for my date when the bell rang.

There were two policemen outside. I had left my address at the warehouse so they could send on my parcel of goods when it came in. It had therefore been easy for them to find me. It appeared that at closing time the mistake in the till had been discovered. As I had been the biggest-spending customer, and had changed a one thousand-guilder note, it was assumed the mistake had occurred while I was doing my transaction. I went through the motions of counting my change. As I had planned to give it to the girl, I told them I could not recall how much had been in my wallet. Then they revealed the missing money would be taken out of the girl's wages, and she might get the sack for dishonesty. Suddenly I recounted my cash and made a great show of remembering – yes, there was two hundred guilders too much! How silly of me not to remember before!

This was all most unconvincing and within a short time I was down at the station – facing charges of swindling. That was the end of my date for the night. I had a lot of explaining to do. They were very suspicious about how a man like me should have so much cash in his wallet. At last they released me on bail. Two weeks later, I was sentenced to two months in prison.

As the fence had not yet sold my jewellery I thought it best not to appeal and I went to jail. After six weeks the fence, however, was arrested with the jewellery on him, and he told the cops where he had got it from. I was really for it now!

They charged me with theft and the court gave me three and a half years.

Most of this time I spent in an open prison where one can work on a farm or learn a trade. I was taught how to sew clothes, and how to repair shoes and clogs.

While I was inside I had much time to think and resolved I would continue my life of crime on my release. I tried, therefore, to get as much information and as many tips as I could from fellow prisoners. One of them told me of an easy haul in a shop – and once I was released I made straight for it.

The shop-keeper used to keep his petty cash and his employees' wages in an iron box, with the key on top, in the drawer of his writing desk. The shop was near where my youngest sister lived with her husband and four children. I visited her and was invited to stay for the night. When they went to bed I said I fancied some fresh air and my brother-in-law lent me his bike. I rode round to the shop. Parking the bike in a street near by I slipped into the premises through the kitchen door. Just as I was removing the cash from the iron box, the lights went on and the old shop-keeper appeared in the doorway. I dived under his arm as he still had his hand on the door knob. Rushing through the kitchen out on to a balcony I leapt into space and crashed through a glass roof up to my waist. The old man was now yelling his head off not three yards from me. Frantically I wriggled free without cutting myself too much and disappeared into the night.

There was no chance of getting my bike back as the streets would soon be swarming with police. I made my way back to my sister's house keeping close to the gardens, and sometimes flattening myself against a door when a patrol car went by. There was only a few hours of the night left and so I did not get much sleep. Next morning my brother-in-law asked me about the bike. I told him it had been pinched the night before and I gave him its worth in cash. I had some cash left but certainly not enough to buy a false passport and to carry out my latest plan which was to go to Scandinavia.

I went back to the Hague where an old cell-mate of mine ran a butcher's shop. He was badly in need of someone to help out both with the clerical and the administrative side of the business. He gave me a small room over the shop, and I stayed there for two months working hard, and waiting for the hue and cry to die down. One day, in the spring, I ran into my sister and her husband while they were visiting the beach at Scheveningen. They told me the police were anxious to see me.

The couple who had told me about the fence now lived at Rotterdam and so I went to stay with them. Although they had given evidence against me at my trial they had also been betrayed by the fence. The fence had revealed that they had given me his address. They had been forced by the police to admit this.

One morning at about five o'clock the police called and arrested me for the shop theft. I swore I was innocent – but the old man insisted he recognized me as the intruder in his shop who had dived under his arm.

I was convicted and sentenced to eighteen months. The police had not found any scars on my legs from the glass roof, and none of my footprints in the garden around. The only evidence was the old man's testimony and the bike I had left in another street. I thought I had a good chance of a successful appeal. I could dispute the man's identification and claim they were convicting me because of my bad record.

I dismissed my lawyer and conducted my own case in the appeal court. Pleading that an innocent man does not need a better lawyer than the truth of his own innocence, I cross-examined the man in the court. I made him re-tell the brief incident in his shop. Then I asked him right out whether he could still swear, hand on heart, and on oath, that I was the burglar. He hesitated a good minute before admitting he might have made a mistake. I was released after having served nine months.

Officially I was not entitled to a passport for five years as I was described as socially unfit to have one. When leaving prison I had been asked where my next address would be. I told them I was going to stay with my mother. All my papers were therefore transferred to the nearest town hall to her home.

I had my birth certificate renewed before leaving prison. I took the certificate to the town hall at the Hague, along with passport photos, and the address of friends in the area. Within three days I had a genuine passport to help me carry out my scheme to go to Scandinavia.

The butcher's son, aged about twenty, was assistant barman at the Seven Club, a fashionable place, used by the very rich. He came up with the idea of getting me a job there as a sort of bar-accountant. The pay was ten guilders a night and I reckoned I could earn enough to live on until the money my friend had invested for me would be paid back. It was not hard work – the hours were from eight in the evening to four in the morning. It was my job to make a note of every drink which was bought and to allow for the free drinks given to the staff. International cabaret artists appeared there and a gipsy band, called Kovacs

Lajos, were booked for a season. Three beautiful hostesses were allowed to entertain the customers, who were mostly directors of companies and diplomats. They rarely left unaccompanied at four in the morning. Two of them told me they took the job because they had illegitimate children to care for, and the third was looking for a rich husband.

While I had this job I visited Louis who had been discharged from the Army after an illness. He had served in the East Indies as an officer. He had been handsomely paid off and was now a buyer for a wealthy firm. Being an affluent bachelor, he was chasing the girls again. At this time he had a problem choosing between two charming women. He was thirty-five now and he thought it was time he settled down. Both the girls, Sonia and Ethel, were anxious to marry.

I was sitting at the bar, thinking about his dilemma, and drinking a few whiskies too many, on the night I got the sack from the club.

For the past two nights we had watched a knife-thrower do his act with his girl assistant. He threw flaming axes as well as knives at her as she stood with her back against a board. At each performance this man would announce at the end of his act that he would give one thousand guilders to anyone brave enough to take his assistant's place. The bar staff were forbidden to get involved in the stage shows but each night I was tempted by this challenge. A thousand guilders was more than enough to buy me a ticket to Denmark.

On this night, therefore, having drunk a little too much, I dropped my pencil, stepped on to the stage, and declared myself ready to have the knives and axes hurled at me. There was a gasp from the rest of the bar staff. Walking across the stage I put my back against the board. The knife thrower picked up his gleaming blades and got ready to throw them. At this moment the manager stepped in. Several customers protested but he was adamant. Staff, he said, were not allowed to take part in the cabaret and the challenge was directed only at the customers. If I was so anxious, he declared, to have axes hurled at me, I would have to do it in my own time. He led me off to his office and gave me my cards.

When Louis heard I had lost my job he came up with a plan which would tide me over until I got some money owed me by the butcher. He asked me to help him choose between Sonia and Ethel. He would pay my expenses for a fortnight and if I managed to seduce either of them he would marry the other. He introduced me to Sonia, a twenty-three-year-old brunette, with Dutch parents, who had been born in the East Indies. She was an art student at the Hague. She was the same size as me and had a figure that would make even Brigitte Bardot jealous. Louis told her I came from Saudi Arabia and, having been bedding brown women in white sheets, was now looking for a white woman to take between brown sheets. She laughed at this showing splendid teeth. I guessed we had a lot in common. Louis had warned me he had failed to get either of the two into bed yet. Both of them were holding out for marriage and he was at his wits end trying to choose between them.

I dated Sonia and we went to a cosy bar. We had a few bottles of wine and got to know each other. She was certainly a delightful girl – fond of everything that was good, exciting and expensive. Her father had his money tied up in Indonesia and she had to exist on a small allowance from the Indonesian Government. Meanwhile she was trying to get a job as a secretary to improve her income. We spent part of the evening making up wild schemes for me to visit her father and to smuggle out gems and valuables. At the end of the evening she was a little drunk and I managed to get a kiss out of her as we said goodnight.

The next night we had a date in her room. Louis came too, with a bottle of Green Chartreuse to enliven the evening. After we had drunk half the bottle he went off saying he had to see his boss and so Sonia and I were left alone. This gave me a chance to see whether the legend of the Marquis de Chartreuse was true. It was said that this Marquis in, I believe, the sixteenth century became a Cardinal after a successful career as a general. He was very fond of women and he thought his new post would enable him to meet them more easily. By this time he was old and almost impotent. His court doctors concocted a brew out of more than a hundred different herbs. This drink seemed to put some new life in him. The story was that after drinking it he was able to satisfy all the nuns who were entrusted to his care.

Sonia and I certainly felt the effects of this drink after a few glasses. She stretched out lazily on the bed as inviting as I could wish. I was not slow to join her. After taking off her shoes and stockings, I removed her pants slowly and gently. Then she sat up and took off the rest of her clothes with a speed and lack of inhibition as though she were alone. I swiftly undressed as well. Soon we were both lying naked on the bed, studying each other.

Her breasts and bottom were as firm and ripe as any man could desire. Her figure was perfectly formed. She caressed me between my thighs and giggled as I stiffened there. Looking radiant and untouched, it was a joy to see her. She was utterly irresistible. I lay with my head near her knees and my thighs by her shoulders. We kissed each other. We both reached a soaring, mind-blowing climax at the same second. After a brief pause we made love again. Then she looked at me seriously and said we must not go on seeing each other. We said goodbye that night and never met again.

Afterwards I told Louis he would never be happy with Sonia as, in my opinion, she would always want luxuries he could not afford or an independence he would not be willing to allow. I still do not know whether he believed me but years later, after returning from my adventures in Sweden, I met his wife – Ethel.

Soon after this incident, in the spring of 1955, I got the money owed to me by the butcher. And so with one small suitcase and a single ticket to Copenhagen, I set off to Denmark.

XV

Secret Agent

I spent my first night in Denmark in a police cell. I was completely innocent of any crime but I had nowhere else to stay.

I had arrived at Copenhagen station from Flensburg in the early hours of the morning, when it was still dark. As I did not have much cash, I went to the police station to ask for help in finding a cheap hotel.

No suitable rooms were available and so they let me stay the night in one of their cells – with the door open. Next morning they even gave me breakfast and let me use a phone to fix up a room! Little did they know they were helping a man who was soon to become the most wanted thief in Scandinavia. Of course, I have never spent a more restful night in a cell in my life, and the irony amused me, even though I could not share my amusement with my unusual 'landlords'!

My train journey had been uneventful, but from Flensburg it had been enlivened by a tall, attractive blonde who had entered my compartment, sat down and started sobbing. As the train eased out of the station I noticed she was furtively wiping away tears while she sat in the corner by the window. When she fumbled for a cigarette, I gave her a light. She smiled weakly and said in a low soft voice: 'I'm sorry to be so childish – but I just can't help weeping whenever I make this journey.'

Her name was Magda. She worked as a nurse in Stockholm, at the Karolinska Sjukhuset. She was about twenty-four, unmarried and the mother of one child. She was on her way back to Stockholm after leaving the child with her parents. When the child was born she decided to escape from the narrowminded society of Flensburg, and to live an independent life in Stockholm. As she earned good money she was able to provide for the child's needs, and to travel regularly to her home in order to see her daughter. 'I've just left her again,' she said, 'so you can see why I have a little cry at the thought it might be several months before I see her.'

By the time we reached Copenhagen, we were quite good friends. As I alighted from the train she gave me her address in

Stockholm in case I ever arrived there and needed a friend. She also gave me the address of a cousin in Copenhagen who was married to a Dane. I promised to visit them and to write to her. It was this cousin I rang from the police station after eating their excellent breakfast.

As I spoke fluent German it was quite easy to persuade her to let me rent a room in exchange for doing odd jobs. Her husband owned a small dairy and I spent my first few days in Copenhagen sorting out empty bottles in their cellar, and taking them up to the street where they were fetched by a van. Her husband, Sven Sorensen, was a kindly fellow, full of laughter and fond of beer. He spoke only Danish, and his wife, Liv, was delighted to have someone around who could chat in German. I told them I was a journalist who had come to Denmark to study Danish.

Every night they scanned the job adverts in the paper for me, because the little help I gave Sorensen would not pay for my room and board, and my cash was dwindling away fast. Finally I got fixed up at a confectioners called Streng. The work was easy. At five each morning I had to be there to deliver fresh buns and bread to customers living quite near to the shop. These rounds were usually over by eight in the morning and I then had to clean plates and dishes left by the nightshift. A few more deliveries, a little more cleaning and my chores were over. I was able to go home at about three in the afternoon, with the rest of the day off.

I used to spend most of my time at this stage in my room studying the language with Liv. To reward them for these lessons I used to give her husband a hand when he closed the shop at six. As it was spring we often went out on Sundays in their car, with me acting as navigator. By using the map on these trips I got to learn the geography of Copenhagen and its suburbs. This stood me in good stead when I started thieving.

I also learned my way about when running errands, and delivering for Streng. Being forced to talk Danish on these jobs I quickly picked up enough to be able to move around quite freely and to feel less of an outsider.

On one of these errands I met Ginger who was to play an important part in the last stages of my criminal career. She was also to be a very good friend who helped me when, later I, made my escape from prison at Malmo. She was arranging the window of a lady dressmaker's shop, when I came in with a box of cakes. It was her birthday. She seemed so cheerful it was quite

easy to start chatting to her. She was obviously a very nice
natured woman and good-looking. She had wonderfully white
skin, a full, generous mouth, and warm dark eyes. Definitely, I
thought, a woman to see again.

At three o'clock I finished work for the day, and went back
to her shop, armed with a bunch of flowers for her birthday. I
had spruced myself up, and with the help of the flowers, soon
got invited to her home that evening. She lived in a suburb, near
her mother's house. We had a pleasant birthday party, but she
firmly sent me home when the celebration was finished. I was
delighted to pursue her, however, especially as there was no sign
of a boyfriend at the party.

My persistence paid off. I soon found out she had an illegitimate child and was glad to have an affair with someone a little
different from her previous boyfriends. Our lovemaking was a
little disappointing but she was good fun and excellent company.
I never really enjoyed sex with her because she usually arrived
at her peak of ecstasy so quickly, when I touched her in the right
places, that everything was over almost as soon as it had begun.
But she took me out, showed me the sights – the Zoo, museums
and so on – and because she spoke only Danish my progress in the
language astonished everyone who knew me.

By July our relationship was still blooming but one evening,
while Ginger was at an evening class, I met Kathy at the Tivoli,
and I knew at once we should have to split up. Like Ginger,
Kathy was to figure in many of my adventures before I finally
gave up my life of crime.

She was a small, slim blonde with a sweet, intelligent face. She
was about forty but looked at least six years younger; the sort
of youthful woman who improves with the years. I had gone to
the Tivoli as it was an exceptionally beautiful evening. Kathy
was strolling on her own, and seemed to invite my company.
She spoke English as well as German, and within three hours
we were cuddling and kissing in one of the Tivoli's many bowers,
as though we had known each other all our lives. She told me
she was divorced, worked as a secretary, and lived in a flat with
her two children in a fashionable part of the town. I took her
home, we kissed goodnight, and she invited me to dinner the
following Sunday.

When Sunday came I made some excuse to Ginger and arrived
at Kathy's apartment loaded with cakes for her children. She had
a boy of ten, and a daughter of twelve. We had a glorious day

together visiting Belle Vue. That evening when the children had gone to bed, I made my first attempt on Kathy.

I was delighted with her reaction. Unlike Ginger she was a skilled and accomplished lover. She was very experienced, knew every trick in the book, and was able to explore and arouse a man better than almost any woman I know. Her breasts were as firm as those of a fourteen year old and she knew how to use her tongue and fingers to maximum effect. I stayed most of the night but left early enough to get to work at Streng's at five.

That afternoon Liv Sorensen shook her finger at me and said: 'At this rate judging by your success with Danish girls your room will soon be empty!' At this time I laughed at the idea, but events were to prove her right. Each time I saw Kathy our affection for each other grew stronger, and eventually she suggested I moved in with her. Ginger had grown suspicious in recent weeks and had guessed there was somebody else. I told her all about Kathy and, although she was sad, she made no attempt to persuade me to stay. We parted good friends and this was fortunate, because the time came quite soon when I needed her friendship.

When I went to live with Kathy she accepted my story that I was a student of languages keen on learning Danish and Swedish. But I had already begun burgling villas around the town in order to keep up my finances and contribute to the household expenses.

The summer passed swiftly as I kept up my studies, and did odd jobs around the house while Kathy and the kids were out. By the second half of August I judged the time was ripe to steal some really big money. I knew my way around Copenhagen and the suburbs. I had made myself a bicycle from various parts picked up cheaply here and there. This would make tracing its origin impossible in case I had to abandon it after a burglary. I had a list of addresses from newspapers and magazines which told me where the rich lived, and where a burglary might be worthwhile. Kathy had quite a few friends and acquaintances so she used to be out visiting about three or four times a week. I picked these times to go thieving.

I hid the tools needed, and the clothes and shoes, for these expeditions in the loft of the tall block of flats. While exploring outside the rear door of Kathy's apartment, I discovered some very nice hiding places, easy to reach and difficult for others to find. The late August evenings grew dark earlier and earlier, and as the weather was still warm, the period was ideal for my purposes. While the rich went out for the evening their servants stayed at home leaving windows ajar to let in fresh air for as long as possible.

My first effort did not produce much. It was a nice house. I got in by breaking a pane of glass. I knew nobody was in as I had checked by ringing both the telephone and doorbell. I found only a few gold trinkets and a bunch of keys, one of which clearly belonged to a safe. It was easy to see the safe was not in the flat, and easier to find the owner's office address. I slipped out and crossed the city to his office. Again there was no sign of his safe. By this time I had to get home as Kathy was soon due back. I tossed the keys in a canal and got home just before Kathy walked in.

My second expedition was more rewarding. A servant was sitting in the kitchen reading a magazine and listening to the radio. I shinned up a drainpipe, entered an open window on the second floor, and got into the bathroom. The place must have been occupied by several women because the wardrobes were full of fur coats and dresses. It took me over an hour to gather all the jewellery from the many rooms. When I left, however, the servant was still enjoying his magazine and the music.

This theft caused a big sensation in the newspapers next day. They said nearly 100,000 kroners' worth had been stolen. They were very angry because there was no trace of the 'thieves'. At the first opportunity, when I was left alone in the flat, I started taking the stones out of their settings, cutting up the gold and putting everything wrapped up separately in my special hiding place.

By the time I had carried out two or three more raids the newspapers were whipping up fury against the mystery burglar, and nagging the police for failing to make progress. I tried several villas and flats in another part of the city but made no more big hauls. I made a few trips to another area and again I did not strike lucky.

So I decided to return to my first hunting grounds in the hope of further success. As soon as I approached I noticed some dark figures hiding in the shadows here and there. I guessed that the citizens had formed themselves into a kind of vigilante group to protect their property as the police had failed to do so. I decided to teach them a lesson and show them they could not keep me out. Throughout all my thieving the excitement of beating the odds meant almost as much to me as the money or jewels I gained. Of course, it was the cash I was after in the first place, but the thrill of outwitting my pursuers gave the real flavour to the exploits.

I left my bike outside the area and started walking in the middle of the roads. Whistling softly, I kept a close watch as I strolled past the villas. Once in a while one of the figures hiding in the dark started moving towards me. But because I kept walking quite briskly, whistling and acting as if worried about nothing or nobody, they shrank back into hiding and I was able to reconnoitre the whole area. When I found what I was after I also knew where each of the vigilantes was concealed.

Sneaking back through the gardens, keeping constant care not to step in soft earth which would leave footprints, I bent very low so that I could spot each shadow against the sky. This journey took me more than an hour before I was back at the villa I had chosen. The lights were on in the living room, the french windows leading to the garden were open, and so were some first floor windows. The walls were in such darkness I would not be spotted as I climbed a drainpipe. An elderly couple were in the living room, chatting and sipping drinks with some guests. Someone was playing a piano. Unfortunately, the drainpipes were set in the walls and could not be climbed.

The latticework around the french windows provided a way in, however, and keeping close to the walls, out of sight of those in the room, I got up to a windowsill of an open bedroom window. The piano-playing and chatter downstairs continued as I started searching. Soon I was in luck, and complete with my haul, I shinned down the lattice-work, and slipped to safety without being spotted by the outraged citizens.

Next day the newspapers announced a 'spectacular' 50,000 kroner theft – 'right under the noses of the police and private vigilantes'. Even Kathy was amazed by the news and she chattered away about how remarkable it was. I decided to lay off for a while. I thought this would give things a chance to cool off, and I also estimated that I now had enough loot to take to a fence in Paris.

Next morning as I was packing things up, and breaking apart gold pieces in the flat, the doorbell rang. I had been sitting on our large double-bed setting out most of the jewels on the sheet covering the mattress. As I went to answer the door thinking it was the postman, I hastily drew the blanket over the sheet. When I opened the door, however, I saw two men – obviously plain-clothes police.

They asked if they could come in and speak to me. My heart jumped as I bade them enter. They said they were inquiring about my visa. My permit to stay had been for only three months, and that period had been over long ago. 'We want to see if you understand the law, and what you plan to do,' said the taller one. His partner was gross – short, with an enormous paunch and squat legs. The tall one said: 'Can we see your passport?' I fetched it for him. He added: 'You'll have to come down to headquarters to make a statement, and apply if you wish for permission to stay another three months.' As I was wearing only my pyjamas I went into the bedroom to dress, and they followed me.

I kept talking in Danish to demonstrate my progress in the language. To my horror the fat one slumped down on the bed, on top of my precious haul! There he lounged with his great bottom over the loot which he and all his colleagues were so frantically searching for. I tried not to stare at him as he shifted position occasionally and seemed certain to tug the blanket off the gold and jewels and give the game away. I dressed as fast as I could, and when I was ready he got up and we left the room together. I still cannot understand why he did not feel the hard objects underneath him. I can only assume that being so heavy, and the bed so soft, they did not come to his attention.

I went to their headquarters and made the statement. They did not detain me for long so I was able to get back to the flat long before Kathy and the children returned. I had plenty of time to arrange everything according to plan. It had been a close shave but this little incident enabled me to give Kathy a good reason for leaving her and Denmark for a while. The police had told me that even though I had applied to stay I could not remain in the country while I awaited the reply. I must leave Denmark within forty-eight hours. I promised Kathy I would write regularly and return as soon as the answer to my application arrived. She and the kids saw me off at the station and I boarded the train with a single ticket to Paris.

My boss at Streng's seemed sorry to see me go. He was very sympathetic. I had not told the cops about working for him, as special permission was required to employ a foreigner without a work permit. I warned Streng about this, but he only laughed and thanked me for being so cautious.

The journey was long and uneventful until we reached Hamburg. I do not want you to think I made a point about never going on a train without picking up a girl, but trains, like air-ports, have a certain romance about them and loneliness is a great matchmaker. As we got to Hamburg an elderly couple escorted a plump, dark-haired woman into my compartment.

They fussed over her like two old chickens as though she was a teenager instead of a woman in her late twenties. She smiled apologetically as the old man asked me where I was getting off, and urged me to look after his niece Elfrieda. I have no idea why he should have thought me a suitable escort, or her in need of protection, but as the train pulled out we both looked at each other and burst out laughing.

She told me she was married to a Frenchman and lived in Provence. She had foolishly fallen in love with him just after the war. He had been in Germany when they met, a member of the Allied Forces occupying Hamburg. After his discharge he had taken her to a tiny village in a forgotten corner of Provence. Their home was attached to a baker's. He had inherited this property and they had been buried there ever since. This trip to see her uncle and aunt was the first chance she had had to see her relatives.

'I feel I'm going back to a prison,' she said. Looking back now I suppose the combination of her feelings about the fate that awaited her, and the emotions that had been stirred by her visit home, made her more daring in her reaction to me than she would have been otherwise. It also came out that her hus-band's relatives despised Germans and barren wives. As she had not yet borne him a child, they had grown apart and this made her more vulnerable to the advances of strange, sympathetic men. As the express rattled through Germany we talked away in German, except when others entered the carriage when we switched to French.

She accepted my tale about being a small-time businessman, dealing in gold and jewels – buying in one country and selling in the next. As we neared the French frontier she sensed my nervousness, guessed I was smuggling something, and offered to help me.

I had most of my haul strapped around my body but there was one bulky parcel of gold, in my raincoat pocket, which was so bulky I had no chance of concealing it. She took it and calmly slipped it down the front of her dress between her breasts.

When we had passed the frontier safely it was dark and we were alone in the compartment. She slowly unbuttoned her dress and, looking coyly at me, pressed her large breasts against the parcel and offered it to me. I could hardly accept it and just say: 'Thank you!' I felt elated at having got over the last barrier between us. I let the parcel fall to the floor, kneeled in front of her, and began kissing her breasts.

Soon we were stretched out caressing each other intimately. We were so engrossed we were not even concerned when the doors were occasionally slid open and quickly closed again. Fortunately the blinds were pulled down and the curtains drawn. Whoever it was who discovered us, it cannot have been the conductor.

When we got to Paris we had to part. Her husband's relatives were expecting her, but we made a date for the next day. I slipped round to my old haunt the Hotel de l'ABC where I met Jeanine who was still following the world's oldest profession. Next day I took Elfrieda back to my hotel room where we made love very pleasantly. Unfortunately we had to be brief because she had to catch a train in order not to arouse suspicions by being late home. She was very sad to leave so soon but I comforted her and let her take the packet of gold. This was convenient for me because I had no idea where or how to sell it.

The jewels were quite easy to sell. Goldsmiths and jewellers were glad to buy the smuggled goods I offered them. I was careful to dress as well as I could, and they seemed to accept my yarn about the items being smuggled. I learned a lot of valuable information during these negotiations. I learned a good deal about stones and their values. Although it was clear that the value of the stolen goods as claimed in the Danish papers was greatly exaggerated, my loot still brought in a nice amount of cash. It was enough to buy me a Renault van, without side-windows, which was fitted out to be suitable for a camper. I also bought a heavy BSA rifle and some fishing gear. The rest of my money I put in a deposit box at a branch of the Credit Lyonnais bank. Nobody was going to steal from me!

A few days later I left Paris because I had sold nearly all the stones, and had discovered how to get rid of the gold. It was time to visit the lonely Elfrieda, but first I decided to look up my Maquis comrades and friends in Salbris even though it was eleven years since I had seen them last in 1944. First, however, I wrote to Kathy and other friends I had made in Denmark sending them presents and telling them how to contact me at the nearest post office.

When I got to Salbris, Dede was still living with his parents, wife and family in the same house with a large garden. Although we had not met for such a long time I recognized him at once. He had two children; the elder was six at this time.

Both Dede and his father were unemployed and living on the dole. They were very hard up but they invited me to stay for as long as I wished. I was determined to help them as much as I could for old times' sake but they were proud and there was no question of my offering them anything that could be seen as 'charity'. I accepted their offer of a room and wrote to Elfrieda saying I'd been delayed.

From the day I arrived I pretended I was on a special diet so I could treat them to wine, meat and other items too expensive for their tiny income. I said the doctor had prescribed the diet because I needed to put on weight. When I travelled to the nearby town of Vierzon to have suits made to measure Dede came with me and I made sure he got fitted up as well.

When Dede saw my new car he came up with the idea of using it and the airgun to poach game. All around his house there was large castles and wealthy homes surrounded by estates literally crawling with pheasants. Each estate had at least one gamekeeper who strove day and night to protect the birds, but Dede had lived in the district all his life and knew every inch of the forests. The odds against us were not all that bad, but we always had to be very careful. Within a short while we were poaching twice a day and the family soon got used to seeing pheasant on the table. The second one I shot I wrapped up and posted to Elfrieda.

Early morning, just after sunrise, and at about three in the afternoon, Dede and I used to set out in search of game. I always drove as he did not have a licence. He was a crack shot and we made a good team.

We also shot pigeons, but the tastiest haul was something I had never tried before during these expeditions with Dede. He taught me the joys of eating hedgehogs! They were really delicious and many times we went out just looking for these little creatures in the bushes and under the roots of trees which had spread over ditches.

These hunting expeditions were not the only pleasures to be enjoyed during my stay with Dede. He was worried from the start about the problem of finding me a girlfriend. After several attempts to fix me up he was successful when he introduced me to his twenty year old niece, Lorette, who had been divorced when her husband discovered she had been unfaithful. She had one child while she was married. When I met her she had just ended an affair with a local doctor in Vierzon. She worked as a nurse in a local hospital. I was charmed by her simplicity, attracted by her soft, white inviting body and long black hair. We were instantly at ease with each other and she climbed into my bed with a promptness which astonished me. Dede's mother and family were broadminded about our friendship and I soon started taking her to and from work each day.

But when Elfrieda replied to my present of a pheasant by sending me a live turkey in a large box, I thought it was time I kept my promise and visited her in Provence. Dede and his relatives promised to feed the turkey until I returned, so I set off south to see the lonely Elfrieda.

Her home was perched on a large hill along the side of a winding country road leading over the hill to the next village. I went into the inn adjoining the baker's and saw an old man sitting at a table peeling potatoes. I asked for Elfrieda and he shouted for her. She came down the stairs into the taproom. As soon as she spotted me she gave a squeal of pleasure and began hugging and kissing me as if no one was watching. As I responded I noticed out of the corner of my eye a tall man had entered the room through the front door. Gently pushing her from me I turned and faced him. It was her husband. He had seen my car parked outside from the window of his shop. Elfrieda was obviously a good actress and a very resourceful woman. She had thought of everything and was not a bit put out by his silent entrance. 'This is my cousin from Germany,' she said. 'He has come to France to study literature and wishes to stay for a while.'

I admired her coolness and was greatly relieved when he appeared to accept this tale. I never found out whether he was fully taken in by her yarn but neither he nor the old man, who turned out to be his father, ever made me feel really welcome. It may have been because of their hostility to anyone from Germany, or just because of their indifference to her – she had of course let him down by failing to bear him a child.

Her husband, Charles, was a surly man with a miserably thin body and dark, shifty eyes. He gave me a limp handshake, a curt 'bonjour', and shuffled off to his shop. It was late afternoon. Elfrieda had made a bed up for me in a spare room at the rear of the inn. Later, that evening, when everyone was in the taproom for some wine and a chat, she invited me upstairs.

'Is it wise?' I asked, feeling rather taken aback by her reckless attitude.

'Oh yes,' she said, 'Charles may be inconsiderate but even he realizes how anxious I am to hear the news from Germany and he understands how much better it is for us not to be chattering away in German downstairs.'

She led me up to their bedroom and showed me where she kept the gold I had given her in Paris. It was clear she had closely examined the lot. The variety of jewellery – all cut up and with the gems removed – had made her guess where it had come from. If I was not a thief at least I must be some sort of international fence, she reasoned. Having helped me to smuggle once, she now begged to be taken on as my permanent assistant.

She grew more and more overcome with emotion and implored me to run away with her. I calmed her down by saying that much as I would like to pair up with her there were others to consider. Did she really think that I was all alone in this business? And I argued for her to think how foolish it was to run off and risk losing half the inheritance of her husband's parents. 'You will be needing some money of your own,' I added. 'For even this sort of crime does not pay off sufficiently to support both of us.'

She sobered up a bit at this but then she began begging me to make her pregnant. She believed her husband was sterile and she pleaded for me to give her a child. Unbuttoning my trousers she seized me and thrust herself on me. The whole incident struck me as faintly ludicrous. There we were riding up and down on the marriage bed, while her husband served drinks only five metres away beneath the wooden floorboards. She was in dead earnest about the whole thing and during my two day stay I was commanded by her to take every opportunity to plant my seed in her. I did my best but I never discovered whether I succeeded. I could not help feeling sorry for her pathetic desire to have a child after she had just made a desperate attempt to break free from her husband.

It began to become oppressive to consider the irony of the fact that she was turning to a man like me for help. I gave her a small gold pendant with the gems intact – it had not been cut up because of its size. After I left I stopped writing altogether. It would have been too dangerous, although I was fond of her. She was the sort of woman who might do something desperate like leaving her husband suddenly, tracking me down and perhaps blackmailing me into taking her on as a partner in crime. Even as I write this, I still feel ashamed of how I handled the situation.

I took the gold back with me to Salbris where Lorette had a week's holiday. We took this opportunity to travel with Madame Rousseau to Paris. She had not seen her sister who lived there for years, and it seemed a good idea for the three of us to take the trip together. Her sister was known as the Mother of the Paris underworld. She had owned a bar and brothel. She used to lend money to crooks so they could finance crimes and pay her part of the proceeds. But when Paris was liberated, her home had been burned to the ground. She had been the only member of her family to survive, and her face had been badly burned while escaping.

I left Madame Rousseau with her sister and drove Lorette down to Brussels. Dede had often said he wanted a .22 rifle. I got hold of one quite easily in Brussels. It could be detached into two pieces and so I had no trouble getting it across the border on the return trip to Paris, where we picked up Madame on our way to Salbris. Dede was overjoyed at his present. He was even able to shoot an occasional deer with his new weapon.

While in Paris I sold the gold Elfrieda had looked after so lovingly. But the price was very disappointing. My funds were getting low and so a plan, suggested by the fence who bought the gold, seemed quite attractive. He said he would pay 200,000 old francs if I picked up some watches in Switzerland. I was to bring them back to him in Paris.

The reward was not so great but I reckoned that while in Switzerland I could pull off a few burglaries and make the visit more worthwhile. And so early in December (1955) I set out for Geneva. When I arrived I took a room in an hotel, bought myself a map and started driving around examining possible properties. My chances of a big haul did not seem very great. At that time in winter, with snow all around, there was little likelihood of windows being left invitingly open. As I was a stranger in this country I had to roam at random, not knowing where the rich lived. I drove around Berne, Zurich and Lucerne for a week.

It is always dangerous to break windows and so I had to concentrate on unoccupied houses. But despite all these difficulties I managed to steal several thousand Swiss francs. One haul raised over a thousand francs, all in small coins packed in bags. This was far too heavy to carry around and so the next day I changed the coins while buying a gold watch, bracelet and an expensive camera.

I finally found the address given me by the Parisian goldsmith, and I arrived with my pockets full of gold trinkets and two large emeralds. The man had the watches ready and I hid them away in my car. Before leaving for France I also bought some perfume, and two bottles of liqueur to help me get past the customs.

When I reached the border the French customs officer asked me if I had anything to declare. I told him I had been visiting my aunt who had given me some Christmas presents. I pretended I did not know whether there would be any duty to pay or not. They asked me to show them the gifts. I opened up my suitcase and there was the liqueur and the perfume on top. Of course there was duty to pay, but they searched no further, thinking I was an honest traveller.

When I got back to Salbris I hid the watches in a deserted farmhouse nearby. It was fortunate that I took this precaution because just as we sat down to dinner a car drew up outside and three policemen got out. Two belonged to the customs headquarters in Paris, and the third came from the station at Vierzon.

They asked for me. It was soon obvious they knew I had been in Switzerland. They searched the whole house and found the rifle I had bought Dede, and my haul from the burglaries. Madame Rousseau came to my rescue and claimed the gold trinkets were family heirlooms. One of them examined the emeralds. He showed it to his companion and revealed how little he knew about jewels by announcing them to be false.

Finally they decided to confiscate the gun, much to Dede's concern, and I was ordered to report to their headquarters in Paris within forty-eight hours. My three month stay was nearly up and I did not have special permission to remain. The worst disaster had been avoided, although Dede was heartbroken at the loss of his gun. I still had the trinkets and the emeralds which I sold later to a jeweller in Paris for 150,000 old francs. When the police left the whole family was in an uproar. 'Who could have given you away?' they asked. Perhaps a neighbour jealous at the good fortune which had come to them during my visits? We never found out the answer but I reckoned it was time to leave again for Paris. By the look of things the fun seemed to be over. My holiday had come to an end; it was time to attend to more serious business in Scandinavia.

Two days later I delivered the watches to the goldsmith in

Paris, after making certain I was not followed. Then I reported to the customs headquarters. Because I had been caught possessing a firearm which I had obviously smuggled into France they questioned me thoroughly about my movements and sources of income.

I told them I was a student in foreign languages, living off some capital left me by my father. I said I had bought the rifle in Belgium and intended to apply for a licence. The sudden trip to Switzerland – due to my aunt, who lived there, being seriously ill – had put the application off. They stopped questioning me and held a muttered conversation at the far end of the room. They discussed me in a most mysterious way for some time, then returned to me, saying they wished to ask me a very confidential question. 'Would you be prepared to co-operate with us?' they asked. I said that I could not see how I could be of much help but I was willing to do what I could. They wanted me to pass on information about any smuggling to and from France if I learned about it in the course of my journeys. I could barely curb myself from hooting with laughter. What a joke for them to ask *me* to aid the police with their inquiries! But restraining myself, I told them good-naturedly that of course I would assist them as much as I could. What else could I say? They gave me a special code number and told me how to contact them by telephone. 'You are now a sort of secret agent in the war against crime!' said the senior officer rather pompously. 'In view of your willingness to co-operate with us we will not pursue the matter of possession of forbidden firearms any further. The confiscation of the rifle herewith is formal and the matter closed as far as we are concerned.'

I took down the details about my assignments and left the building a free man.

XVI

The Panther Strikes Sweden

I had promised Kathy I would spend Christmas with her and the children. We had a marvellous traditional Christmas. The children enjoyed my dressing up as Father Christmas, and bringing out lots of presents. We danced round the tree and they taught me how to sing their carols. We were a real family and I contrasted the love and warmth in that small flat with the gloom of my own childhood Christmasses.

That winter passed swiftly and pleasantly. I had not taken up my old job at Streng's. With enough money to last me until the spring I took it easy doing odd jobs in and around their home, and taking the children out. I also worked on the interior of my car preparing it for future exploits.

The rest of that time I passed studying and reading about Sweden. The language being very much like Danish did not give me much trouble and soon enough I was able to verify all I heard about the golden opportunities there from former prison mates.

Swedish burglars seemed only to dynamite safes for the money in them. They would even steal liquor but never touched jewels. The market for stolen jewellery was non-existent. Rich people in these parts simply had no use for safes or alarm systems in their homes to safeguard their valuables. This decided me to open a whole new field, a virgin one so to speak and all to myself. The Swedish magazines offered splendid material for my hunting trip. In nearly every one some rich dwelling was described minutely with pictures also. Enough details were included to judge whether it was worth a visit in the future.

When Kathy was out during the daytime I was also busy inventing some contraptions to make burglaring a little easier. One in particular needed a lot of time, patience and experiments before it was finished. I put a light hook on the top of a telescopic fishing rod. It was possible to hang this hook on the rim of a balcony two floors above me. This done I could collapse the rod, and climb the rope attached to the hook quite easily.

Once I was on the ground again, after paying my visit to the rooms above, I had a special way of retrieving the hook from the balcony rail. An exceptionally strong, but very thin, fishing line was twisted here and there through the rope so that it did not hamper me as I descended. Jerking this I was able to unhinge the hook, which was made of very light, but strong plywood. I usually managed to catch it, but if it dropped, it was so light it made very little noise in the dark. I was very proud of this contraption. It was so made as to be easily wrapped around my waist under my coat.

Each part was packed away in different places in my car. When finally I was captured these sections puzzled the police. It took them many weeks to work out how to re-construct my climbing contraption, and to learn what it was used for. When they did solve this problem they were as proud as Punch, and because they had found it so hard, they placed it on display in the Stockholm police museum – where it can be seen today.

Meanwhile I was also preparing a foothold in Sweden. During those winter months I often wrote to Magda, the blonde nurse I had made friends with on the train from Flensburg, and she promised to let me know when there was a job for me near her home. My relationship with Ginger being much less official than the one with Kathy, gave me the idea of improving my strategy. In case of emergency her address, unknown as it was to both Kathy and the immigration officials, could be an excellent place to lie low. Mainly for this reason I continued cultivating her by taking her out in the car when Kathy was visiting friends. I had installed a nice comfortable pneumatic mattress in the rear of the Renault, and Ginger never said 'no' to an evening's lovemaking. She was working shifts at a factory and on a few afternoons when the weather was fine and she had the time off, we would take a trip. It was good to know that if we felt aroused a bed was so near!

Early in May 1956 Magda wrote to say she had discovered a job. My three months in Denmark being up anyway, I had little trouble explaining to Kathy the offered job in Stockholm was just the chance I had been looking for to learn Swedish the quick way. Of course I promised to return to her after and meanwhile we would write each other and even meet occasionally whenever I could find the money to pay for the trip. Although sad, she accepted this. The day I left I would not have her see me off. This gave me the chance to transport my big trunk to Ginger's house first. After taking leave from her too with exactly the same yarn and promises, I crossed the Oresund by ferry and arrived in due time in Stockholm.

Magda lived in a suburb called Solna in a large block of flats. Only nurses from the Karolinska Hospital were allowed to live there – I was not even allowed to go in. One of the nurses, however, told me Magda was on duty till the evening. I waited until she came out of the hospital. She was with her friend Ina and was delighted to see me.

Magda was even taller than I remembered – perhaps her white nurse's uniform made her look even taller – but Ina was even bigger by a good few centimetres. Magda, slim and blonde, used padding to bolster her tiny bosom but Ina, dark and plump, had breasts to make a milkman jealous.

As male guests were not allowed in their flat we first went shopping in my car. Then the girls went home while I waited outside until the coast was clear.

Their balcony was on the fourth floor. When Magda came out and gave the signal, I swiftly entered the building with a key they had given me. Ina had the lift waiting and I reached their flat without being seen. It was a very cosy one-roomed apartment, a bedroom and sitting room combined. There was also a small kitchen and toilet.

Neither of the girls had dared to have a man stay with them before. The regulations were strict, and they risked being thrown out if they were caught. So they decided to turn me into a girl! I had a shower then put on some dark stockings to cover my hairy legs and Magda tried to make my hair look feminine. Ina glued some pads on my chest – a bra and a slip completed my disguise. We decided always to talk in whispers. If anyone came to the door I was to show just a glimpse of myself and then go into the shower-room. We agreed to speak in German so that most Swedes could not understand us.

I chatted to Magda while Ina showered and changed into a loose-fitting dressing gown. She told me she had seen the man in charge of the laundry department at the hospital and he had agreed to give me a job. Then I told her all the news from the Sorensens, and gave her a parcel they had asked me to deliver.

Ina then came into the room and began pouring drinks while Magda took a shower. She said she had come to Sweden to get a rich husband. 'I don't give a damn how old or boring he is,' she said, 'providing he's rich enough.' She was about twenty-five, a boisterous, daredevil of a woman, attractive despite her unusual height and plumpness. Magda was more reserved and inclined to bouts of melancholy. She would go silent for ages and then start sobbing her heart out.

These fits of crying were brought on by her missing her little child or by thinking of some German who it seemed had broken her heart. When she and Ina were together they were a lively pair, however, and usually up to something. Their efforts to find Ina a rich husband often resulted in a lot of fun.

As the night wore on the problem of where I was going to sleep was discussed. As the nights were still quite chilly they would not hear of me sleeping in my car. They decided, amid much laughter, to throw a dice to see whose bed I shared. Finally I found it was clear Ina had won and she lent me one of her nighties. Then we all began undressing and larking about. Suddenly Ina shot out her hand and lifted up my nightie. Making a big show of measuring me she declared: 'Oh dear! This won't do at all – you're much too small!' Then in one movement she picked me up as if I were no bigger than a puppy and dumped me on Magda's bed. She was as strong as a bull.

And so I spent the night with Magda. It was so unexpected for both of us that we did not make love at all. She cuddled up to me, sobbed a little and then we fell asleep.

Next morning I drove them to the hospital where Magda introduced me to the woman in charge of the laundry department. She telephoned the immigration officials to sort out the work permit. I went along to their office and filled in the necessary form, but it was obvious it would take some time before the permit came through. They were very short handed at the laundry and they were glad to have me signed on. They gave me a key to a flat – similar to Magda's – at the back of the laundry. After dumping my gear in the flat, I parked my car in a quiet spot, and went to use the meal vouchers they had provided me with in the canteen. That afternoon I started work hauling heavy bundles of clothes in and out of the spin driers, loading them on trollies, and pushing these into the ironing room. It was very hard work and very sweaty too because of the heat from the machines, but I did not mind this.

It was the end of June before I got a reply to my application for a work permit. They said I had to return to Holland to apply in person at the Swedish Embassy in The Hague. This meant I would have to give up my job in the laundry. I was paid off, and I handed back the key to the flat. As the weather was fine,

I started sleeping in my car. I told the girls I would go back to Holland and do as the immigration people asked. They were very sad to see me leave, and said that they hoped I would return as soon as possible. I would like to feel they did not feel too badly about me when the story of my life of crime appeared in the newspapers.

The nights were still too short for me to get into houses through open windows, so I went on a camping trip. I realized there would be all sorts of difficulties living and sleeping in the car; I thought it would be best to solve these problems out of town in the countryside. In the next fortnight I roamed around, fishing and managing to poach, among other birds, a giant turkey. Of course this huge bird was far too much for me, and it was spoiled before I had a chance to eat all of it.

About the middle of July I moved back to Stockholm to do my first 'job'. I had met a German girl at one of the dances. She had asked me to join her in a 'ladies excuse me'. We chatted during the dances and over a drink, and she let slip that a friend of hers did some housework at the home of a rich Consul, who always left Stockholm in the final week of June. This meant her friend was able to visit her relatives at this time. I had carefully memorized the Consul's name, and it seemed his house would be a good start for my career of crime in Sweden.

The Consul lived in the top flat of a very high building in Kungsgatan overlooking Kungs Treadgarden. This was good for me because, being so high up, no one would be able to spot me if they glanced up at the tall, closely-packed trees in the park. During the day I reconnoitred. The only way to get into the flat seemed to be from a house in the street behind the apartment building. Three buildings to the left of the block there was a garden which would suit my purpose. I had noticed through the windows of the apartment building that there was a winding staircase which looked like a fire-escape leading to the roof. I studied the block through my binoculars while well-hidden in a narrow passage. When I had seen enough I put the binoculars away and returned to my car.

It was now that all my preparations in Kathy's flat came in useful. I had parked the car in a street on the far side of the park so I could leave or enter it without being seen. By the time it was dark I had changed into my 'working' clothes – I was dressed entirely in black. Around my body I fitted the packages containing the tools of my trade. I carefully wiped each one clean of fingerprints in case I lost one or had to leave it behind while making a quick getaway. I knew on this job my specially designed hook would not be needed, and so I left it in the car. Into each piece of clothing I had sewn a zipped pocket which contained a copy of the car key, and some change. After putting on some thin cotton gloves I pulled an unlined leather pair over them and left the car.

Noiselessly I slipped across the park moving swiftly in my gym shoes. I entered the street at the back of Kungsgatan and went into the passage leading to the gardens. It was easy to climb on to the low building next to the garden.

I edged along the low roofs in the adjoining backyards on tiptoe until I was in front of the window leading to the fire-escape. Suddenly I heard voices behind me. I ducked down and turned to see. One of the many windows was opened and two people were leaning out, laughing and talking. After a few minutes they withdrew, leaving the window open.

I tried the window in front of me. It unfastened easily. I climbed in, closing it behind me. There was enough light on the staircase for me to see what I was doing. I went up. As I passed each floor the lift occasionally went up or down but no one could see me. I soon reached the top floor. The backdoor of the Consul's flat was locked of course but by opening a window I was able to reach a drainpipe outside. Shinning up two or three metres of pipe I got onto the roof. It sloped up to the centre of the building quite gradually, and was not too steep to climb safely.

Bent double, I went over the top and slid down the other side which overlooked Kungsgatan. I edged cautiously to the gutter and peered over, looking down at the traffic racing up and down below like streams of children's toy cars. For a moment I felt frightened, not because I was in danger of falling but because I thought I had made a mistake in thinking the Consul's balcony went all around the front of the apartment building. Gripping hard I stuck my head further over the gutter until I saw the balcony rail I was looking for. Inching round on my belly and clutching the edge of the gutter, I got into position so I was hanging only by my fingers above the balcony. Holding my breath and trying not to think of the mess my body would make if I crashed over the rail into the traffic below, I landed softly on the balcony floor – well out of sight of the people in the street.

Glancing in each of the Consul's windows I suddenly stopped

dead in my tracks. In the third window I came to I could see an elderly woman reading in an armchair beneath the intimate light from a lamp.

As she seemed to be all alone I ducked down out of sight and crept on. At last I found the bathroom window unlocked and I climbed into the flat.

Using my thin, small pocket torch I started to investigate the apartment. I kept my fingers over the torch's glass and pointed it towards the floor to make its light too weak to be spotted from outside. Before searching for valuables I tried to make sure I would have an escape route. I looked for the back door leading to the fire escape. When I found it, its key had been left in the lock. I turned it softly.

Then I had to make sure which of the doors led to the sitting room where the old lady was reading. After studying them all as I crept up the hall, I decided to peer through the keyhole of one of them. I could see the woman very clearly and hear the sound of a violin concerto playing quietly on the gramophone. After this it was easy to find the bedrooms. Hers was next to the living room. The dressing table was unlocked and I was soon able to start loading the pouch strapped round my waist. There were so many small boxes to examine; this took a lot of time, and so I had to keep checking to make certain the old lady was still enjoying her concerto. At last all the boxes were empty and I was able to investigate the Consul's bedroom. There was only some cash in a wallet and a few gold trinkets. After taking one final peek at the woman I gently opened the rear door and slipped out of the flat.

Within a few moments I was down the stairs and out of the building. I raced across the empty park, found my car and drove well away from the area to another part of town. There I parked the van and drew the curtains around the windows in the rear. Then I locked the doors, undressed, and went to sleep on the pneumatic mattress where Ginger and I had enjoyed so many hours of pleasure.

Next morning the papers already carried the news of my break-in. The evening papers that day contained a complete list of the property stolen. They claimed I had got away with jewels worth 50,000 kroner (about £4,000). As the police found no evidence of my trip across the roof they were baffled about how I had broken in. They assumed the thief had entered by the unlocked rear door but they could not work out how he had known the door would be open. The housekeeper was on holiday so could not have given him inside information, and the door was usually locked. The Consul's wife was pretty certain she had turned the key that evening when her husband had left the house. It was also revealed that if it had not been for some unexpected business appointments cropping up at the last minute, they would have left for their holiday together that very morning.

If I had removed the gems from their settings and put them, say, in a deposit box in a Hamburg bank, the loot would never have been found, and the police would remain mystified to this day. But I didn't and my fate was decided – we all run towards our destiny and cannot run from it.

I had not planned to start my thieving interest until the second week of August when it was dark by eight o'clock and the weather still warm for about one more month. I needed something to do to kill the time until then and I thought a trip to Norway could be interesting as well as beneficial. Next day I left Stockholm but went to Halsingborg first to reconnoitre Sofiero, the summer residence of King Gustav. A detailed description in one of the Swedish magazines I had read in Denmark had made this address top of my list. I had fallen in love with the Queen's diamond necklace. I had sworn to myself I would not leave Scandinavia without it. It was part of her personal jewellery and it consisted of about sixty diamonds, all of the same size and just the right size for easy selling once they were removed. She was always seen wearing it at houseparties and when she stayed at Sofiero. If I could steal it I reckoned I could sell it for enough cash to last me the rest of my life.

When I got to Sofiero I was told that its grounds were open to the public when the royalty were away. I bought an entrance ticket and, armed with a camera and binoculars, mingled with the tourists. I took pictures of anything that might prove useful when I wanted to break in, and studied the bedroom windows through my binoculars. I was not able to enter the castle, but the guards and flunkeys were very helpful. They told me details of the Royal Family's habits. After walking all round the park I had a note of the places where guards were posted. At this time the royal guards were not on duty but were replaced by policemen in white caps.

When they shut the park I left with the rest of the tourists and examined the area outside near to the grounds. That night I slipped into the park unseen by the policemen. It was quite simple to keep out of their way because their caps were easily spotted even in the dark. Inching forward on my belly, propelled by my elbows, I moved towards the castle. Occasionally I had to dive under a bush when a watchman passed on his rounds. When the coast was clear I raced across the vast lawns as fast as I could in the light of the moon. Whenever I could I ducked under trees or bushes before darting off again. My eyes were always seeking out the best hiding places, and parts of the lawn where the earth was not so soft that I would leave footprints.

Finally I reached the rear of the castle. There on the third floor with a magnificent, panoramic view of the park, and the surrounding woods, was the Queen's bedroom.

As I stood there in the shadow of those ancient walls, gazing at the sturdy-looking drainpipe which led all the way up to the balcony outside the rooms, you can imagine how excited I was. This was the path to my beloved Queen's necklace! Even now, here on the ground, I was near to the reward which would enable me to end my career of crime. No more being on the run. No more messing about under beds for a few shillings. No more racing up and down stairs with trays of cakes or sweating away in a stifling laundry. No more rawlplug factories, and no more prison cells. The route to riches and freedom was short and easy.

There was little time for such anticipation and so I set off to check whether there were guards posted close to the castle walls, or even patrolling the grounds. Sliding near to the walls in the shadows, I went on my tour of investigation. When I reached the large, white steps leading up to the terrace I stopped in complete astonishment. There, in the light coming from the drawing room windows, were the Royal Family! I recognized several of them from pictures I had seen in papers and magazines. They must have arrived that afternoon just after the last of the tourists had left the park. Now I recalled how reluctantly the visitors had departed. They must have been disappointed at not seeing their King or any members of his family. Reading Swedish was a lot different from understanding what those visitors had been talking about and living the life of a wanderer had made me forget to check the date. It must have been either the last day in July or the first of August.

Standing on tiptoe and stretching I caught a glimpse of the Queen, but it was impossible to see whether she had on the necklace I coveted so much. They were chatting and strolling about. I thought it best to retreat in case they decided the weather was so warm they would open the french windows and come on to the terrace.

After checking there were no guards nearby to the castle, I returned to the drainpipe. It was fastened to the wall by heavy plugs which made it stand away from the stones leaving a small gap. Such a pipe cried out for a man to clasp his hands around it and heave himself up!

As soon as the watchman had passed me, and would not be returning for another fifteen minutes, I grabbed the pipe, as far up as I could, put both feet against the wall, and climbed the forty feet or so up to the balcony. It took barely two minutes to reach it and once I was over the rail, the watchman would not be able to spot me, even if he peered closely. A little later I saw him passing on his rounds. The bedroom windows were closed, but a window to an adjoining room opened quite easily. With one last glance at the darkness of the park behind me, I slipped into the room. With a throbbing heart I opened the side door leading to the bedroom. As the venetian blinds were shut, it was very dark inside. Keeping the beam of my pencil-thin torch away from the windows, I made a quick survey of the room.

The bed was not made and there were some large trunks standing in the dressing room. It was clear everything had still to be got ready for the Royal Couple. Suddenly I heard voices in the corridors outside, and glimpsed a light appearing under the door. I swiftly moved to the balcony and shinned down the drainpipe as there was still five minutes to go before the sentry passed by again.

When I reached the car and began driving north to Norway I felt buoyant. The necklace was as good as stolen! In two or three weeks' time it would be there for the taking. For a fortnight the servants would put it away on time but as the holiday drew to a close they would get lazy and leave it on a dressing table or chest of drawers. Then I would return and the Queen's necklace would be mine.

XVII

The Panther is Captured

My brief trip to Norway was exciting but unprofitable. Although I could understand the language, as it was so similar to Danish and Swedish, I did not know the country well enough to know where to find rich houses. In both Denmark and Sweden I had had plenty of chances to spend time preparing my raids but here I had to act fast and hope I would strike lucky. Only wishing to cover my expenses during a short stay, I was not too optimistic, but little did I realize how quickly I would decide I had had my bellyfull of Norway.

In Oslo I bought a map and found out where the villas were. Most of them were quite unsatisfactory. The gutters were too weak to climb and the general state of dilapidation of these homes gave the impression that the rich had fallen on hard times. Little care was taken of the gardens and grounds, and the exteriors needed a coat of paint. On the second night I found a very large villa, half stone and half wood, which rose up from a sort of cliff on one side and sloped down to a wide garden and lawn on the other. It would have been impossible to approach from the garden because several women were sitting on the verandah, and in the drawing room, doing needlework. The cars parked outside and in the garage indicated it was one of those clubs-for-the-girls which married Scandinavian women go in for.

An open toilet window on the second floor seemed the only way in. To reach it I would have to climb a drainpipe running up the middle of the wall past the window and bending sharply upwards to the roof. As the first floor was made of stone there was a narrow ridge where the timber of the second storey rested. It was about five centimetres wide and I was going to have to stand on tiptoe on it. Then reaching upwards I would just be able to balance by holding on to the drainpipe.

To reach this spot I had to climb on to the verandah roof, shin up the drainpipe and struggle hard to get into the right position. As there was a drop of about sixty-five feet to the street below, and I could see the steep drop of the cliff to the side of the house, I felt as if I were mountain-climbing. As there were no street lamps there was no danger of my being spotted by passers-by. Working my way, inch by inch, I managed to move the twenty-five feet or so to the toilet window. Looking back now I still recall, with some surprise, that at such times one does not think about anything but the job in hand. I became like a kind of robot that has been programmed; the thinking part is finished and I just press on. Next day when I drove past this villa I must confess, however, that in broad daylight I would not have had the nerve to attempt such a foolhardy climb. But when it is dark one sees only half the danger.

After reaching half-way I rested as best I could, then reached the toilet window and climbed in. I found myself in a corridor on the second floor with a number of closed doors running on both sides the length of the house. There were about a dozen of these rooms. The first one led to the linen cupboard and so I tried the next. Both this and the next were obviously spare rooms. Then there were two rooms knocked into one, making a bedroom for about six sleeping children. It was nearly ten o'clock and as this was the fourth house I had tried that night, I was determined to get a good haul here.

Leaving the door to the children's room ajar. I went on down the corridor, and found several furnished rooms. Hurriedly I ransacked drawers finding cash and gold trinkets. 'Obviously,' I thought later, 'one cannot have both jewels and six children.' Just as I ended exploring the last room I heard someone coming up the stairs. The corridor was divided by a staircase and I was standing near the nursery. I slipped into the room opposite the nursery. There was so little time I was unable to shut the door and I saw a young woman pass on her way to the children's room.

As soon as she entered I went back into the corridor and crept to the bannisters. I had to go round them in order to reach the top of the stairs. Later at my trial this woman gave evidence she had spotted me as I did this. She said she had come upstairs after thinking she had heard a noise. In case one of the children had woken up, she had gone to look, as quietly as she could. After glancing in their room she saw they were all fast asleep. She had then investigated the adjoining room to see if the sound had come from there. At this moment she had seen me tiptoeing down the stairs. At the time it had not seemed extraordinary as her brother often used to slip down to the kitchen to have a snack, moving as quietly as he could to avoid bumping into any of the women

attending the hen-party. The next day, however, when the burglary was discovered she had asked him whether he had gone
for a bite, and found he had not returned until after midnight.
Then she realized she had seen the thief! She was only the second
person who ever spotted me during all my exploits in Scandinavia, and she created a minor sensation at the trial by insisting
she was certain it was me because I looked so much like her
brother. 'If he did not resemble him so nearly,' she declared, 'I
would have sounded the alarm at once.'

But this astonishing coincidence saved me, I got out of the
house via the front door and found my parked car. Next morning
I examined the trinkets and counted the kroner. Then I treated
myself to a slap-up meal and went shopping. I had promised
myself one of those handmade, knitted sweaters which all tourists
love to buy when in Norway. At the main shop for such goods
I found what I was looking for – and also discovered Ester.

She was English, about twenty-five and red-haired. As we
stood at the same counter we started chatting and soon we were
choosing sweaters for each other. A slim, well-dressed woman
with a very good figure, she behaved rather primly when I asked
her to join me for a cup of coffee. I soon learned she was single,
a private secretary to some important civil servant, and now
thoroughly enjoying her holiday. I told her the usual tale about
my being a student and sleeping in my car to save money. Gradually she thawed out and became less reserved.

She agreed to let me walk with her to her hotel before lunch,
and when we reached it she went up to her room to have a shower
and change. We had arranged to have lunch together and so I
went back to the car to get into a fresh shirt before taking up her
offer of using the shower in her room. As I had her room number
I went straight up and knocked. Wearing only a long bath robe
she opened the door and invited me in.

I soon undressed, washed, but decided the bathroom was too
narrow to dry in. Wrapping the towel round my hips I went in
search of my clothes and a place to dry in.

Probably because I was so quick she was still wearing her bath
robe as she sat at her dressing table fixing her hair. She looked
so attractive, being fresh and warm from the shower, I found
myself going up to her and kissing her impulsively. She returned
my kisses but it was obvious something was bothering her. Suddenly she turned away from me as I persisted. 'I like you very,
very much,' I said.

'That's easily said,' she replied, 'but I don't believe you mean it.'

I went on: 'It's quite true that it is easy to say these things but think how well we got on in the shop.

'We talked as though we had known each other for ages and now here we are, just the two of us alone in your room. We aren't strangers so why don't you relax and be more friendly?'

We started to kiss again and she responded more than before. It was clearly time to encourage her to go further. Kissing her and caressing her passionately her robe burst open, and I saw she wore a bra and slip. I unfastened her bras and pressed her naked breasts against my chest. She had relaxed a great deal up until now but as she saw and felt the power of my lust she tightened up and drew away from me. When I said I had no intention of doing what she suspected she said mockingly: 'What did you have in mind then?'

I replied earnestly: 'I only want to make you happy and to show how much I like you.'

Obviously she was puzzled by this but she did not resist as I urged her to trust me, and edged her nearer the bed. As she sat on the bed I slipped her pants off with one smooth movement and unhooked them from her feet. Then, urging her backwards, I knelt and assured her I would not go further if she did not want me to. Slowly she lay down and gazed at me with a wondering look. I began by kissing her mouth and moving downwards, all the while stroking her breasts, I started kissing her between the thighs. At first she made some attempt to push me away but when I persisted she grabbed my head and pressed me closer. Growing more and more excited she finally writhed in ecstasy and then soared to her climax. When it was over she looked a little shyly at me. It must have been that she had never experienced a thing like this before that made her express the wonder of it by saying: 'I am speechless!'

Touching her lips to silence her, I then eased upwards and made love to her. She urged me to be careful and then she relaxed and we both reached our peak in a glorious moment. Then we lay back, satisfied and exhausted. After lunch we strolled round the museums and saw the famous Oslo folk village and Viking ships.

That evening I told her I had to be off to Bergen. She gave me her address in London so that I could visit her. Later, when I was arrested, the Swedish police found this note on me and they had her interrogated to establish the precise time of my trip to

Norway. When it was found she had nothing to do with my crimes she was left alone.

I had not lied to Ester. I had heard about the rich ship-owners in Bergen and wanted to investigate their homes. After setting out that evening along the tortuous road across valleys and mountain passes, I stopped to have a sleep. In the middle of the night, somewhere high up in the mountains, amidst the snow and ice, I tried to get warm in my sleeping bag in the few hours left until sunrise. I was appallingly cold but when the sun burst through I felt much better, and able to cope with the last part of the journey to Bergen. When I arrived it all looked very beautiful but the city turned out to be bad for thieving.

I made only one attempt on a house. It looked promising but I nearly broke my neck trying to break in. As soon as it was dark I tried a house set on the side of a mountain. The only way in seemed to be up a drainpipe to the roof where an attic window had been left open. The drainpipe led up from a garage roof and it was luckily in the darkest corner of the house. As the gutter jutted out about fifteen inches I thought it would be strong enough to hold my weight if I had to hang from it while trying to find the open window with my feet. It was easy to climb on to the garage roof and it was also fairly simple to get up the drain-pipe. But when I reached the gutter the drainpipe jutted out sharply and it was difficult to find the edge of it with my fingers. For a time I hung halfway on the bend from one arm while I attempted to grab the gutter with my other hand. Suddenly the drainpipe broke without warning.

The next thing I remember was lying sprawled on the garage roof with a piece of broken drainpipe in one hand and wondering whether I was still alive. A window opened at the back of the house where there was some light, and someone leant out. I had the presence of mind to imitate a cat mewing and after a few seconds the window closed again. After discovering I had nothing broken or damaged I decided I had had enough of Norway.

Without stopping to sleep I drove all the way back to Stockholm. On arriving there I reckoned I was so stiff and weary that a nice hot bath would do me good. I found a place run entirely by women which really gave value for money. They cleaned, ironed and washed all my clothes, gave me a fabulously close shave and then an elderly lady ordered me into a bath tub and scrubbed me all over. Totally refreshed after this I did some shopping, had lunch and began making plans to raid the home of the King's son, Prince Karl Johan Bernadotte.

He had a summerhouse, a sort of semi-bungalow near a fjord, along a narrow, winding road. It was dark when I reached it and so I drove past the first time, having to come back. It was about twenty yards below the road, half-hidden amid the bushes and trees. Worried that my car might block the road if I parked there I drove on till I found a suitable spot to leave it and had to walk back a couple of kilometres. The drive sloped down steeply to an open garage where a Volvo sports car was parked. It was the sort of expensive, fast model to quicken the heart of any car enthusiast. As the garage was open and the keys in the ignition, the owner had to be nearby. The house was in darkness except for a light in an upstairs room where the curtains were drawn. Approaching the house I noticed the revolving windows – the lower part came outward and the upper part went inward. One was unfastened except for a hook inside, which was easily removed.

I slipped in through this window without making a sound and stood listening for any noises. From upstairs I could hear the muffled voices of a man and a woman. Occasionally there was a giggle and a creaking sound which could have been bedsprings.

The Prince was reputed to be more interested in booze and affairs of the heart than affairs of state. It seemed probably an intimate party was going on upstairs and I reckoned I was in little danger. Switching on my pocket torch I found the room was quite long. One part was furnished as a sitting room, and the other a bedroom, with a beautifully carved oak cabinet standing against the wall in the middle.

The door opposite me was ajar and I decided to close it before searching this cabinet. I almost had my hand on the doorknob when an alarming thing happened. The door suddenly moved towards me – nudged open by the muzzle of a Great Dane. Growling, the dog, as big as a young lion, strode into the room towards the beam from my torch. Switching off the beam I re-treated cautiously to the open window with the dog following me step by step. When I put out the torch, the room was only lit by the soft light from the moon and the monstrous beast stopped growling, but his ears jutted up, erect like accusing fingers, and I did not feel reassured.

With one hand behind my back I hoped to find the window-sill and make a quick dive to safety. But as soon as I formed this

plan I rejected it. The dog was so close he would have to open
his mouth to seize my legs, if I made any sudden move. Then
I found my back was against the wall beside the window.
Weak with fear, I sank to a crouching position in front of the
dog.

He was so near now I could feel his breath on my face. My
heart seemed to have risen to my throat. I was trapped! All I
could do was to stare into the beast's eyes and pray. Then to my
immense relief he suddenly squatted down on the floor in front
of me. There we sat, each waiting for the other to make the next
move. Terrified as I was, I realized my brain was still working
because I noticed the animal had not even barked. Then I remembered big dogs are prone to rely on their strength and size,
and are less likely to bark than small ones. I also recalled that
Danes are reputed to have kind natures. As I watched this dog
sitting peacefully on his haunches, I remembered the fun I had
had as a boy trying to entice police dogs away from their masters'
bikes when they were guarding them. I had learned several tricks
which enabled me to stop them making an attack. Dogs, I had
found, grew puzzled if I squatted down to their level. And in this
case it worked – the dog stayed calm and friendly.

This was all very well but my mouth was still dry with fear.
Feeling for some peppermints in my pocket I popped one into
my mouth while thinking furiously how to get out of my plight.
Then the dog started wagging his tail. He opened his jaws, licked
his lips, swallowed a few times and gazed relentlessly at me. The
taste of the peppermint gave me an idea. Not daring to risk
stretching out my hand to him, I leaned forward with the sweet
on the tip of my tongue. The dog stood up, sniffed, examined the
peppermint, drew back and then sniffed again. His head seemed
so big when it was that close I imagined he could have swallowed
my head if he wanted to. After three inspections he took the
sweet from my tongue and started munching it.

He enjoyed it so much he began nudging me – asking for
another. The next one I handed him. Then I threw a third
towards the door and while he retrieved it, I found the nerve to
follow him. As close to the door as I dared go I threw the fourth
sweet into the dark hall. He shot after it and as soon as his long
bony tail had passed the doorpost, I swiftly shut the door on
him. Leaning against the door, and breathing more easily, I
could hear him chewing away. When he had finished he tried to
open the door again with his muzzle and then, when that failed,

with his paw. I kept shushing him but as he scratched the door I ordered him in Swedish as loudly as I dared to lie down. Then he went quiet and with a huge sigh of relief I turned away. During this tense encounter I could hear the sounds again from upstairs. The giggles had changed to moans, heavy sighs and cries of excitement – it was clear they had their minds absorbed and I was in no danger.

Switching on my torch I hurriedly ransacked the cabinet in the few minutes left for me. I knew the dog would not stay quiet for long. If he did raise the alarm I was in deep trouble as my car was parked so far away. My luck was in. I found a pair of gold cuff-links, studded with two large deep blue sapphires, a gold cigarette case and monogram and an enormous pearl set in a tiepin. But there was no money, no women's jewellery and no other valuables. While the dog was still silent I slipped out of the window and back to my parked car.

As my car needed several repairs after the rough journey from Norway, and the garage said these would take two days, I knew I was going to have to sleep rough. This also meant I would have to hide my loot. There was no question of my taking a hotel room as this would entail having to show a passport when signing the register. I found a hiding place on one of the many islands around Stockholm, Djursholm. As one crossed the bridge to this island there was a junction of main roads running to right and left. On the right was a car park cut out of the rocks. The steep slope from this car park was covered with bushes and rocks. At the top of a winding footpath up this slope one could get a panoramic view of the fjord, and in the other direction you could see the edges of the Stockholm suburbs. There was a spot among these bushes where I could bury my gold and jewels. As I would have to take the car into the garage next morning I decided to spend the evening trying to add to my loot.

Driving towards Stockholm I came across a really huge mansion set in the middle of a vast park. There was a river at the back. Moored there was a large luxury cruiser with two Rolls Royce engines. As the boat proved unlocked I investigated it partly out of curiosity and partly to verify the owner's wealth. When seen from a distance the back of the house looked like a small palace. From the glass windows on the third floor there was a balcony lit up by lights from within. As there were several cars in the locked garage it was clear the inhabitants were at home but I decided, however, to have a go. I could not see if anyone was up on the ground floor because there were too many trees and bushes. I set off cautiously towards the house.

I reached the house, shinned up a drainpipe, and got to a balcony by edging along a gutter, and dropping on to it. The glass windows leading to the balcony were open, the light was on, but the curtains were drawn. Tiptoeing over and parting the curtains slightly I saw right in front of me a woman of about forty was lying in bed propped up by pillows, reading a book. A radio at the bedside was playing soft music. This probably explained why she had not heard my drop to the balcony. I let the curtain fall gently back into place.

To reach an open window I had to step on the iron joints between the panes of a glass roof. They looked quite substantial and I decided to risk the four yard trip. After swinging over the balcony rail I put my fingers in the brickwork and rested the balls of my feet on the joints. Moving centimetre by centimetre I reached the window. The curtains were drawn here too so I parted them and climbed into the room. As I landed I immediately heard the sound of a man snoring. There in a large bed at the far end of the room he lay and seemed unlikely to wake up. Shielding the beam from my torch I studied the room. On the right the door to the woman's bedroom had a light under it. On the left was an open door and to reach it I had to pass a dressing table. On the top were the contents of the man's pockets. I took his wallet, pushed the open door and entered the room which was obviously a study. The walls were covered with bookshelves up to the ceiling and in the centre of the room there was a huge writing desk.

It was covered with postage stamps and letters from nearly every foreign country in the world. There was some loose change in foreign currency and I pocketed it. The wallet contained 3,000 kroner in notes, and having removed them I put it back on the dressing table. The man was still snoring and so I went back into the study to look for a safe or more valuables. As the furniture and oak panels round the walls creaked as I touched them I did not persist with my search. The light in the woman's bedroom was still on and therefore there was no chance of my exploring there. I went downstairs and slipped out of the house by way of the front door which was a lot easier than the way I had entered.

Months later in prison I was browsing through the telephone directory of the warden's office and I discovered I had missed the opportunity of a lifetime that night. Leaving the house I happened to notice the number of the house and the name of the street. That directory told me it was the home of Thorsten Krueger, the brother of the 'Match King' Ivan Krueger. He was one of the world's leading stamp collectors and if I had been brave enough to go on with my search I would have found a fortune. This theft never came to the attention of the police because Krueger preferred not to report it in order to avoid the publicity. I learned a lesson from this raid. It is essential to investigate not only the layout of a property but also the personality of the owner before rushing to raid it.

Next day I hid the loot in the spot by the car park and as soon as it was daylight I took the car to the garage for repairs. I went into Stockholm and passed the day changing the foreign currency. I bought some new underwear and shirts. After a damned good meal I felt an urge for some nightlife. But after going to a few night clubs with that oppressive atmosphere of rationed drinks, bad artists and members of the public unable to entertain themselves, I started to roam the streets. There was only one side street where the two or three whores available were so ugly and badly dressed that only the very drunk would fancy them. Alcoholism being the natural vice of Sweden (hence the rationing) the black market flourished in alcohol and there were so many drunks about these tarts really did business by the score.

In the early hours of the morning I walked around the parks, ate a hearty breakfast as soon as the restaurants were open, and then I investigated the jewellers' shops. I had already noticed the protection against burglars was very poor. I discovered two or three jewellers with a small fortune lying about in uncut stones and diamonds which were strewn around on the velvet cushions in the windows. I thought it would be amusing to figure out how to get hold of these gems and I even went so far as to look around the inside of the shops, study the people working in them, and work out the best get away routes after a robbery.

At about five o'clock I picked up my car from the garage after paying over 1,000 kroner in cash for its overhaul and repairs. After dinner I found a place to park, crawled into my sleeping bag and went to sleep – dog tired. Next morning I had to fetch the laundry and afterwards drove into the centre of town. There was parking space in front of the jewellers where the largest amount of diamonds lay so invitingly. There was also plenty of traffic so I decided to put a plan into action. With the rear door of my car open I fired my air-gun at the window, intending to rush out, grab a handful of stones, and make my getaway, but the raid was a flop.

When I fired I had the engine running for a smooth escape but all that happened was the pellet just bounced off the window causing a puzzled jeweller to come out and investigate. I jumped back into the driving seat promising myself I would try again with a more substantial gun or a brick at some later date. When it got dark I drove off in the general direction of the rock car park at Djursholm, to collect my loot. On the way I spotted a large mansion in a quiet street somewhere far from the city centre. It had the air of affluence about it. The handforged iron railings, and the street number in wrought gold made me decide to park the car and explore. The drawing room was ablaze with lights and the guests talking and drinking were clearly too engrossed to worry about the odd sound outside. It was simple to sneak unseen through the garden, climb up the drainpipe to a balcony and climb into an open bedroom window on the second floor. Once inside the light from the street lamps made my torch unnecessary. Crossing the room I reckoned it looked too small and uninteresting so I slipped out on to the landing where I could hear the guests speaking in English.

I had just started to turn a door handle when someone began to come upstairs. Noiselessly I hid in the room and watched a female servant pass into the bedroom through which I had made my entrance. I could hear her closing windows, putting out lights, and shutting doors. By the time she reached the large bedroom I was hiding in, I was inside a wardrobe with the door shut. She finished her rounds and returned downstairs.

After searching all the bedrooms I had a large amount of jewellery and trinkets. One item in particular was interesting – a heavy silver cigarette case with a coat of arms engraved on it. I put everything in my pouch round my waist as usual. Later this case turned out to be Sterling silver and a personal gift from the Queen of England. I had raided the home of the British Ambassador but I did not realize this until I examined my treasures more closely. I got out of the house safely, reached my car and drove to Djursholm.

As I drove over the bridge the moon lit up the car park, but the spot where I had buried my loot was in shadow. I parked the car and sat there for some time making sure there was no one about. Then I took a small trowel and started to climb up the slope. When I reached the spot where I had buried everything,

I found to my horror the hole was uncovered, my loot was gone.

Frantically I scratched around in the bushes to make sure there was no mistake. Furious and confused, I thrashed at the bushes hoping to find the fruits of so many risky raids. Then I stopped charging about and realized I was not alone. Several cars screeched to a halt in the car park and policemen, in uniform and plain clothes, swarmed everywhere. Brandishing torches, shouting and running, they went checking the other cars on the car park. These were empty, I knew, as I had checked before starting up the slope.

At first I did not realize they were after me. For a minute I thought they must be pursuing someone who had just escaped. Then they began to climb up towards me. The only thing I could think of was to lower my trousers and pretend I had chosen that place to relieve myself. It was a pretty flimsy alibi but there was nothing else I could try. Then several shots were fired and I grew so alarmed I began shouting in English. Standing and clutching my sagging trousers I tried to explain to the police that I had been in desperate need to meet the call of nature. But they gathered around me and just shouted to each other in Swedish. Then one of them realized how ridiculous I looked and burst out laughing!

A senior man in plain clothes ordered me to button up and come down the slope. I had to obey. There was no escape. Police were even sliding down from the top of the rise towards me. Others were by now examining my car in which I had left my papers, money and the loot from the last burglary. The game was up. The Panther was captured in a scene of farce and confusion. Once they had found I was unarmed they drove me off to the nearest police station, where they locked me up in a cell after thoroughly searching me.

As the key turned in the lock I sank on the bunk, stunned and frightened. I reached for some cigarettes or even a peppermint but they had emptied my pockets. There was no time to think of alibis or explanations before the door was opened again and I was taken off to be interrogated. Seeing my passport was lying on the detective's desk I said: 'I'll tell you anything you want to know tomorrow. I'm far too tired to endure all these questions now. You must all be pretty tired too. Let me have my peppermints back and a good night's sleep.' They agreed and led me back to my cell, after making sure the peppermints were not poisoned.

Once back in my cell I knew there was no question of my going to sleep. As I undressed I thought frantically how to concoct some tale which would satisfy their questions next morning. I decided to tell them a cock-and-bull story about a mysterious man called Maurice. I would say I was not a burglar but a contact man who had been told to take the goods abroad. The incriminating equipment and the stolen goods in the car had been given to me by 'Maurice', I would claim. It would then be up to the police to find out what had really happened.

Next morning I told this tale and learned how I had been caught. I had been very unlucky. Some kids had been playing cowboys and indians and had decided it would be fun to pretend they had to bury the cash from a bank raid. While digging around they had discovered some real loot.

They took the jewels and trinkets to the police, who posted a lookout at the car park to watch for when I returned. He had been across the stream with a powerful pair of binoculars. The rest was patience.

Soon public opinion was aroused by the papers and the discovery of the film I had taken at Sofiero inflamed their patriotic outrage even further. The newspapers gave me the nickname of 'The Panther' because of my obvious skill as a cat burglar, and ability to scale walls. The worthy citizens recognized the police force at Djursholm was under strength and so they formed a vigilante force. Two extra locks were put on my cell door and from the window I could see the vigilantes with shotguns which they used for hunting. They were anxious I should not escape and raid their summer cabins. They were also frightened for the safety of their beloved Royal Family after hearing about the evidence of my plans to steal the crown jewels. After several weeks I was transferred to Langholmen prison where I was kept in strict seclusion whilst awaiting my trial. At the trial the evidence against me, especially the testimony of the one eye-witness, the maid who spotted me in Oslo, was damning. The police had by this time discovered how to reconstruct the climbing apparatus and the black clothes, body pouch and other gear clearly belonged to a man of my size. It was obvious to the Judge that it was more likely that I was the thief, and the owner of these things, than the mysterious 'Maurice'. They sentenced me to four and a half years.

I appealed but the sentence was confirmed. For the first eighteen months in Langholmen I moped about – stunned by the loss of my freedom and the suddenness of my capture. Although I spent this year and a half in solitary confinement they allowed me writing materials and books. I used the time to write a crime novel loosely based on some of my experiences called 'When the Fox Starts Preaching . . .' and I still have the manuscript.

I also passed the time by collecting information about Sweden. The chief Warden went to town each week with a list of books to get from the library. He never queried the titles I asked for. My interest in Swedish culture and history was not entirely without an ulterior motive – I was collecting addresses of large houses where I had a good chance of stealing treasures which were easy to sell. I planned to make a new tour of the country one day – and this time I vowed I would not get caught!

Eventually my good behaviour was awarded a removal to the main building. I was allowed to join my fellow prisoners in community life. With two and a half years of my sentence to go I started thinking about escape. It was out of the question, however, to make a break from Langholmen. Even if I got out I would have to travel more than 1,000 kilometres across Sweden to reach Denmark. In view of the public interest in me the entire police force would be on my heels. It was clear, therefore, that I had to get transferred to another prison and so I thought up a scheme to get moved to Malmo, only a short distance from Copenhagen.

When I heard about an escape plot among the Finnish safe-breakers I realized how my plan could result in a transfer. I told them I would join them but I had no intention of doing so. Their idea was simple. On Sundays all the cells were open, the prisoners roamed the corridors, and the guards went into an office to drink tea. The guards on the outside also had a rest from their duties and it was obvious that this was a good time to get over the wall to freedom. The Finns had sawed through most of an iron bar in the window of a cell overlooking the lowest part of the prison wall. Near the wall they had hidden a broomstick, a large stone and a rope. I had agreed to be the last one over the wall. I said this was not only sensible but fair. I pointed out that I was the most agile and so grateful at being asked to join them I was willing to keep watch until they were safely away.

The Sunday of the planned break-out came. Everything went according to plan. A few friends who knew of the plot walked about keeping prisoners away from the cell with the sawn bar in its window. We yanked out the bar and one by one they dropped

and the rope. Then they hurled the broomstick, with the stone
attached to it, over the wall. When the first man started to pull
himself up the rope the broomstick held firmly in place by the
heavy stone enabled them to get to the top without sliding back.

But when the second Finn reached the top, the alarm was
sounded. The other prisoners were in two minds whether to join
them or not. Then the guards started to rush in all directions. I
made sure they saw me standing quite close to the route to freedom, pointing like the other prisoners at the escaping Finns. The
third Finn made it over the top and soon I saw the loose end of
the rope slither over the top of the wall. They were on their way.

Next morning I asked to see the Governor. I asked if I could
be transferred to Malmo so that it would be easier for my fiancée
Kathy to visit me. He smiled and said: 'I suppose you too want
to escape.' Then calmly and firmly I told him that if he thought
that he did not realize how easily I could have got my freedom
the previous day. He looked astonished. Then I went through
the whole progress of the Finn's getaway. I pointed out how long
I had been near the open window with every chance of making it
over the wall. He looked thoughtful and said he would let me
know his decision. Two weeks later came the good news. I was
on the train, accompanied by two armed guards, to Malmo.

XVIII

Lust for Freedom

I had not been in prison at Malmo very long before I began planning to escape. My cell was on the top floor, the fourth, about forty feet from the ground. The staff treated me very kindly, but they had been given strict instructions to watch me with extra care. It was not going to be easy to get out.

My exploits had been so well publicized in the newspapers, everyone knew about the daring 'Panther' and the other long-stretch prisoners seemed quite honoured when I sought their help in my escape plans. I knew I needed a great deal of information before I could slip away, reach the ferry, and sail safely to Copenhagen.

First I got hold of a timetable for the ferry and learned it by heart. Then I made maps of the grounds in and around the prison, and studied them thoroughly. Next I compiled a timetable of the night guards' movements. I watched when and where they went, and I checked and re-checked from time to time to see they did not alter their routine.

For the price of a large amount of tobacco, I got hold of a saw which would cut through iron bars. It was about six inches long, and it was smuggled to me from the workshop below, where I was forbidden to go. My eager helpers also managed to get me a large piece of soap to make the sawing operation a smooth one. The soap would also make it easier to reduce the noise while I worked on the bars. I also had the promise of enough rope for my needs. It would be delivered on the day I decided I was ready to break out.

As soon as I had learned the maps and the timetable by heart, I destroyed them. I hid the saw inside my mattress, the straw inside being excellent cover for the short blade. I also managed to obtain a pair of blue trousers, a sports shirt, and gym shoes. I planned to leave behind my prison garb. I did not want to be once again accused of stealing government property. I learned this lesson after I deserted from the Dutch forces. I knew if they hung such a charge on me I could be facing extradition. My mates swore they would pass over these vital clothes when I required them. I had no place in my cell to hide them. The guards were under orders to search my cell every day. They were so efficient they even tapped each iron bar in the cell window – to test whether I had been tampering with them. They made this inspection every day but Sunday, and so it was certain I would have to escape on a Sunday.

Kathy used to visit me. It was a simple trip for her to come over on the ferry. On one of her visits she passed me a ten kroner note (about 76 pence) in Swedish money which was more than enough to pay my fare if I reached the ferry. I probed her cautiously on her visits and decided it would be too risky to ask her for any more help. She seemed too frightened to be reliable. And so I settled for getting her to pass the note unnoticed into my hand, saying I needed it to buy some extras. I did not tell her anything about my plan.

With Ginger, however, I was not so timid. I confided in her when she came to the extent of asking her to forward my trunk of clothes to Louis in Holland as soon as she heard I had escaped successfully. I intended to return to Holland from Denmark, knowing they could not extradite me just because I had escaped from prison. Then I planned to lie low for a while, before going back to Sweden. There I thought a little disguise and some false papers would give me time to make one big haul, before disappearing to South America for good.

Once Ginger was convinced I was determined to go through with my plan, she stopped trying to talk me out of it, and promised to do as I asked. When we settled this a good-humoured guard allowed us ten minutes to say goodbye in the prison doctor's consulting room. The examination table made a convenient 'bed' and so we were lucky enough to be able to make use of those few brief minutes together.

The guard, chuckling to himself, placed a screen between the door and the bed. He chortled away as he stood at his post – tickled by the notion of the joke he was helping us to play on the prison authorities. We made love as best we could. Ginger was a little hesitant at first, but soon she saw the funny side of the situation, and was relaxed by the guard's obvious amusement. Her underwear was loose fitting, and I was soon able to enter her. I have often noticed how such situations stimulate some women. If there is a danger a husband or boyfriend, or even a father will be heard on the stairs, a woman gets excited by the danger, and reaches her moment of pleasure much quicker than if she knew a whole, leisurely weekend at a luxury hotel stretched before her. She had always been easily aroused, and rarely took long to feel satisfied, but on this occasion she finished more swiftly than usual. This was very fortunate for me. I had been without love for over eighteen months, and it would have been impossible for me to restrain myself. Almost as soon as it had begun, our 'goodbye' was over. Even the guard looked a little astonished by our speed. But he soon changed his reaction to one of relief. He had endangered his job by his good-natured act.

I had planned to escape the following Sunday. It was the second Sunday in September. I had six days to go. Six days to prepare myself and make my final arrangements. Ginger insisted I took another ten kroner note. She also had a useful idea to help me get from Copenhagen to Louis' home in Holland. She had a friend who drove a truck which left Copenhagen for Holland every Monday morning. She gave me the address from which the trucks used to start, and promised to speak to her friend on my behalf. She was confident he would not refuse me a lift. I was very grateful for this assistance. Without such aid I was going to have to risk trying for a lift from a stranger when I reached Denmark. Of course I would still have two frontiers to cross but, as it was peacetime, this should not be difficult. There was still the problem of getting a lift once I had crossed the German-Dutch border, but there was a good chance her driver friend would be able to advise me about that.

The day before I was going to make my attempt I started sawing through the bar in my window. They inspected our cells just before lunch, after our daily exercise session, and I knew the next full inspection would not be until Monday morning, or until they discovered my escape in some other way. After lunch on Saturday, we finished work. The weekend's recreation began. Each prisoner started relaxing in the different ways allowed by the authorities. Some prisoners had more privileges than others, of course.

My neighbour on my left knew about my plan. He spent most of his free time downstairs playing cards in another cell. My neighbour on the right asked permission to play cards in my cell. He spent the afternoon at the door listening for guards as I sawed away at the bar. I stood on a chair, which I had placed on a table, in order to reach the bar.

I wrapped the saw partly in a piece of cloth in order to protect my hand. With my other hand I gripped another bar to steady me on my unstable platform. From time to time my look-out heard an approaching guard. As soon as he gave me the tip, we had to move with lightning speed. I had to leap down from the chair and put both chair and table into position. Then when the guard looked through the peep-hole, he saw us sitting at the table, cards in our hands, apparently engrossed in a game.

As the afternoon wore on, I became quite pleased to get the news that a guard was on his way. These brief interludes were a pleasant way of interrupting the tedium and strain of sawing away at the bar. After an hour or so I began to get cramp in my arms. It got so bad I could hardly hold the tiny blade. From one o'clock until six, I worked away until finally the top of the bar was sawed right through. Fortunately it was entirely made of iron and not steel. The bar was about one and a half inches thick. It was hard to get at it. There was little room for my hand. Every four or five thrusts with the saw, I had to pause and run the blade through the bar of the soap.

My difficulties were further intensified by the size of the window. It consisted of three rows of five small panes. The centre panes of the two upper rows opened as one, leaving a gap of ten inches by twenty. These panes opened outwards and hung downwards. The bars outside, one of which I had just sawed through, stood in the centre of each of these panes. I could not do anything with the framework of the window as that was cast iron. And so only this one square had to be sawn through. Once this was done I estimated there was enough space for me to squeeze to freedom. Many times since my early youth I had regretted being so small, but for once I was glad I was no bigger. I was certain I would be able to slide my tiny body through that ten inch gap.

After supper my neighbour was again allowed to join me in my cell. We kept up sawing the other end of the bar until ten o'clock. As the prison radio was broadcasting music, and the loudspeakers were in the corridors, the rasping sounds from our sawing were fairly well drowned. But although nearly every prisoner within ear-shot was aware of our efforts, it was essential we finished the job as swiftly as possible. Although we still used the soap to soften the sound of our sawing, the noise could be heard as it rumbled down the walls.

My 'opponent' at cards, and former look-out, noticed how much the effort of sawing through the top end of the bar had taken its toll of me, and he volunteered to finish the job, while

I kept an ear open at the door. There I rested my muscles, and listened intently. Nobody disturbed his work – and the bottom end was sawn through a few minutes before ten o'clock. We kept the bar in place with a mixture of kneaded bread and pencil shavings. Soon after this 'cementing' had been completed, all prisoners out of their cells were taken back to their own and locked in for the night.

I had been in some tense situations since I ran away from home to Paris, but I shall never forget the tension I felt as the guard, who had come to lock my cell, looked round and glanced at the window. It was open as the weather was warm. If I had closed it, I would have run the risk of arousing suspicion. The security procedure at this time of night was for prisoners to put their clothes outside the cell door, before being locked in. I placed mine in the corridor, and bade him good-night. He locked the door. I was left inside – lying on my bed. Underneath me was my escape kit. The trousers, gym shoes, shirt, and rope had all been delivered as promised. These essential items had been smuggled into my cell by my neighbour on my left. He was a corridor cleaner and therefore easily able to move from floor to floor. After the last inspection that day he had, piece by piece, smuggled everything into the cell belonging to my neighbour on the right. The door of this cell had been left open and so this part of the operation was simple. When my 'opponent' at cards returned to my cell after supper, he brought the rope and clothes to me.

As soon as the lights went out, and everything was quiet, I started my preparations for the last stage of my breakout. First I changed my underpants and vest. I had pinched extra underwear during our weekly shower, at the clothes store. Then I put on the blue trousers and sportshirt. These had been made for me by a friend in the tailor's workshop where uniforms were sewn. As the night was quite cool I was glad the trousers were made of rather thick material. I put on an extra pair of socks, and the gym shoes, which were rather too large, but I could not complain about that. I have no idea where they managed to get hold of them.

Most of these items had been obtained or organized by one man. He was a prisoner who had been present in the office when I had been transferred to Malmo. He showed immediately he was one of my greatest admirers. It was very fortunate for me that I met him at that time. During the train journey, with my guards, from Stockholm to Malmo, I had managed to regain my passport. My guards were very friendly and trusting. They treated the trip as a day's holiday. They both knew me very well. They made me give a solemn promise not to try to escape. I gave my pledge and they trusted me so much that they even left me on my own in the carriage, while they strolled down the train to stretch their legs. My prison papers, money and passport had been placed in a large envelope, fastened with a brass pin. They left the envelope, lying with my suitcase and their luggage in the rack over our heads. I took the passport from the envelope while they were on one of their strolls.

When we arrived at Malmo prison they had signed and received a receipt for me, but the envelope was opened only after they had left. Surprisingly there was no list of contents for the envelope. So no one asked me where it was. As the prisoner in the office welcomed me so enthusiastically, he seemed a man sent by heaven at just the right moment to help me. I passed him the passport when the chance came, and he hid it furtively. No one noticed this move. After this he heard about my escape plan, and he proved invaluable in getting hold of the more difficult items. He even provided some useful ideas which assisted me when I completed my scheme. A few days before that fateful Sunday, he had returned the passport, as we were out exercising together. Now, thanks to this admirer, I had, with 20 Swedish kroner from Ginger and Kathy, enough to get me back to Holland, and to save me spending the last two years of my sentence in prison.

When the guards finished their rounds at eleven o'clock, I knew the time had come. My chance of freedom was there for the taking. There would not be another tour by the guards until one o'clock in the morning. And so there was ample time for me to slide out of the window and cross the courtyard in the direction of the Prison Director's villa, which was separated from the rest of the grounds only by a low fence. Once through his garden, it was a simple matter to reach the open road, the ferry, and freedom!

I put the table into position, and placed the chair on it. Removing the sawn-off bar, I threw it on to the bed, and stuck my head out into the open air. My heart was racing, my hands clammy with tension and fear, but the chilly air calmed my nerves considerably. As I looked down at the courtyard, forty feet below, I smiled at the thought that the next tour of the guards, in two hours' time, would pass along that route, and they would have no idea that one of the prisoners they were guarding so carefully had escaped from right under their noses.

I climbed down from the chair, and began sorting out the rope which I had hidden under my blankets. One piece was almost the right length to reach the ground. It was attached to several shorter pieces. The knots fastening these pieces together, plus the knots that had been tied, would make the descent easier. I tied a few more knots at regular intervals and took the whole piece up to the window. I had knotted the end with a huge knot to give it weight. I threw this knotted end out of the window.

It was so dark I could not see how near the end was to the ground. But I reckoned that even if it was a few feet too short, I could drop without too much risk. The longest piece I had left without knots. I curled this round one of the bars. This meant I had two pieces of rope dangling out in the darkness, one with knots and one without. If I kept hold of both, and if I remembered to hold on to the knotted stretch if I had to jump, I should be able to pull the rope down after me. The smooth piece would slip easily round the bar, and there would be no sign, for the guards to see, that anyone had left that cell.

Once the rope was in place, I started to squeeze through the tiny opening in the window. As I had nothing to hold on to, up there on the chair, pressed against the ceiling, I had to go out head first. Like a high board diver, with my arms stretched alongside my ears, I tried to edge through the opening. It was soon obvious my chest was too broad, and so I was forced to start again. I then approached it sideways. I got as far as my armpits. My arms were now free to grab the remaining bars and pull.

I had little strength left after almost a day of continuous sawing and effort. I quickly realized I must stop and take a rest. The iron framework, which was only about a foot wide, cut into my ribs, pressing the air out of my lungs. It felt like a vice. Sweat poured into my eyes making them sting like hell. I rubbed them, and started to pull again. One edge to the left, one to the right, another to the left, and then to the right. Each movement was agony. Each huge effort brought so little reward. Then as the pain grew, I felt my chest just move a tiny fraction through. Gasping for breath, feeling as if a dozen daggers had been stuck in my back and chest, I was now dangling at the waist, forty feet in the air, with the yawning abyss of inky blackness below.

Everything was so silent my gasps, groans, the pounding of my heart and the blood throbbing in my ears, seemed to make a thunderous noise which would be heard by someone, sooner or later. Then I saw, at regular intervals, the rectangular shapes of the cell windows below me. I thought of my fellow prisoners who would be soon standing on their tables, gazing out into the night, willing me on, and watching me pass to freedom. I had to smile at the thought. Then I began the final stage of this part of my escape. It was, if anything, even tougher than before. As my legs were no longer on the chair, as I had to make sure I did not kick the chair over and attract attention by the noise of its clattering to the floor, I had from now on to use only the remaining strength in my arms.

I turned on my side again, using the oblong shape of the window, and started to pull and push. My hips and bottom proved less pliable than my chest. Although I pushed with all my strength, all that happened was I got stuck tighter between the edges of the frame. I had to stop to regain some strength in my arms. I clutched at the bars, and looked up at the distant, twinkling stars. Those tiny lights had a soothing effect on me as I rested. They looked like the welcoming, beckoning lights of some far off but approaching town, after many hours driving on a cold, dark, winter's night. A driver knows then the hostile, dangerous darkness will soon be replaced by the cosy warmth of companionship, and the sight of loved ones who have awaited one's return with impatience.

Suddenly, I realized with a shock I was dreaming away and forced myself back to consider my plight. I gripped the bars tightly with both hands, I turned on my side, and pushed and pushed, realizing my life and hopes of freedom depended on making a supreme effort. But all my pushing was in vain. I sobbed from the exertion. My arms were nearly without any feeling. I had to give up trying. It was no good, I could not get my hips through. It was hopeless.

Then I realized the worst part of my predicament. I could not get back either. I could never get the upper part of my body through that bloody gap. I lay on my back and took stock of my position. First I had got rid of the grey, despairing picture of total failure from my mind. Now I had to confront the probability I would be left hanging, like some wet rag, from the window, waiting to be spotted by the next round of guards. It was a ghastly farce. What a way for the notorious, the daring, the inimitable 'Panther' to end up! It was a prospect that seemed a near certainty. But there *had* to be another end to this story.

I found my brain working normally again. I had passed through despair, panic, hysteria and now I was examining each of the facts about my plight to search for a way out. I could not go forward. I could not get back. What was really wrong? Suddenly the answer came to me. It was so obvious – once I had thought of it. My clothes were keeping me from freedom. That thick underwear, those bulky hand-made trousers; it was the thickness of my clothes that trapped my hips. They would have to come off. Clutching the bar with one hand, I pushed the other back through the window to reach the top of my trousers. After a desperate, sweaty struggle, I finally managed to undo the buttons both of the trousers and the old-fashioned shorts underneath. I wriggled and pushed frantically and at last my bottom was bare and free! The cool night air caressed my skin, which seemed scalded with sores and scratches. Now I was filled with an increased sense of urgency. There was no time now to dream about warm firesides, welcome mats, hot soup, and homecomings.

Once more I turned on my side. This movement loosened my trousers even more. As I pushed away from the iron bars with all I could muster, the iron sides of the frame cut into my skin. What a complacent fool I'd been to think edging through that gap was a straightforward matter! I curved my back, stifled a scream of pain, and pushed, and pushed. Suddenly I was out!

I am certain that the final effort brought such an agonizing stab of pain, which cut into my side, I would have yelled – if I had had the breath to do so. As it was I hung in space, near fainting, saved from severe injury, or even death, only by my numbed and enfeebled arms.

I cannot tell how long I hung there. I just kept telling myself I had to find the dangling rope, and get down to the courtyard as swiftly as possible. I had no idea how long I'd been twisting and sweating up there, and for all I knew the guards might be along any minute.

Having conquered the difficulties so far, and suffered so much pain, I had no intention of being detected now. To ease the stiffness of my arms and hands, after grabbing at the bars for so long, I started letting go with first one hand, then the other, until I could move my fingers more easily.

When I thought I was up to it, I began groping for the rope. I found it. Now I took the bar it hung from with both hands, and as I was to the side of the section of the window I had emerged from, I found enough room to get my legs out and was soon hanging, full length, down, outside the bars. All that was left was to take the rope, and clamber down to the ground. But I waited. Some vague uneasiness held me back. Without knowing why, I felt for the wall with my feet. I again flung my armpits round the bars, and exercised my hands and fingers one by one. They were numb, and my muscles cramped. The hours sawing at the bar, the time spent straining to force myself through the window, had drained the last grain of energy out of my body.

But gradually this feeling of total weakness passed. The thought of the freedom that was so near, and for the taking, stimulated me. I was spurred into taking the ropes at last. As I let go of a bar with one hand and grabbed the knotted rope, and then took the smooth rope, steadying myself with my feet against the wall, I suddenly realized what had held me back before.

My trousers were still unfastened, and now sagged down below my knees. They stopped my legs parting and taking the rope between them. As I realized this, I also recognized that my plight was even worse. This situation meant the position was one of absolute disaster. As the gym shoes were too big, I could not kick off the trousers.

Slowly at first the knots came up to my hands as I slithered down. I had to try to save my neck with only my weakened arms to hold me up. My legs dangled farcically with the trousers flapping about. Like a slow motion picture showing the unavoidable impact of two cars, I careered towards the courtyard. The rope went faster and faster, burning its way through my palms and torn fingers. Halfway down, one of the ropes slipped free and, after what seemed an eternity, still frantically searching for the loose rope with my feet, I crashed into the ground below.

The impact must have knocked me out for a while. When I came to, I found my hands still clamped round the rope. It had fallen with me, just as I had hoped, and it now lay round my head and shoulders. I lay half sitting, half toppled over sideways, with my right leg underneath me. My first thought was: 'What a ridiculous mess I must look! Sitting here with my pants down, on my bare behind, looking like some lunatic playing with a piece of rope.' Next I thought of the guards and their one o'clock tour. I had had to barter my watch for my extra clothes. I had no idea what time it was. I hastened to get out of that courtyard as fast as I could. I started to get up. At the first movement, I fell back in agony like a maimed duck. My right leg just didn't seem to go along properly. Then the first searing flame of pain flashed through my leg. Panting for air I took the limp leg with both hands, and slowly straightened it out. I became aware of an ominous throbbing in my foot. Feeling along my leg gingerly there seemed to be no sign it was broken. But when I reached my foot, I felt a big lump.

It was where my big toe should have been. It bulged out of the side of my shoe. I sighed with relief. No dislocated big toe was going to stop me going out of this prison. I must have damaged it when I hit the ground feet first. Knowing my leg should hold me, I scrambled to my feet. I had to get on to the open road *now*. Later I could examine my foot in some safer place. I ground my teeth to keep back a cry of pain, put the rope over my shoulders, and limped across the courtyard.

As I left the protective shadows of the wall, I heard some muffled voices at my back; it was my fellow-prisoners, who must have heard the crash of my fall, and were now wishing me good luck. I gave a general wave in their direction, and staggered as fast as I could to the Director's villa. Luckily his fence had no spikes or barbed wire, and once over I was out of sight behind the trees and bushes.

I flopped on to the grass. I found I was trembling all over from my exertions. The throbbing in my right foot had not only got worse, there were now sharp pains shooting up my leg. Without fear of being spotted by a guard, I took off my right gym shoe. Perhaps because it was too large it was possible to do this, despite the bulge in my foot. I began to fear I would never be able to put the shoe on again. As I took my sock off, I saw, in the feeble light of the stars, my foot was already changing colour. The swelling around my toe was growing visibly. I decided now was the time to put the bone back into place.

Bending my right leg, as I sat on the ground, I pressed down on the bulge of the dislocation, while pulling the top of it with my other hand. After trying this operation in different positions, I had to stop.

Sweat gushed from my face and back of my head on to my neck. The pain was unimaginable and unendurable. I leaned back on my elbows, closed my eyes, and thought hard. Pulling away from my body I could not exert enough strength to put the bone in place. I *had* to get it back. If I failed, I would be easy prey for the police, as soon as my escape was discovered. I had little time at my disposal. I had to get the next ferry over the Oresund. At six o'clock when the ferry left, my escape should not yet have been discovered, and at eight o'clock Ginger's truck-driver would be setting off for Germany. I must get moving at all costs, no matter how much pain my foot gave me.

I sat up, placed my left knee on the flat ground, and placed my right leg forward, making the foot rest flat on the ground. Having the weight of my upper body to help me, I felt better able to exert more pressure. Again using both hands, one pressing the bulge, the other pulling at the toe; I pressed and pulled with all the strength I had. Gritting my teeth, tensing my muscles against the scorching pain, I kept trying desperately to put that damned bone into place. It was no use. It was hopeless. I could not manage it. Perhaps it was because I was too weak. Sobbing with fury, pain and despair, I sank back on the grass. At that moment, footsteps approached.

The sound came from the yard. I peered through the bushes. A guard was walking leisurely beneath the cell window I had just emerged from. He stopped. My heart missed at least two beats. He looked up for a few seconds. Then he carried on, and disappeared round the building. Until that moment I had not realized I was holding my breath. Now, immensely relieved, I fell back again on the grass.

This interval, frightening as it was, seemed to give me a boost. I started to think: 'To hell with my toe! If I could not help myself, surely some doctor would. Maybe the emergency ward of a hospital would put it back into place. A visit to a doctor or hospital would not take long, and I would still have time to catch the ferry.'

With more agonizing pain, I slowly pulled on my sock and shoe. I found a broomstick in the unlocked shed in the Director's garden. Using it as a walking stick, I hobbled along. I began to feel better, more assured, more hopeful of reaching that truck driver on time. The villa windows were still dark. I crossed the garden and reached the public road, after walking through the garden gate.

Once in the street, I had to force myself to walk in the street-lights. I brushed off some dry leaves, combed my hair with a small piece of comb I had brought with me, and started off in the direction of town. There was little traffic but, before I had travelled more than a few hundred yards a taxi came along. I hailed it with my hand. The driver opened the passenger door, but kept to his seat. I slumped into the cushions and asked him to take me to a hospital.

I began thanking my luck in having learned Swedish rather well during that eighteen months in prison at Stockholm. I was able to spin the driver some yarn about having been on a cycle trip and having had a collision with a drunken driver, who had not even stopped to help me. When he asked what had happened to the bike, I told him it was so smashed up, I had thrown the pieces in a ditch. I told him I had the car's number and would be reporting it in the morning to the police. I could not tell whether he believed me or not. But he took me to the hospital, and I paid him with one of my two ten kroner notes.

He was even kind enough to help the night sister get me inside. Medical help in Sweden is free to everyone. I gave a false name at the registration desk. I told them I was a Dane. This helped my tale about having had an accident on a cycle tour, because the Danes are notoriously keen on cycling. My story was accepted. After the GP on duty had examined me, I was put on a mobile bed. The doctor firmly announced no one must touch my foot until the specialist called in the morning. He said I could have a sedative to help with the pain, but I had to wait until the specialist arrived on duty.

Of course this was out of the question. I started telling them I absolutely had to get to Copenhagen and be at work by eight in the morning. I said I worked at the city's electricity works. Several of my colleagues, I explained, were on holiday, and if I did not get back in time, part of the city, including a hospital, would be without electricity. After stressing and repeating the urgency of my need for instant attention, they agreed to ask a surgeon, who had just finished an emergency operation, to look at my foot.

He immediately ordered X-rays to be taken. When this was done, he studied them, and then showed me I had a broken shinbone, a dislocated big toe, and two other toes broken in two places. This took several hours. It was now four o'clock. The surgeon started work on me. First he took hold of my big toe. Telling me to bite on my tongue, he jerked it into place with one short pull. Then he said it would be months before the swelling would disappear, and years before I could trust its strength again. Then he injected a needle into the joints of the two broken toes. For a few seconds the pain was quite vicious. All this time the surgeon gave me a lecture on my folly in walking with a damaged toe.

Then he said my shin would heal by itself. When the injections had had their effect, he reset the pieces of the smaller toes. Then he put plaster round my foot, leaving a hole for the big toe. When this had hardened, he told me cheerfully I could be off, on my way to Denmark to save the people of Copenhagen from hours of cold stoves and darkness.

He told me to take it easy for six weeks. He said I should see my own doctor without delay when I got home. In fact he advised my staying in bed for this time, to give my body a chance to put things together properly. Then he said goodbye. It was twenty to six when the taxi I had ordered arrived. It took me, with my broomstick, to the docks where the ferryboat lay waiting to take me to safety.

The driver got my ticket for me. I was blessing dear old Ginger for that extra ten kroner. Without it I would have been stuck for the cost of the ferry, after paying for the two taxis. He insisted on helping me aboard. There were very few other passengers. They were mostly workers with jobs in Denmark. When I was sitting in one of the chairs, the driver wished me *bon voyage* and left.

Turning to one side, so I was not seen clearly by anyone coming on board, I sat waiting through the longest minutes of my life. Just because I had a valid passport, I was by no means safe. I had to check with the immigration officials to get a visa for leaving Sweden, as well as for one to re-enter Denmark. But this would only happen if the immigration officer noticed I was not a Scandinavian. Inhabitants of Denmark, Norway, Sweden and Finland were allowed to travel from one country to another without a visa. Out of the corner of my eye I spotted the immigration officer amble through the different lounges until he passed me.

Sizing me up he obviously did not think of me as a foreigner. He gave me a friendly nod as he passed me. I smiled back. Then at that moment, as he crossed the deck to tell the captain we could sail, two men rushed up the gangplank, calling to him.

They were policemen. I could sense it. I turned further away from their view, but within seconds they were at my side, asking to see my papers. The game was up. I handed them my passport. I could have cried there and then. It had all been for nothing. All my planning, my sawing, my sweating through that damned window, my struggling to put my toe in place, my quick thinking in the taxi, and in the hospital, all for nothing. I was to be back in my cell in Malmo, when I had hoped to be driving out of Copenhagen on my way to Germany.

The two policemen helped me out of my chair, and ashore into their car. It was clear they felt more than a little sorry for me. They offered me their cigarettes as consolation. Then they told me just how bad my luck had been. It was the first taxi-driver who had unwittingly given me away. When taking his coffee-break he had chatted to the other drivers about my plight. A passing policeman on duty had heard the story. On the hunch that it might be an escaped prisoner, he rung his station. They called the prison. And of course mine was the first cell they looked into. A talkative taxi-driver, and an ambitious copper, were enough to smash my attempt for freedom. I was soon back in prison with two years still to serve.

XIX

The Running Stops

When I found the first woman I really wanted to marry – she was married already. Her name was Jo. I was back in Holland, living at Doorn, and she used to camp with her friend, Mary, on a site just outside the town. Aged about thirty, tall, slim, with a wonderful figure, she was far and away the finest woman I had ever met. But it took a long time to woo and win her, and, at least once, it looked as though we had parted for ever.

I had been released from prison in Stockholm, with a year of my sentence still to serve, on the condition that I never set foot in Scandinavia again. I was warned that if I did return not only would I have to serve out the rest of my sentence, but there would be extra added. I had been given time off for good behaviour but it had not been easy to sweat out the days after being captured on the ferry. I had gone through several moods lying there alone in my cell, counting off the days, and although sometimes I had great hopes of some future coup, which would set me up for life, often I was plunged into the blackest despair.

When they got me back to jail in Malmo I was interrogated. They wanted to know where I had got the passport, cash, rope, saw and clothes to make my bid for freedom. They had found the rope where I had left it hidden under some bushes in the Director's garden. But their greatest worry was: 'How had I obtained the passport?' They were anxious to explain to their superiors, and the press, how I had regained the passport when it should have been locked in the prison safe. At first they thought it was a forgery, but the Dutch Consul in Malmo soon confirmed it was genuine. I told them they had never believed my explanations before, and I was keen not to upset them, so I suggested they made up any tale they liked, and I promised not to challenge it. This baffled them even more, but when I stuck to my guns, they took me back to my cell.

The prison doctor ordered complete rest, and it was clear to everyone I was in no condition to try to escape again. The Director came to my cell and urged me to reveal how I had obtained the passport, but I kept to my line that it was up to them to find a suitable cover-story. He was furious. He said that for at least a month I was to be in solitary confinement, without books, visitors, writing paper or tobacco. So there I was left, with nothing to do but gaze at the ceiling, and plan my future.

After a period of gloom when all seemed lost, and the bad luck which ended my escape-bid appeared a sign that I would never do the big job that would fix me up for life, I began to think more constructively. Soon I was viewing my re-capture as an unfortunate set-back rather than the end of the world. I realized my toes would heal and I could get some strength back in the big one by exercising it each day. I recognized I still had two years to serve, but I grew more confident I could pull off a really big haul.

I still had some loot hidden in Denmark and I planned to use it to buy a boat. When they let me read again I could study navigation, and I reckoned I could slip in and out of Sweden making a few break-ins, and leaving loaded with treasure. This idea seemed so attractive, as the days went by I was enthusiastically filling in the details in my mind. When they took the plaster off and sent me to the top security wing at Stockholm, I was able to start a correspondence course in coastal navigation. With the help of books from the public library I was able to pass this exam, and I began feeling more confident about the future.

They soon saw my conduct was exemplary and they relaxed their restrictions to allow me to play chess or bridge at the weekends with other prisoners. During the week I worked with Fred, a British-born, naturalized Swede, who had been a skin-diver. We earned quite a bit making toys and I was able to use this money to pay my course fees, and buy books which were unobtainable at the library. Fred had nearly murdered his brother-in-law and had been given a year's stretch. He had escaped, been captured, and as a punishment been put into the security wing. We became very close friends. He had married a Swedish girl, and they had two children. One night returning from a diving job it seemed she had left him for another man. Her brother had always hated him, and he started to jeer at Fred for being unable to keep her happy. This was too much for Fred who was very strong and fit. He flew into a terrible rage and beat up his brother-in-law to within an inch of his life.

Soon I decided to tell him about my plan, and we agreed to set up a salvage business together. We thought we would make a fortune diving for sunken treasures on the bed of the seven seas.

I disclosed my scheme for returning to Sweden and we estimated we could buy the equipment for our business venture out of the proceeds from robberies. I already had addresses which looked promising enough to raise the sum needed. There was the Hallwylske Museum in Stockholm which had been given to the Swedish State by the late Countess of Hallwyll, one of the richest women of her day. I had incomplete details of the museum's lay-out but the catalogue showed where the valuables were. The Countess had insisted that all the items must be kept where she had left them. Her jewellery, for example, was still laid out on the dressing table and was worth several million kroner. Then I knew of a summerhouse owned by Marguerita Wennergren. It was up in the Stockholm Skargard and among the many attractions there was a complete dinner set for twenty-four people, all in solid gold. I also had on my list the jewels of Princess Ann, as well as Ann-Ida Bostrom; the famous Stephanson stamp collection, housed at Huseby; and the summerhouse belonging to Sarah Leander, which was easily reached from the sea. There were rumours that she had in her cellar some of the treasures hoarded by Hermann Goering. These jewels and works of art had vanished mysteriously after the war. I even had a plan to break into the tombs of a mediaeval family who were said to have been buried with their jewels. Freddy was not a thief, but he agreed it was a waste to leave such wealth lying around, unused by anyone. If I could pull off any of these raids we would have enough cash to realize all our dreams.

He was released about six months after we met, and I grew depressed again when he was gone. He was the first real friend I had made inside, and, left on my own, I started to grow suspicious and cynical. I thought perhaps I had been a fool to confide in him and I knew I had to occupy my mind to shake off this melancholy. I took out the manuscript of 'When the Fox starts preaching . . .' and began revising and re-writing whole chapters. Gradually I got over my moodiness.

Soon I made new friends. A rich, but crooked stable-owner, a bank robber, and a young safe-breaker, asked me to make up a four at bridge. For about five months I worked with each of them during the days, and played cards with them at the weekends. Although I got to know them well, I never felt I could confide my secret to them. They, however, talked freely about themselves, and their lives were interesting enough to help pass the days.

Then came the good news of my release. I was taken to the airport amid some fuss and massive press coverage. They took pictures as I entered the plane. And I heard later the stories were carried at some length, with editorials saying how the Swedes could sleep soundly as their cash and jewels were safe from the infamous 'Panther'. When I reached Amsterdam they confiscated my passport but said I was free to move around Holland. I had kept in touch with Louis while I had been in both Swedish prisons, and he met me at the airport. He drove me to the Hague where he lived with his wife and two-year-old son. I soon got a job as a sales representative for a large international engineering firm. My salary was 400 guilders a month with a four per cent commission on any orders I got. Louis and his wife were very sympathetic and helpful. They let me stay with them for a month until I had my first pay-cheque. Then I moved to a small room in Doorn to be nearer my office.

It was very hard work. As I had no car I travelled by train and usually rented a bicycle when I reached the station. Soaked when it rained, frozen in the winter, dripping with sweat when it was hot, I biked around the factory areas in search of orders. I was quite successful and my boss was satisfied with my efforts. Although I was so busy, and often exhausted, I did not for a moment forget my scheme to go into business with Freddy. I kept in touch with both him and Kathy. They were happy and doing well. He had got a diving job with the Government, and she sent her love, promising to visit me as soon as she could get a short holiday from her job as a secretary in Copenhagen.

In order to be better prepared to carry out my plans I had to get a new passport. It would have been hopeless to apply for one in the normal way. They had told me this was out of the question for at least three years. Luckily I knew how to get round this. This was one of the reasons for my moving to Doorn. Soon after settling in I went to the Town Hall and asked for my birth certificate. In order to provide this my papers had to be sent from The Hague. On my next business trip to the Hague I applied there for a passport saying I had moved back into the area again. I gave my brother's address, paid the necessary charge, provided the photographs, and within ten days heard from my sister-in-law an official envelope had arrived asking me to come to the Town Hall to pick up my passport. I must have been the happiest man in town the day I stood there watching the clerk witness my signature on the new passport.

It was soon after this that I met Jo. I had contacted a large firm at Rotterdam and was expecting to settle a big order of more than a million guilders. The deal was taking some time to arrange and so my boss decided to take a fortnight's holiday in Switzerland – leaving me in charge, helped by his son, Charlie, who was a bright young man of about twenty. Charlie wanted to be a painter and played the piano in his spare time. His father said he should look after the house while I stayed in the office (which was part of the same villa) in order to answer the telephone and keep the business ticking over. I was also supposed to look after administration and keep the store room tidy. I stood to gain nearly 40,000 guilders when the transaction was completed with the firm in Rotterdam. We were all very excited about it.

While I had been staying at Doorn I had met a man called Walter who was in his early thirties, and a bachelor like me. At the weekend we used to go out dancing or walking in the many woods in the area. He told me of a camping-site nearby and said there were two married women, Mary and Jo, who used to camp there every year throughout the summer. They had no children, and Mary was his girlfriend. Both were in their mid-thirties. Mary was plump, and not very bright.

But, as I have said, Jo was a different proposition. Although her friend often spent the night with Walter, when her husband was away, Jo was faithful to her husband, an ugly, loutish drunk called Tim. She used to shake her glorious long, brown hair and join in the fun with the rest of us, but when bedtime came she managed to sleep alone. It was hard to understand her fidelity to her husband, not only was he disgusting and uncouth he also beat her up if she did not jump to obey him, or if she failed to have any housekeeping money left to supplement his bouts of drinking. I never heard her complain.

The notion of leaving this bastard never seemed to enter her mind. Tim and Mary's husband, Donald, worked as mechanics in Rotterdam, and came to the site only at the weekends. After meeting her I quickly decided she was the most wonderful woman I had ever met – I worshipped her. She seemed the living symbol of everything that was pure and honest in the world. I even (and this still astonishes me) adored her without feeling the urge to sleep with her when we first met.

My feelings must have showed because Tim grew very jealous. Towering above me, he used to sneer and give me menacing looks, but he never raised his fists to me or to Jo, while I was about. It is probable he feared I would break his fingers as easily as I had once – while we were all horsing around – lifted his huge bulk on my shoulder and dumped him on the ground much harder than I had intended. During the week, while the husbands were at work, and Mary and Walter were in bed, Jo and I used to take a stroll through the woods and have long talks. I had no idea whether she really liked me or just liked talking to me.

But we soon became good friends. When my boss took the fortnight off, while we waited for the Rotterdam deal to come through, I introduced Charlie to her and Mary. He immediately fell head-over-heels in love with Jo, which rather amused Jo and I because of the moonstruck way he behaved. Charlie invited us to his father's house and the women helped us to tidy up. They even cleaned and cooked for us. One evening, as we all sat there sipping cold beers, my boss returned unexpectedly. Ignoring my attempts to introduce him properly, he scolded Charlie for having guests, ordered the girls out of the house, and gave me the sack.

Next day I went and pleaded with him to see reason, but he would not listen. He said I had abused his trust by leaving the office while he was away, without telling him, and he would not take me back. I refused to lie down under such an injustice. Luckily I had had the sense to join the union some time before and our dispute reached the industrial court. He was fined and forced not only to pay me three months' salary but also what would be owed me when the Rotterdam deal came off. Unfortunately it fell through, but at least I had cleared my name and I had in my pocket some honest money for a change. There was enough to tide me over for a month or six weeks while I was looking for another job.

By now it was July, 1960 and Kathy sent me a telegram announcing she would soon be arriving. I met her at the station, and took her to my room. I had told my landlady she was my fiancée and she raised no objection to our sharing a room. Jo, however, reacted rather strangely when I told her about my girlfriend. Later she told me how jealous she had been and admitted she had felt both guilty and silly about it. But for the time I put thoughts of Jo out of my mind and dedicated all my attention to Kathy. While I had been writing to her I had not mentioned the jewels I had hidden in her flat. I had told her about them when she visited me at Malmo but I was afraid to talk about them in the letters in case the cops were opening the correspondence. She had not known the loot was there when I left to see Magda in Stockholm.

As we had not seen each other for so long our first thoughts were to satisfy our passions and I did not say anything about the jewels. But gradually, in what I thought was a diplomatic way, I worked the conversation round to this problem. She reacted in a most unexpected way. First she denied knowing anything about the jewels, then, when I pressed the point, she burst into tears and said I was only interested in her because of the loot I had left behind. This was nonsense, of course, as we had been friends long before I hid the valuables in her flat. But there was no reasoning with her. She got up, put on her coat and announced she was going home rather than discuss the matter further. Still sobbing, she packed and I took her to the station. After having got her tickets there were still several hours to go before the train came in, but I was so angry I left her to sit it out in the waiting room.

Back in my room I thought frantically how to solve this problem. I decided to write to Fred and ask him to investigate what had happened. I finished the letter but went to bed before posting it. At breakfast however my landlady brought the mail and there was a letter from Sweden. Thinking it was from Fred I opened it eagerly. It was from his mother. He had been staying with her since his release from jail. The poor woman had written to tell me her only son was dead! While finishing a diving job, helping to build a bridge, a disaster had occurred. His equipment must have failed him and he was dragged from the water already dead.

Stunned I wandered from my lodgings not really knowing where I was going, or what to do. I roamed about aimlessly unable to think straight or make plans. Suddenly I found myself at the camp site with Jo running towards me. Seeing how distressed I was she took my arm and led me deep into the forest. Her sympathy was obviously genuine and quite touching. I managed to explain Kathy's betrayal, and Freddie's death, without disclosing my life of crime. I said, however, the goods had been smuggled and that I had a reputation as an international smuggler.

She was silent for a while, then she outlined her plan. It was out of the question, she said, for me to enter Scandinavia and put myself at Kathy's mercy. She had let me down once and it seemed likely she would contact the police, said Jo. No, the best solution was for her to travel to Copenhagen, if I could pay the fare, and she would see Kathy to find out what had happened to the jewellery. I tried to talk her out of this, arguing that she spoke no Danish and only a little German. But she was determined to go through with it and at last, as we walked back to the camp, I agreed.

Next day after hearing all the details of the gems I had left behind, and the whereabouts of Kathy's flat, she set off. It was possible for her to be back in thirty-six hours and I promised to be waiting for her at the station. As soon as she left I began reproaching myself for letting her go and take such risks. I called myself a cad and a coward. I reckoned my weakness and selfishness made me unfit to clean her shoes or even wash my own dirty linen. How I lived through those thirty-six hours I will never know. At last, however, the long wait was over and there was the train from Copenhagen steaming into Utrecht station with Jo on board!

I helped her down, kissed her and took her on the bus to the camping site. Dog tired but smiling, she seemed to have got through her mission safely. Mary had gone to Rotterdam so, for the first time, we had the tent to ourselves. She had not slept at all while she had been away, so I made her undress and get a rest. After some hot milk and brandy she fell asleep and lay like a log all night, and well into the next morning. Then, as I was making coffee she awoke. We had breakfast and then she got up, went into the tent, and returned with two small packets she had hidden in her bra. 'This was all we could find,' she said.

I opened the packets. There were no pearls, no large stones, just some diamonds and several small gems. The whole lot was worth only a few thousand guilders. When Kathy had reluctantly let Jo into the flat, Jo had gone straight to my hiding place, a secret hole underneath the top of the dining table. I had left several hundred pearls there and many other jewels. The gold pieces and trinkets I had buried in a spot outside Copenhagen. When Jo saw that a great deal was missing, she questioned Kathy as well as she could in her poor German, and in a little English. At this Kathy had flown into a rage and threatened to call the police. Jo decided it best to leave. At the station she had put the jewels into two equal-sized packets and slipped them into her bra.

Now the story seemed clear. Kathy had found the loot and sold the best part of it to pay debts. She must have felt safe to come to Holland because I had not mentioned the jewels in my letters. When I raised the matter she probably thought I would either forgive her or forget the whole business. She must have hoped I would be so confident of future hauls I would not be too worried about what she had stolen. She may also have thought I intended to go straight and would not want to start my new life on stolen money. Whatever her motives my feelings for her were now dead, and I began to grow even more attached to Jo.

When Walter and Mary returned, Jo astonished me by telling Mary some tale about having spent the night in an hotel with me. This gave me an idea. I could take her to Paris for a few days and sell the jewels to the fence there. He still owed me some money and there was a good chance he would pay up. After some hesitation Jo agreed to come along with me, and, as it was Monday, we could set off right away. Mary and Walter obviously had no objection to being left on their own in the camp. We took the night-train and were soon in Paris. There, after booking into a cheap hotel, I went to find the fence. He was glad to see me and quickly paid what he owed. But he said it would take a few days to raise the cash on the jewels Jo had brought from Denmark. He said he would have the money ready by Friday. For the rest of the week I took Jo around Paris, showing her all the sights most tourists miss. At night, perhaps influenced by the romance of Paris, the champagne and delicious food, she responded to me in a way I had scarcely dared dream of.

But our happiness lasted a mere three days. On Thursday morning at about four o'clock there was a thump on the door and a shout of 'Police!' and then 'Open up!' When I let them in two plain clothes detectives asked to see my papers. Then they ordered me to get dressed and took me down to the station. They did not ask Jo for her papers. Obviously it was only me they were interested in. After keeping me in suspense for several hours at the station they said I had no right to be in France. I had been kicked out as an undesirable alien in 1937. They wanted to know what the hell I was doing back in their country. At this my breath came more freely. At least they knew nothing about my visit to the fence! I argued furiously about their charge of illegal residence but it did not do me much good. They agreed, however, to drive me back to the hotel to explain to Jo what was going on. As she did not understand a word of French she was most distressed. The hotel owner's wife agreed to take her to the station and buy her return ticket. She would be able to catch the evening train. As the cops with us did not understand Dutch I was able to ask Jo to go to the fence. She agreed. Because she could not quite remember how to get there I persuaded the cops to drop her near the address. This daring move made her smile a little and the detectives softened up when they saw her a little happier. They explained that I was in custody only to ensure that I left France as fast as possible. At this Jo looked even more cheerful and we said good-bye.

It took until Monday to sort my case out. The immigration office was closed for the weekend and so I had to hang around awaiting my fate. They handed me an official paper saying I was, for the rest of my life, an undesirable alien in France, and if I ever returned I would get at least a three months' stretch. Handcuffed, they put me on a train from the Gare du Nord and they kept the cuffs on till we reached the Belgian frontier. As the Belgians had nothing against me they let me finish my journey in peace and I got back to Holland in the afternoon.

Back at the camp site I found Jo, Mary, Walter and Charlie. They all knew most of the story, except, of course, my real reason for visiting Paris. As soon as we were alone Jo told me the fence's shop had been empty when she got there, and there had been no reply to her rings on the bell. I said this was not important as we could get in touch with him at some future date. She had the cash, several thousand francs I had got from the fence, in her purse when I was arrested. This would last me until I obtained what he owed me.

Relieved at our safe return and delighted at our reunion we began to horse around, doing hand-stands and a little Judo. This caused a disaster which changed my whole life. While Charlie was trying out a clumsy stomach throw on Jo, he fell while attempting to get her over his head. She crunched to the ground and nearly broke her neck. She remained very still on the grass and appeared unconscious. We sent for a doctor and he said she was suffering from severe concussion. He ordered us to make sure she stayed in bed in the tent.

After several hours she regained consciousness. She complained of a terrible headache and was very sick. I told Charlie and Walter to leave so that she could have complete quiet. Mary acted as nurse for the first week. When the husbands arrived at the weekend Tim took the news very coolly. He seemed more worried about the possibility of expenses for a professional nurse than he was about his wife's plight.

Mary, Donald, Jo and Tim had planned to take a trip to Austria. Mary said she could not go on looking after Jo, and Tim announced he had no intention of giving up his holiday either. He suggested taking her home and asking his sister to care for her. At this I stepped in and pointed out that I had had some hospital experience and could well look after her as I was unemployed.

They all jumped at this suggestion. It was quickly agreed I should nurse her while they were all off having fun. Jo regained consciousness at this time and stayed awake long enough to nod her agreement. The sadness in her eyes showed how hurt she was at their callousness. As everything had been settled I cycled into town, collected my things from my digs, explained the emergency to my landlady, and returned to the camp. While I had been away Charlie had come back to find out how Jo was. The others had been quarrelling. Mary had rather belatedly criticized Tim for his heartlessness. Tim, who was by now in an ugly mood, was getting rid of his guilt feelings by abusing Charlie for causing the accident. At this I flew into a rage.

Calling them selfish brutes, I ordered them to pack their bags and get out of the camp as fast as possible. When Tim offered me money to cover any expenses I refused to take it, saying there would be plenty of time for that later. The patient's needs must come first, I said, and right now all she required was peace and quiet. They left but Charlie stayed, still full of remorse. He offered to leave me his bike in case I had to fetch a doctor in a hurry. Then he went off too. Jo managed to doze a little despite her fearful headaches. When she woke up she would cry or groan, and refuse all food. I managed to persuade her to drink a lot.

For the first week the doctor came every day. On his first visit he was amazed by my presence and by the absence of the others. I explained the situation and, as he soon saw how well the patient was cared for, he became co-operative and friendly. After ten days Jo was still weak, and in some pain, but the crisis was over. I felt happy and proud when the doctor congratulated me on my nursing.

But there was still a long way to go before the patient was fit. I had an idea to relieve the monotony for Jo. As she had to rest all the time and be comfortable I fixed up a hammock between two trees to save her having to spend the days in the tent. Each morning I carried her out and the hammock made a cosy outdoor bed for her. The other campers knew she was sick and they left us in peace. Our only visitors were a few squirrels who came to look at her when she was asleep. I used to sit about twenty metres from her, smoking my pipe, and watching the view.

As I sat there during these idyllic days I slowly started to change my plans for the future. I cannot tell why I began to think differently. It might have been simply that I was in love with Jo. It was true, I was in love with her. But other factors and feelings conditioned my thinking and gave me a new attitude, and new ambitions. Here I was at thirty-nine with a whole fresh future opening up before me. I was experiencing love, loyalty and honesty from a woman as I had never known them before. Fred's tragic death had removed one possibility from my thoughts. My bad luck in Sweden when the children stumbled across my loot had shown me how easily the best-prepared thief can be caught. Was it always to be like that? Would my grand plans for sailing on hit-and-run raids round Sweden, stealing from Royalty and the very rich, also end in disaster and a prison cell? Kathy's treachery contrasted with Jo's constant loyalty, and seemed to make it even more valuable.

Whatever the strengths of each argument, whatever the power of each mood, I came to a conviction: 'It is time you stopped being a bloody fool.' Glancing over at Jo as she slept in her hammock I made up my mind, my future lay with her. If I could only rescue her from the mess her life was in we could make a good future together. Of course, my life of crime had stemmed partly from my father's lessons in hate, and the disruptions of the war, but I had had many opportunities to go straight and had preferred to go for a life of adventure and quick riches. Now I had a chance, perhaps my last, to dedicate myself to Jo's happiness.

Tim arrived on Saturday with Donald and Mary – as though none of them dared to come alone. After the first greetings and conventional questions, Tim said he was taking Jo home. He had rented a car and was going to drive her himself. He thanked me for caring for her, and proposed he settled our account by paying the expenses. Jo put a stop to this by announcing she would not budge from her hammock until the doctor said she was free to walk wherever she wished. This was a new Jo. Before her accident she would not have spoken out with such firmness and courage. Tim was quite taken aback. Then she added that as she had done so well under my care, she had no intention of changing her nurse now. 'If you were so keen to look after me,' she told Tim, 'you should have done so when I needed you, instead of going off to have your holiday.'

Tim went into a fearful rage. He threatened to leave her penniless unless she did as he ordered. I remarked quietly: 'She seems to have managed well so far without your money.' Then I added she was just as free to stay here now as he had been to take his vacation. I also pointed out that it was better for her to recuperate here in the heart of the forest than in a stuffy flat at Rotterdam where her sister-in-law would occasionally come to her room with food, and Tim was out all day. Tim was beaten – and he knew it.

All he could do was to threaten Jo with divorce for staying and living in a tent with another man. He told Mary and Donald they were witnesses to his wife's infidelity, and with this he left. When he had gone Mary, who had decided to stay for the week-end, took over the household duties. Donald, who had known Tim for ten years, decided it was time to have a serious chat with me. He pressed me about my intentions. I told him if Jo ever had the courage to divorce that brute of a husband of hers it must be of her own free will. I did not want to force her into anything. He thought this was unfair, and said a woman in such a situation needed the help and encouragement from a man who loved her. I pointed out a woman leaves her husband because she is fed up with him, not because there was another man round the corner waiting to take her to bed.

Then he said: 'If you're not going to persuade her to leave Tim, why the hell did you take all this trouble to nurse her through her illness?' At this I got quite annoyed and gave the only answer: 'I was the only one available to care for her – you'd all gone off to have fun.' He gave a shrug, and it was clear the interrogation was over.

When they left on the Monday I made a count of the cash we had left. The cost of the past few weeks since our trip to Paris had thinned my reserves. Although Jo had changed the francs into guilders when she returned from France I had no intention of breaking into that capital. I decided some new source of food was needed in order to cut down our expenses. On a nearby pond there were about fifty or sixty wild ducks. It was time I brought my experiences in France with Dede into good use. I made a catapult and using pebbles as bullets I managed to kill one or two ducks every day. At first there was no need to use the catapult. I merely had to walk from the pond towards our tent dropping bread or crumbs of boiled potato behind me. The ducks waddled along in the right direction. Then, with Jo watching fascinated, I threw the last piece of bait into the tent through the open flap. When the duck went after it (sometimes three or four went in at a time!) I quickly closed the flap.

But after a few days they grew to suspect me and I had to go out hunting. If another camper was near the pond the ducks stayed away and I had to look for other game. One night I captured and killed a big hedgehog. Without telling Jo I prepared it next day. She was delighted with the succulent meat, and asked what it was. Wisely, I just smiled mysteriously until a few hours had passed, and she had had time to digest the meal. The wisdom of this was proved when I told her what she had eaten. She was shocked and started retching at the thought. But intelligent and realistic as she was she soon got over her inhibitions. Soon she was eating crow's breast, owl soup and roasted sparrows! There were plenty of wild berries around and the fields nearby were full of carrots, potatoes and onions.

We lived a good life and by October, when there were few ducks left, she was up and on her feet again. But we still pretended she needed all the care and attention in the world. Our pastoral life was by now so attractive we were both loath to leave it. We had long talks and of course by now we no longer hid our feelings from each other. Although I tried to make her realize Tim was not worthy of her, I made no promise or proposal. I was still determined that leaving Tim had to be a decision she took on her own. This made everything very difficult for her. She had been brought up strictly and thought of divorce as some kind of blasphemy. Having been married in church she had been taught to think it really was ''Till death us do part'. At the age of thirty-four, and without children, she still shied away from breaking a promise she had once made to a man even as unworthy as Tim. I sometimes lost my patience with her but I knew how hard it was to act against deeply-ingrained principles, and I also recognized the uncertainty such a step would bring, as I had not promised to take his place.

Finally the day came when she had to return to Rotterdam. We closed up the tent and travelled to her flat. As it was late in the afternoon she invited me in for dinner and said I should stay for the night. This, she said, was the least she could do, and she was certain Tim would agree when he came home. At about nine o'clock he arrived, slightly drunk. He greeted his wife cheerfully, and even had the grace to thank me for what I had done. He had no objection to my staying the night, and Jo had already

made up the couch for me. He offered me a drink but of course
the conversation was strained. After a bit, Jo, who looked
exhausted, said she was going to bed. Tim urged her to stay on
for another drink but she refused, and disappeared into the bedroom. He offered me another drink but I turned it down saying
I too was very tired because of the change of air, the journey and
the difficulty of getting used to the noise of the city after the
peace of the woods. He scowled at me, finished his drink and
went to join Jo in the bedroom. After a while, although their door
was closed I heard the murmurs of an argument, and then he
began to sing and bawl like a man who was totally drunk.

Although I was undressed and a guest, I opened the door and
asked Jo if she needed any help. He started to shout insults at
me, and ordered me out of the apartment. He seemed in such
a bad way, as he lay there stretched out on the bed, it looked
likely he would vomit all over the room. I calmly told him we
would talk things over in the morning and shut the door. All
through the night he kept getting up and coming to the door
shouting in a mindless, drunken anger. Neither Jo nor I could
get any sleep. Finally I told him, if he did not stop, I would ring
the police and have him taken to a mental hospital. This sobered
him up no end and we managed to get a couple of hours' sleep.
Next morning I was shocked to see how pale Jo looked after
such a dreadful night. When Tim left for work, I kept telling
her to leave him, but she refused. At last I got so impatient I
said goodbye and left the house.

I went to see Louis and his wife. They did not give me much
of a welcome. I soon found out why. My ex-boss had told them I
had been living in the woods with some godless woman who had
been neglecting a husband and children for my sake. Louis would
not listen to my side of the story and he said: 'From now on –
you're on your own.' I contacted Tony, a friend of Walter's,
whose mother had been my landlady at Doorn. He very kindly
got me a job selling cash registers. Soon I had a secondhand car
and was able to set up in business as a travelling salesman on my
own. One night while having dinner with Tony and his girlfriend
in her flat I told them all about Jo and Tim. Walter had already
given them some idea of our situation. When they saw how worried I was, Tony decided to help me. Next day he went to see
Jo in Rotterdam and learned that Tim was drinking more than
ever. He was abusing her and even threatening her life. Jo was
frantic and her doctor thought she might have a breakdown if

this was allowed to go on. But she had nowhere to go if she left Tim as her family would not take her in if she deserted her husband.

The next day I went to Rotterdam to see her. I told her she could come with me and stay at my digs. I offered her shelter, and food till she felt able to stand on her own feet. She came and my landlady welcomed my new fiancée. Tim soon discovered where we were living and one day he appeared at the door. For once he was sober. Jo told him calmly but firmly he was wasting his time. She would never live with him again. After one more meeting on neutral ground they came to an agreement. Tim would start divorce proceedings and would pay for the lawyer. Jo would admit to being the guilty party. She would also agree to taking no more than her clothes from their flat.

That night she cried till morning and I went to get a doctor. He said she was too mentally and physically weak to even be up and about. He ordered her to rest fully for a fortnight. Then he said she needed a complete change in her way of life to keep her mind off the ordeal she had endured. For two weeks I looked after her night and day, reading to her, making her drinks every hour or fixing refreshing, nourishing meals. When the doctor said she was well enough I started looking for a job for her. Soon she was working as a saleswoman in a large store. I managed my selling tours so that each evening I could meet her outside the shop as it closed. Then we would eat out and go straight home.

In January 1961, however, my landlady told us we could no longer live in that tiny room without getting married. Jo's divorce had still not come through. Desperately we searched for another home. As we were short of cash I remembered the money the fence still owed me in Paris. Once again Jo volunteered to fetch it, and this time she was successful. She returned with about 5,000 guilders. Meanwhile I had two attic rooms in an old house in the red-light district of Rotterdam. The tarts paraded up and down outside, but we did not mind that.

Finally her divorce was approved and she was free at last. But still she often woke at night screaming from the frightful nightmares caused by her life with Tim. Whenever this happened I used to get her up and dressed, and drive her to the beach at Scheveningen where we would walk until she felt calmer and ready for sleep. Gradually these attacks grew less frequent, but it was years before the scars and memories of her loutish husband stopped causing her pain.

After several months she was promoted to branch manager of the shop, and became quite a business woman. But she hated the idea of earning more money than me, as I got little from selling those beastly cash registers. Every day, however, I kept trying for a better job. But each time either my age, my lack of experience, or my prison record meant I was rejected. One day while we were on holiday at Lake Konstanz I made a call to hear the result of my application for a vacancy as a sales representative in a large international firm selling women's undergarments. My luck was in. They had decided to give me a try. From now on I was to have a good salary and expenses, as well as a house in southern Holland. Now we could think of starting a family.

That night we celebrated and later in our bedroom, holding Jo in my arms – I told her the story of my life. To her, as to you here in this book, I omitted nothing. When I finished I proposed to her.

She accepted on one condition. I was never to act as 'The Panther' again. I swore there and then never to do so, and I have kept my word. Once back in Holland, after waiting out the time prescribed by law for those who have been divorced, we were married in a registry office. In December, 1961 we moved to a cottage in the woods and a whole new wonderful stage of our lives began. After a year she presented me with a son, and our happiness was complete. Now after fourteen years we are just as happy.

After years of running from police and soldiers, years of escapes in strange countries and brief encounters with lonely women, years in prison cells and squalid camps, I was lucky enough to get a chance to live a decent life without fear or shame. I have never regretted the decision I took in the forest while Jo slept soundly, watched by the squirrels.